BOEING 747

The first twenty years

JIM LUCAS

· B R O W C O M ·
London · England

Published by:

Browcom Group Plc,
Browcom House,
Browells Lane,
Feltham, Middlesex,
TW13 7EQ, England

ISBN 0 946141 37 1

Distributed in the USA/Canada by:

TAYLOR & FRANCIS. IPS,
242 Cherry Street,
Philadelphia,
Pennsylvania 19106-1906,
USA

Telephone: (215) 238-0939
Toll Free: (800) 821-8312

1st Published 1988

Printed in Great Britain by:
Browcom Group Plc
Browcom House, Browells Lane, Feltham, Middlesex, TW13 7EQ, England

Contents

Spanning forty years of air travel, a well-preserved United Air Lines' Boeing 247 of the 1930s viewed from under the nose of the airline's first Boeing 747. *(Boeing)*

Pedigree

It is difficult to believe that Boeing, the major producer of today's jet airliners, was better known during the 1920s and 1930s as a supplier of fighter aircraft and during the 1940s and 1950s as a builder of big bombers for the US Air Force. However, the company did build a few airliners during that period and, although not produced in large quantities, each type served as a significant stepping stone in the progress of air travel.

Air travel was late arriving in the United States after World War I, the main air transport activity during the first few years being devoted to the carriage of mail. Under the control of the US Post Office, a coast-to-coast (New York to San Francisco) route was established using war-surplus de Havilland DH4 aircraft, a British-designed single-engined biplane which had been built in large numbers in the USA powered by the American Liberty engine. Initially, flying was performed only during the hours of daylight but a considerable time-saving was achieved from 1923 when sections of the route were equipped with flashing beacons and well-lit landing fields and emergency landing fields to permit safe night flying when weather permitted; by 1925 the Lighted Airway, as it was called, extended over the entire 2400-mile (3862 km) trans-continental route.

The US Post Office was by then looking for aircraft capable of carrying greater loads of mail, but still powered by a Liberty engine, and Boeing built a **Model 40** biplane for the competition. This had a fabric-covered wooden structure and was equipped with a large mail compartment between the engine and the pilot's open cockpit. Boeing didn't win the competition but the design formed the basis of the Model 40A mailplane which the company produced in 1927.

During 1925 the Contract Air Mail Act was passed to transfer the carriage of air mail from the US Post Office to private companies. Bids were invited initially for Contract Air Mail (CAM) routes which served as feeders to the trans-continental route and numerous small airlines were formed to operate them. Then in 1926 bids were invited for the trans-continental route in two sections — New York to Chicago (CAM 17) and Chicago to San Francisco (CAM 18). Boeing won the CAM 18 section and formed Boeing Air Transport to operate it with 24 Boeing Model 40A mailplanes which were built between January and June 1927 and located at the main landing fields along the 1918-mile (3087 km) route ready for the take-over on 1 July.

The Model 40A had a wing span of 44 ft 2 in (13,46 m), a length of 33 ft 3 in. (10,13 m) and a maximum take-off weight of 5600 lb (2540 kg); cruising speed was 105 mph (169 km/hr) and its range was 650 miles (1046 km). The aircraft

The two-seat passenger cabin on the Model 40A mailplane of 1927 was located between the mail compartment and pilot's open cockpit but was totally enclosed. *(Boeing)*

differed from the earlier Model 40 in having a welded steel-tube structure for the fuselage and power provided by one of the new 420 hp Pratt & Whitney Wasp air-cooled radial engines. This engine was lighter than the water-cooled Liberty engine and enabled the fuselage to be re-arranged to provide an enclosed two-seat passenger cabin between the metal-lined mail compartment and the pilot's open cockpit, in the hope of gaining revenue from passenger carrying in addition to that from the 1000 lb (454 kg) of mail.

Passengers were able to wear ordinary clothes but had to step up on to the lower wing and take up the crouch position to enter the cabin through a door on each side. Each door was fitted with a sliding window for ventilation and the side-by-side seats were upholstered, which was better than the wicker chairs used in some early European airliners. A woman reporter from a Chicago newspaper flew the whole route on the first day, starting from Chicago at 9.15 pm and dropping in at Iowa City, Des Moines, Omaha (for a change of aircraft and fresh pilot), North Platte (at dawn), Cheyenne (for another change of aircraft and fresh pilot), then over the mountains to Rock Springs, Salt Lake City, Elko, Reno and Sacremento to San Francisco. From Chicago she had logged 23 flying hours, an event which received considerable publicity, following as it did a better-known event in May 1927; this was the incredible 33½-hour non-stop flight by Charles Lindbergh from New York to Paris in his single-engined Ryan monoplane *Spirit of St Louis.*

When the more powerful 525 hp Pratt & Whitney Hornet radial engine became available in 1928, the Model 40As were re-engined to provide improved performance and their model number was changed to 40B.

Further development of the type led to the Model 40C which had a four-seat passenger cabin, reducing the mail load to 500 lb (227 kg), and was powered by a Pratt & Whitney Wasp engine. Ten were produced in 1928, nine for Pacific Air Transport which had been taken over by Boeing Air Transport (together with CAM 8 from San Francisco to Portland and Seattle, home of the Boeing Airplane Company) and one for National Park Airways.

The final version of this aircraft was the Model 40B-4 which had the four-seat passenger cabin of the 40C with power provided by the more powerful Pratt & Whitney Hornet engine. A total of 39 of these was built, plus four built by a Boeing subsidiary in Canada. Deliveries were made between 1929 and 1932 to various airlines, including Pacific Air Transport, Varney Air Lines and National Air Transport, all of which, with Boeing Air Transport, were to be grouped under the general title of United Air Lines from 1931. Varney Air Lines (together with CAM 5 from Salt Lake City to Seattle) was bought by the United holding company in 1930 shortly after United had taken over National Air Transport with its all-important CAM 17 from Chicago to New York, which then gave United the complete trans-continental route.

With the increase in the number of passengers being carried by the Model 40s came a requirement for a bigger aircraft with the emphasis on passenger accommodation instead of mail. To meet this need Boeing designed the

The prototype of the Model 80 airliner of 1928, which provided more space and comfort (and a toilet) for its 12 passengers. *(Boeing)*

Model 80, a big three-engined biplane airliner capable of carrying 12 passengers in reasonable comfort. It had a wing span of 80 ft (24,38 m), a length of 54 ft 11 in. (16,74 m) and a maximum take-off weight of 15,276 lb (6929 kg); cruising speed was 115 mph (185 km/hr) and range was 545 miles (877 km). Its basic structure was of metal tubing with fabric covering and power was provided by three 425 hp Pratt & Whitney Wasp engines. Four Model 80s were delivered to Boeing Air Transport during 1928, followed in 1929 by 10 Model 80As.

The Model 80A was a more powerful version, powered by three 525 hp Pratt & Whitney Hornet engines, and it had a slightly longer fuselage with accommodation for up to 18 passengers. Production of the Model 80 was limited because it appeared on the airline scene after the Fokker and Ford Trimotors which several other airlines had ordered. However, two additional aircraft of the type were built, one as an executive transport for an oil company and the other, designated Model 80B, with an open cockpit for the two pilots in place of the enclosed one on the other aircraft. This aircraft was delivered to Boeing Air Transport for the pilots who preferred to fly with the wind in their face and be able to look over the side; it was later modified to Model 80A standard probably because communication radio for weather reports and early radio beacons for navigation were introduced about this time and these were found to be more reliable than contact flying.

Stewardesses (all trained nurses) were introduced on Boeing Air Transport's Model 80 airliners in 1930, using the best china and silver coffee pots. *(Boeing)*

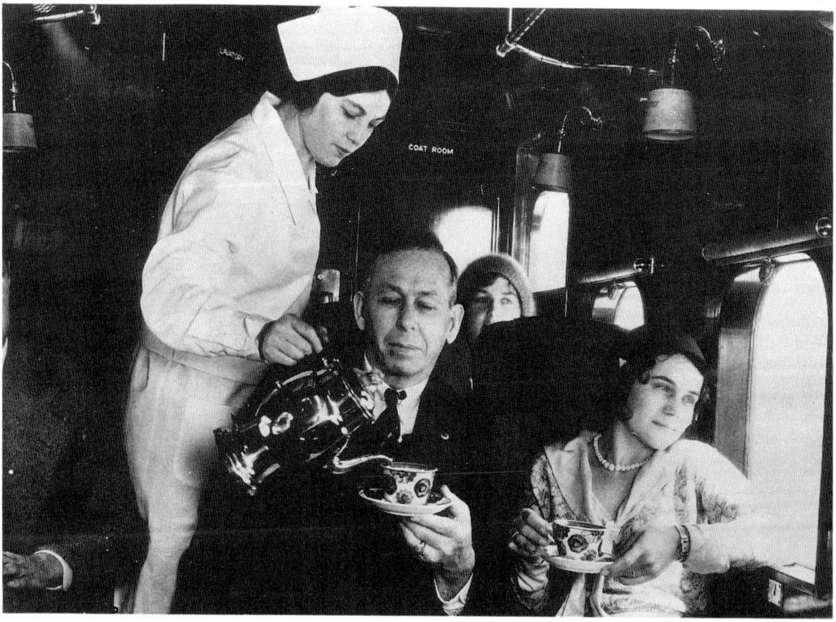

The Original Eight – the world's first stewardesses – from left to right: Jessie Carter, Cornelia Peterman, Ellen Church (chief stewardess), Inez Keller, Alva Johnson, Margaret Arnott, Ellis Crawford and Harriet Fry. *(Boeing)*

One area in which the Model 80 achieved fame was in its cabin service. Boeing Air Transport was the first airline to introduce a stewardess on its aircraft to replace the part-time administrations of the co-pilot. At the start, eight young women were selected, all trained nurses, and Ellen Church (the chief stewardess) took the first turn of duty between San Francisco and Cheyenne on 15 May 1930. The passenger cabin of the Model 80 was big enough for this treatment, being 5 ft 3½ in. (1,61 m) wide and 6 ft 1½ in. (1,87 m) high. The upholstered seats were arranged three abreast, with a single seat on the right-hand side and a double seat on the left of an offset aisle, with large windows on each side. At the rear of the cabin was a toilet, with a wash basin provided with hot and cold running water.

The basic idea of this stewardess service was to provide an air of confidence for the travelling public, especially first-time flyers. In addition, stewardesses were expected to perform various duties which added interest and comfort to the trip, including attention to women and children who may be travelling unaccompanied, describing interesting landmarks along the airway, serving coffee and sandwiches or cold fried chicken lunches, helping the airsick passengers (who were probably quite numerous in those days of low-altitude cruising in turbulent conditions), and handing out chewing gum to clear passengers' ears when it was time to land.

A proposed freighter version, the Model 80C, was not built but in 1929 Boeing produced the **Model 95** mail and cargo aircraft to serve on Boeing Air Transport's routes where the passengers were being carried by the Model 80s. Similar to the Model 40 but with no passenger cabin, the Model 95 had a wing span of 44 ft 3in. (13,49 m), a length of 31 ft 11 in. (9,73 m) and a maximum take-off weight of 5840 lb (2649 kg). Power was provided by a 525 hp Pratt & Whitney Hornet engine. Of the 25 built, 20 went to Boeing Air Transport, four to Western Air Express and one to National Air Transport.

The next mailplane built by Boeing was very different. This was the **Model 200 Monomail**, a single-engined, all metal, stressed-skin, cantilever monoplane with a retractable landing gear. A revolutionary aircraft in 1930, it proved that it was possible to achieve performance increases by structural and aerodynamic refinement rather than by the addition of more horsepower. It retained the familiar mailplane layout of the Model 40 with a mail compartment between the engine and the pilot's open cockpit but otherwise it was a forerunner of things to come.

Powered by a 575 hp Pratt & Whitney Hornet B engine with a special anti-drag cowling, the Monomail had a wing span of 59 ft 1½ in. (18,02 m), a length of 41 ft 2 in. (12,55 m) and a maximum take-off weight of 8000 lb (3629 kg). Although it had a cruising speed of 140 mph (225 km/hr) its full performance potential could not be realised because it arrived on the scene before a reliable variable-pitch propeller had been invented: with the type of propeller it had it was possible to adjust the pitch of the blades on the ground to provide a fine setting for a take-off with full payload or a coarse setting for a high cruising speed when airborne, but not both, and for general use it was necessary to select a compromise setting.

A second Monomail (Model 221) built in 1930 had a fuselage arrangement even more like that of the Model 40 because it had a cabin for six passengers, who would have reverted to the old-style cramped conditions (and no cabin service). Even so it was delivered for use by Boeing Air Transport and later both Monomails were modified (into Model 221As) to have longer fuselages to provide a cabin for eight passengers and they served with United Air Lines between Cheyenne and Chicago. Although offering an express service they were probably not all that popular with passengers.

Boeing got the mix right for its next airliner, the twin-engined **Model 247**, which combined the technical innovations of the Monomail with the full-size passenger cabin of the Model 80. In fact this was a world leader, the first of the 'modern' airliners, with a general appearance that was to be copied by other manufacturers for many of the piston-engined airliners that were to appear during the years that followed.

The twin-engined, low-wing monoplane arrangement had originated in the experimental B-9 bomber which Boeing had built earlier for the US Army Air Corps and which utilised the all-metal, stressed-skin construction, cantilever wing and retractable landing gear of the Monomail. Not quite as big as the Model 80, the Model 247 had a wing span of 74 ft (22,56 m), a length of 51 ft 4 in. (15,65 m) and a maximum take-off weight of 12,650 lb (5738 kg).

Power was provided by two cowled 550 hp Pratt & Whitney Wasp engines which gave the aircraft a cruising speed of 155 mph (249 km/hr). United Air Lines, in the form of its four constituent airlines, placed an incredible order for 60 of these aircraft while the project was still in the mock-up stage and deliveries were made during 1933 and 1934 to completely re-equip the fleets.

Crew for the Model 247s was two pilots, in an enclosed cockpit having an unusual forward-swept windscreen, and a stewardess transferred from the Model 80s. Accommodation in the cabin was for ten passengers in individual upholstered seats down each side of a central aisle at 40 in. (102 cm) pitch for ample leg room and each had a large window. The cabin was heated, ventilated and equipped with a degree of soundproofing which provided less noisy travelling conditions than the earlier fabric-covered aircraft. A toilet was located at the rear of the cabin which had a width of 5 ft (1,52 m) and a height of 6 ft (1,83 m) except for the unfortunate intrusion of the two main wing spars which had to be padded and equipped with a step each side where they crossed the aisle floor to allow passengers (and the stewardess) an easier passage up and down.

With a cruising speed some 50 mph (80,5 km/hr) faster than most other types of airliner then in service, the Model 247 was an immediate success on United Air Lines' trans-continental route where it reduced the coast-to-coast journey time to under 20 hours with seven stops en route. Unfortunately, the success was short lived because when competing airlines had learned of the advanced airliner that Boeing was building and had tried to order some they were told they would have to wait until the United order had been completed. Rather than suffer such a disadvantage they looked elsewhere, and TWA (then known as Transcontinental & Western Air), by then a trans-continental

The first of the 'modern' airliners, the 10-seat Boeing 247 of 1933 provided increased speed and additional comfort for United Air Lines' passengers. *(Boeing)*

route operator, turned to Douglas who designed the DC-1 (that company's first airliner) which followed the basic twin-engined, all-metal monoplane formula of the model 247. The production version, the DC-2, entered service with TWA in July 1934 and was slightly bigger than the Model 247, having accommodation for 14 passengers. Powered by 710 hp Wright Cyclone radial engines driving variable-pitch propellers, the DC-2 also had a higher cruising speed of 170 mph (273 km/hr) and had an additional advantage of being equipped with trailing-edge wing flaps to reduce its landing speed.

To compete with the DC-2, Boeing produced the Model 247D which was powered by supercharged Pratt & Whitney Wasp engines with reduction gearing to drive variable-pitch propellers, and thus increase the cruising speed. Improved engine cowlings and a rearward-sloping windscreen were among minor modifications in the Model 247D of which 13 were built as new in 1934, with the earlier Model 247s being brought up to a similar standard later.

The Model 247D and the DC-2 were in direct competition in October 1934 when one of each type took part in the MacRobertson England to Australia air race. The Model 247D was leased from United Air Lines and flown by Roscoe Turner and Clyde Pangborn while the DC-2 was the first to be delivered to KLM Royal Dutch Airlines and flown by Captain K.D. Parmentier and J.J. Moll. Both aircraft completed the 11,300-mile (18 185 km) course from Mildenhall, Suffolk, to Melbourne and, with extra fuel tanks as their only special equipment, showed the world the capability of 'modern' airliners. The race was won by a specially-built de Havilland Comet racer but the two airliners were not far behind it, the DC-2 coming second and the Model 247D third.

Although offering improvements over the original Model 247, the Model 247D did not match the size or improved performance of the DC-2 so the orders went to the latter, other airlines anticipating the future growth in air travel on the US domestic routes. When American Airlines, who had also started a trans-continental service by then, asked Douglas for a bigger version of the DC-2 to accommodate sleeping berths, the Douglas Sleeper Transport (DST) was born, followed by the day plane version, the 21-seat DC-3. And so started the Douglas line of successful piston-engined airliners.

Another line of successful piston-engined airliners which started at this time was that of Lockheed who, following the basic Model 247 formula but with the DC-2 refinements, produced its first 'modern' airliner in the form of the L10 Electra which entered service with Northwest Airlines in August 1934.

While producing its various mailplanes and airliners, Boeing had also been busy building fighter aircraft for the US Navy and US Army Air Corps, the latter preferring to call them Pursuit planes. Originally these were biplanes but, following its experience with the Monomail, Boeing designed an all-metal, low-wing monoplane fighter: the Navy considered it too advanced for operation from existing aircraft carriers and the Army preferred externally wire-braced monoplanes which appeared to have greater structural integrity in violent aerobatics such as dogfights.

With military fighter orders hard to come by and having been temporarily nudged out of airliner production, Boeing accepted the challenge of an Army Air Corps design study into the feasibility of a very big, long-range heavy bomber. After a lengthy gestation period the company received an order to build a single prototype of what was to be the four-engined XB-15 which made its first flight in October 1937.

Meanwhile, Boeing entered an Army Air Corps competition in August 1934 for a smaller multi-engined bomber and designed a four-engined version of its all-metal, low-wing cantilever monoplane with a retractable landing gear, sized between the Model 247 and the XB-15 – the B-17 Flying Fortress. After passing through the prototype stage and building small batches of development aircraft there came the B-17E, F and G versions, the famous daylight bombers of World War II, which gave Boeing useful experience in mass production. Boeing built 4035 B-17Gs and the old rivals Douglas and Lockheed built 2395 and 2250, respectively; at the peak of B-17 production in June 1944, Boeing's Seattle factory was rolling out 16 aircraft every 24 hours. Production of the great bomber totalled 12,731.

In the early days of the B-17, Boeing considered the commercial possibilities of the basic design. As with the B-9, a new fuselage was designed to mate with the wings, engines and tail of the military version, resulting in the **Model 307 Stratoliner.** Although not the first four-engined, all-metal, low-wing monoplane airliner, the Stratoliner was nevertheless a pioneer in being the first airliner with a pressurised cabin to enter service. The pressurisation was only moderate, providing 8000 ft (2440 m) conditions in the passenger cabin when the aircraft was cruising at 14,700 ft (4480 m) but it enabled the Stratoliner to fly above the worst of the rough weather, providing a smoother flight for its passengers and giving it an improved performance with a better clearance over any mountain ranges along the routes.

During 1934 United Air Lines had been separated from the Boeing Airplane Company so that when the Stratoliner design was completed there was no airline in the family for which it could be produced. Eventually, Pan American Airways and TWA decided to go for the big, four-engined over-the-weather airliner and in 1937 ordered four and five aircraft, respectively. The first Pan American Stratoliner crashed during a demonstration flight, which delayed development, but the others were delivered, together with a tenth for multi-millionaire Howard Hughes.

The Stratoliner had a wing span of 107 ft 3 in. (32,69 m), a length of 74 ft 4 in. (22,66 m) and a maximum take-off weight of 42,000 lb (19 050 kg). Powered by four 9-cylinder, 1100 hp Wright Cyclone engines, it cruised at 220 mph (354 km/hr) and had a range of 2390 miles (3846 km). The flight crew was three, a flight engineer being aboard to attend to the pressurisation system as well as the engines, and two stewards or stewardesses were carried.

Passengers were seated four-abreast in its large-diameter fuselage. For daytime flights, 33 passengers were carried in an unusual arrangement of nine individual seats down the left-hand side of the cabin and four groups of facing triple seats down the right-hand side, with an offset aisle. This arrangement simplified the conversion for night-time flights when the nine passengers down the left-hand side had reclining seats and the four groups of seats on the right-hand side were converted into 16 berths, in groups of four (two curtained-off double-tier berths) arranged laterally. This cabin layout resulted in the exterior of the aircraft having an odd appearance, with nine equally-spaced windows (plus one in the entrance door) on the left-hand side and eight windows arranged in widely-separated pairs on the right-hand side. Amenities included a ladies' room at the front, a gents at the rear and a galley for heating food.

It was not until 1940 that the Stratoliner entered service, TWA being first, in the July, with an inaugural flight in both directions on its Super Sky Chief coast-to-coast service. The eastbound flight from Los Angeles to New York took 12¼ hours and the westbound flight 14¼ hours, both making only one stop, at Kansas City, en route. Pan American introduced the Stratoliner on its Latin American routes out of Miami in September 1940. However, the aircraft had little time in airline service before the entry of the United States into World War II in December 1941, when the Stratoliners were transferred to military duties. The aircraft bought by Howard Hughes was equally unfortunate because he had planned to use it on a round-the-world flight in an attempt to beat his 1938 record-breaking flight of 91 hours but the start of World War II in Europe in September 1939 caused this to be abandoned, his Stratoliner not being delivered until July 1939 and his first planned stop being Berlin. Although not a commercial success, the Stratoliner indicated the direction in which air travel would be going once the period of bombs and guns was over.

Another Boeing airliner that had its airline potential thwarted by the start of World War II was the impressive **Model 314** flying boat. It was designed to meet a Pan American requirement for a four-engined, ocean-going flying boat and this challenging requirement was met by mating the wings and tail of the big XB-15 bomber with an equally big flying-boat hull. The result was an aircraft that crested the wave of the pre-war golden age of civil flying boats.

Pan American had developed an extensive route network from Miami across the Caribbean and around much of South America with early-type flying boats during the late 1920s and early 1930s. The airline's president, Juan Trippe, then set his sights on conquering the oceans on each side of the United States. The Pacific came first because of its less severe weather conditions and its less complicated landing-rights situation, the mid-Pacific islands of Hawaii, Midway, Wake, Guam and the Philippines all being US territories at that time. Survey flights were started in April 1935 and the first scheduled air-mail flight across the Pacific was made in November 1935 using four-engined Martin M-130 strut-braced monoplane flying boats. Three of these aircraft were available for the start of a weekly island-hopping, scheduled passenger service from San Francisco to Manila in the Philippines which was inaugurated in October 1936 (with an extension to Hong Kong in April 1937).

With the route across the Pacific established, Pan American turned its

When Stratoliners entered service with Transcontinental & Western Air (TWA) in 1940 they were the first airliners to have a pressurised cabin for their 33 passengers. (TWA)

attention to the North Atlantic, which took rather more time and effort to conquer because of its strong prevailing westerly winds, often with stormy weather and severe icing conditions, and also because most pieces of land around it belonged to a different country. Two routes between the USA and Britain or France were planned, the more direct northern route from New York via Shediac (New Brunswick, Canada), Botwood (Newfoundland) and Foynes (Eire) to Southampton, which would be suitable only for summer services, and a southern route from New York via Bermuda, the Azores and Lisbon to Marseilles (with extension to Southampton in winter). Survey flights and experimental mail-carrying flights were carried out from 1937 onwards by Imperial Airways and Pan American, using Short C Class and Sikorsky S-42 flying boats, respectively, but scheduled passenger services had to await the delivery of a bigger and better flying boat – the Boeing 314, the 'jumbo' of the golden age of civil flying boats.

In 1939, when the first of the Model 314s was delivered, this was the biggest and most advanced aircraft produced up to that time in the United States. It had a wing span of 152 ft (46,33 m), a length of 106 ft (32,31 m) and a maximum take-off weight of 82,500 lb (37 422 kg). Powered by four 14-cylinder, 1500 hp Wright Double Cyclone engines (the most powerful engines to be fitted to a pre World War II airliner), it cruised at 188 mph (303 km/hr) and had a range of 3685 miles (5930 km). The flight crew was seven, comprising captain, first officer, navigator, flight engineer, radio officer and junior flight officer, plus reserve crew members (with crew rest area) for long flights, who were all located on an upper flight deck.

Up to 74 passengers could be accommodated on the main deck in the deep hull but for long trans-ocean flights this was reduced to 35 passengers, who enjoyed spacious living with full facilities, including a separate dining room.

The passengers sat (or slept in berths) in five compartments and there was also a promenade area and a self-contained suite at the rear. Forward on the main deck was a big galley in which two stewards prepared hot meals, and a dressing room/toilet was located fore and aft.

Pan American's initial order was for six of these big flying boats, at a cost of $550,000 each, and deliveries were made at monthly intervals from January 1939. The first two were allocated to the trans-Pacific route, which was by then in need of bigger aircraft, and the remaining four to the trans-Atlantic route. After a survey flight to Southampton via the southern route in March 1939, a mail flight to Marseilles was operated on the route on 20 May 1939, the 12th anniversary of Charles Lindbergh's famous flight from New York to Paris. This was followed by passenger flights on both the southern route to Marseilles and the northern route to Southampton carrying invited guests of Pan American. Then on 28 June 1939 Pan American's Model 314 *Dixie Clipper* operated the first fare-paying passenger service by flying boat on the southern route to Marseilles, and on 8 July 1939 the airline's Model 314 *Yankee Clipper* operated the first fare-paying passenger service by flying boat on the northern route to Southampton.

The civil flying boat operations over the North Atlantic were cut short by the outbreak of World War II in Europe, which led to the closure of the northern route and the curtailment of the southern route at Lisbon (neutral territory), and the eventual transfer to military requirements. Civil operations

Passengers arriving at Lisbon after the first commercial trans-Atlantic flight by Pan American's Boeing 314 flying boat Dixie Clipper in June 1939. *(Pan American)*

The dining room aboard one of Pan American's Boeing 314 flying boats in which hot meals were served by two stewards. *(Boeing)*

continued on the trans-Pacific route until the Japanese attack on Pearl Harbor, Hawaii, in December 1941, when these too became a military operation.

Six more Model 314s, with improved range and performance, were ordered by Pan American. Designated Model 314A, they had increased fuel capacity, an increased maximum take-off weight of 84,000 lb (38 102 kg) and were powered by four 1600 hp Wright Double Cyclone engines. The war in Europe had started before these were delivered and three of them were diverted to British Overseas Airways Corporation (BOAC), as Imperial Airways had become. The earlier aircraft were later modified to this standard.

The tide of progress flowed against the big civil flying boat during the six war years, when the faster and more economical landplane achieved a state of development where it could take over the trans-ocean and other long-haul routes. The four-engined Douglas DC-4 and Lockheed Constellation, both of the 'modern' standard with the additional improvement of a nosewheel landing gear, were initially built as military transports. War surplus, unpressurised DC-4s became the choice of many US and other airlines when peace returned, to be followed quickly by improved Constellations and DC-6s (both pressurised) as production lines changed over to civil airliners again.

These four-engined landplanes were used by most of the US and European airlines who started operating services across the North Atlantic after World War II, alongside Pan American, and they were joined in 1949 by a new Boeing airliner – the Stratocruiser – for a share of what was to become the golden age of the long-range, piston-engined airliner.

During the war, besides mass producing B-17s, Boeing also designed and built the B-29, a four-engined, long-range, high-altitude (pressurised) bomber and put this into full production to serve over the Pacific, where it ended the war by dropping the atomic bombs. In the midst of all this activity, Boeing had designed a military transport, based on the wings and tail of the B-29 but production of this, the Model 367, or C-97 Stratofreighter as it became known, did not start until the war was over when it came into its own serving mainly as a flight-refuelling tanker (KC-97), and 888 were built.

From the C-97 came an airliner counterpart, the **Model 377 Stratocruiser,** another big one from Boeing. It had a wing span of 141 ft 3 in. (43,05 m), a length of 110 ft 4 in. (33,63 m) and a maximum take-off weight of 145,800 lb (66 135 kg). Power was provided by four of the most powerful piston engines ever made, the 3500 hp Pratt & Whitney Wasp Major, which had 28 cylinders arranged radially in four banks of seven, an arrangement that earned it the nickname of Corncob. Cruising speed was 300 mph (483 km/hr) at 25,000 ft (7620 m) and range was up to 4200 miles (6760 km).

A total of 56 Stratocruisers was built for five airlines: Pan American 21, American Overseas Airlines 8, Northwest Airlines 10, BOAC 10 and United Airlines 7.

Entering service in 1949, the Stratocruisers arrived when competition between trans-Atlantic airlines was hotting up. At that time there was only one fare (equivalent to today's first-class fare) and the passengers –film stars, politicians, businessmen and the otherwise wealthy – were offered a variety of 'extras' by the airlines vying for their custom. The Stratocruiser was ideally suited to this situation, having a spacious and comfortable interior which is best described as the landplane equivalent of the big flying boats. The passenger cabin was wider than those of the DC-6 and Constellation, allowing ample elbow room with the normal four-abreast seating (pairs of seats on each side of a central aisle), and the interior was divided into three compartments separated by dressing rooms/toilets forward and a galley towards the rear. In addition, because of the aircraft's unusual 'double-bubble' fuselage, there was a lower-deck lounge, located just behind the wing and reached by a spiral staircase from the main deck, which was equipped with 14 seats and a bar. This lounge was very popular with passengers, giving them the opportunity to stretch their legs and have a change of scene to break the monotony of long flights (London-New York in the early 1950s took about 17 hours with one stop, weather permitting), there being no in-flight entertainment at the time.

The normal accommodation was for 60 passengers but this was reduced for trans-ocean, over-night flights according to the number of berths required in the forward compartments. The ultimate in Stratocruiser trans-Atlantic flights was reached with Pan American's *President* and BOAC's *Monarch* luxury services, aboard which, for a surcharge, passengers were really given the treatment, including a seven-course dinner with champagne and a berth for the night. Cabin staff on these services comprised four stewards and a stewardess, with one steward on duty in the lower-deck bar.

Such luxury was, of course, available for only a few, but two events in May 1952 marked the beginning of a major change in air travel. The first of these was the introduction of 'second class' (but given the name of Tourist class) and the second event was the introduction by BOAC of the world's first jet airliner service.

Pan American was first to operate a trans-Atlantic tourist-class service with a DC-6B between New York and London on 1 May 1952, for a fare of $270 single compared with $395 single first class. At that time, separate aircraft were used for the two classes, and to get the same revenue from a tourist-class aircraft an additional line of seats was added down the cabin, making it five-abreast instead of four (reducing elbow room) but still retaining the 40 in. (102 cm) seat pitch (for ample leg room), and the cabin service was reduced to meals and beverages, with alcoholic drinks having to be purchased. Pan American DC-6Bs carried 82 tourist-class passengers or 52 first-class, and in BOAC's Constellations the figures were 68 and 43, respectively.

Another fare cut came in 1958 with the introduction of a 'third class' (called Economy) which further limited comfort by reducing the seat pitch (and leg room) to 34 in. (86 cm) and therefore adding more passengers. The New York to London fares then became $435 first class, $315 tourist and $252 economy but 'economy' soon displaced 'tourist' and became the standard for second class.

Another big one from Boeing, the spacious Stratocruiser of the 1950s was powered by four 28-cylinder Pratt & Whitney Wasp Major engines. *(Boeing)*

Jet airliners were a long time coming because in the early post-war years the fuel-guzzling jet engines of the time were suitable only for short-duration fighters and bombers, certainly not for long-range airliners. However, rapid development of the jet engine for military purposes soon made it suitable for short-to-medium range airliners, and the de Havilland Comet 1 introduced by BOAC on a stopping service from London to Johannesburg on 2 May 1952 demonstrated the pleasures of smooth, fast travel by jet airliner. The bigger, extended-range Comet 3 was in the early production stage to meet a Pan American order for a trans-Atlantic version when the Comet 1 ran into trouble in 1954 and the type had to be withdrawn from service.

Meanwhile, Boeing had continued to build bombers for the US Air Force, producing its first jet-powered type, the six-engined B-47 Stratojet, from late 1947 and following this with the bigger eight-engined B-52 Stratofortress from 1952. Both designs had swept-back wings with their jet engines in 'pods' mounted on pylons beneath the wings, an arrangement which set the pattern for many future military and civil designs. With the increasing number of jet-powered fighters and bombers entering service, there was a requirement for a jet-powered flight-fuelling tanker to support them and therefore Boeing set to work designing one based on the earlier Model 367 KC-97. The final design had swept-back wings with four jet engines in pods mounted beneath them and when the company-funded prototype appeared in 1954 it had the almost window-less fuselage of a military tanker but carried a civilian registration N70700, for it was to serve as a prototype for both the KC-135 Stratotanker and the Model 707 airliner.

The military version was the first to be ordered (given a separate model number 717) in late 1954, and 820 were eventually produced. The airlines at the time were content with their fleets of piston-engined airliners so were in no hurry to make the change to jet airliners, considering them to be too big and to have doubtful operating economics. Then, in October 1955, Pan American took the bold step and ordered 20 **Boeing 707s** at a cost of just over $4 million each, plus 25 Douglas DC-8s, the first of which was not due to fly until May 1958 but appeared to offer better range. Most of the trans-Atlantic airlines, and others, soon followed Pan American's lead and ordered jet airliners. And Boeing was back in the airliner business – this time to stay.

The first 707 to be produced was the 120 series, a US domestic version intended for non-stop coast-to-coast services. It had a wing span of 130 ft 10 in. (39,88 m), a length of 144 ft 6 in. (44,04 m) and a maximum take-off weight of 257,000 lb (116 575 kg). Power was provided by four Pratt & Whitney JT3C turbo-jets, each giving 13,500 lb (6124 kg) of thrust. It cruised at between 550 and 600 mph (885 and 966 km/hr) at 30,000 to 35,000 ft (9144 to 10 668 m) and it had a range of 3217 miles (5177 km).

Although BOAC was first to introduce jet airliners on the trans-Atlantic route when it started de Havilland Comet 4 services between London and New York on 4 October 1958, Pan American followed soon after with its first service with a Boeing 707-120 from New York to Paris on 26 October 1958. These early services were of an interim nature, requiring one refuelling stop

Pan American introduced its first Boeing 707-121s on trans-Atlantic services in 1958 at the start of the jet age for long-distance air travellers. (Pan American)

on the way, but the higher cruising speed of these jet airliners reduced the westbound journey time to around 9½ hours and the services paved the way for the eventual non-stop flights of the extended-range 707-320 (Pratt & Whitney powered) and 707-420 (Rolls-Royce powered) which took over the route in October 1959 (Pan American) and May 1960 (BOAC), respectively.

The 707-320 Intercontinental was the main production version. It had a wing span of 142 ft 5 in. (43,41 m), a length of 152 ft 11 in, (46,61 m) and a maximum take-off weight of 317,000 lb (143 790 kg). Power was provided by four 15,800 lb (7167 kg) thrust Pratt & Whitney JT4A turbo-jets which gave it a cruising speed of between 550 and 600 mph (885 and 966 km/hr) at 30,000 to 35,000 ft (9144 to 10 668 m) and its range was 4235 miles (6815 km). The 707-420 was similar but was powered by four 17,500 lb (7938 kg) thrust Rolls-Royce Conway by-pass engines (an early version of the turbo-fan). The later production versions, the 707-320B and 707-320C were powered by four 18,000 lb (8165 kg) thrust Pratt & Whitney JT3D turbo-fans and had an increased wing span of 145 ft 9 in. (44,42 m), a higher maximum take-off weight of 336,000 lb (152 410 kg) and an increased range (707-320B) of 6160 miles (9913 km). The flight crew on trans-Atlantic services was four, comprising captain, first officer, flight engineer and navigator.

Tourist/Economy class had been introduced by the time the 707 arrived, so the aircraft's passenger cabin was designed to suit the new way of life, with a row of small, closely-spaced windows down each side, ensuring that every economy-class seat row was adjacent to at least one window, and a cabin width to accept six-abreast seating (a triple seat on each side of a central aisle). Generally, the aircraft were operated in a mixed-class configuration from the start with, typically, a small first-class compartment (seating about 20 passengers arranged four abreast at 40 in (102 cm) pitch) at the front, and a large economy-class compartment (seating about 125 passengers arranged six abreast at 34 in. (86 cm) pitch). The usual cabin crew was five who, depending on the airline, could be stewardesses or stewards or a mixture of both.

The combination of economy-class fares and fast big jets (the Boeing 707, Douglas DC-8 and the British Super VC 10) resulted in a considerable increase in the number of passengers crossing the Atlantic (and travelling elsewhere). The non-stop flights had reduced the journey time between Europe and New York to about 8 hours and the time passed easier with the help of in-flight movies, first introduced by TWA in 1961 and quickly followed by most other airlines.

By the mid-1960s these so-called big-jets were showing signs of not being big enough. The forecast of the growth of air traffic indicated a 12 per cent annual increase and to meet future demand bigger aircraft would be required on long-range routes instead of continuing to add to the number of existing aircraft, which would lead to congestion of airways and airports. Both Boeing and Douglas tried to enlarge their existing aircraft, and Douglas introduced a 250-seat version of its DC-8. The design of the 707 did not lend itself to a simple 'stretching' operation and therefore Boeing took the major step and went for the really big one.

During the early 1960s Boeing, Douglas and Lockheed participated in a US Air Force design competition for a very big transport aircraft, twice the size of existing transports and equipped with engines giving twice the power of the then current turbo-fans. This gave the aircraft and engine manufacturers the incentive to think big and evolve technology to meet the new challenge. Lockheed won the competition with its C-5A Galaxy powered by General Electric big-fan engines, but that turned out to be a good day for long-distance air travellers because all the effort expended by Boeing designers and engineers on the military transport project was then utilised in the design of a very big airliner, the mighty 747.

One of the initial designs of the **Boeing 747** featured a mid-wing and a double-deck fuselage with a width not much greater than that of the 707. However, airline reaction was not favourable from an emergency-evacuation viewpoint, and the design was finalised around a low-wing aircraft and a fuselage with a single main deck much wider than that of the 707 – in fact, 20 ft (6,10 m) wide providing for up to 10-abreast seating, arranged 3 x 4 x 3 with two aisles – the first of the wide-bodied airliners. In this arrangement, up to 500 passengers could be carried in a high density layout (10-abreast, all economy class) and the lower part of the fuselage provided large holds for cargo as well as the usual baggage and mail. To meet the requirement for a freighter version, the flight deck was located on a level above the main deck so that the front of the fuselage could be hinged upwards to provide easy access to the main deck; the 20 ft (6,10 m) fuselage width also suited this requirement, allowing two 8 ft (2,44 m) wide containers to be accommodated side-by-side along the main length of the fuselage. Fairing the lofty flight deck into the top of the fuselage, to give the 747 a distinctive hump on top, left a compartment behind it which Boeing advertised as an upstairs lounge in the passenger-carrying versions and linked it to the main deck by a spiral staircase, similar to that of the Stratocruiser.

The other dimensions of the 747 were to be equally impressive. It was to have a wing span of 195 ft 8 in. (59,64 m), a length of 231 ft 4 in. (70,51 m) and a maximum take-off weight of 680,000 lb (308 448 kg). Power was to be provided by four of the new 41,000 lb (18 597 kg) thrust Pratt & Whitney JT9D-1 big fan engines which would give the aircraft a cruising speed of 600 mph (966 km/hr) at an altitude of 30,000 - 40,000 ft (9144 - 12 192 m) and it would have a range to match that of contemporary long-range jet airliners which could fly non-stop from Europe to the US west coast.

In April 1966 Pan American placed an incredible order for 25 of these very big airliners at a cost of $20 million each. As with the airline's pioneering order for 707s eleven years earlier, other airlines soon followed its lead. In July 1966, William M. Allen, president of Boeing, announced that the board of the company had decided to go ahead with the development and production of the 747.

At the time of the go-ahead announcement, a Boeing advertisement described the 747 as "Ushering in a new era in jet transportation. For passengers - an entirely new concept in air travel comfort and spaciousness. For airlines - the fastest, quietest, most profitable airliner in commercial aviation history".

Construction

Following the go-ahead to produce the 747 in July 1966, Boeing was faced with the gigantic task of not only building the world's largest airliner but also producing sufficient 747s in a short period of time to satisfy the demand from the numerous airlines (particularly those on the trans-Atlantic route) who could see the competitive threat of the order from pacemaking Pan American and had to order some 747s of their own. In 1966 the orders totalled 88 from 11 airlines, and the mighty airliner was still at the drawing-board stage. Programme target dates were: late 1968 for completion of the first aircraft; September 1969 for first deliveries to airlines; and December 1972 for the delivery of the 200th aircraft.

From 1966 onwards there was intense activity in the State of Washington, located in the north-west corner of the United States. This had been the home of The Boeing Company since 1916 when William Edward Boeing started building small biplanes at Seattle. Expansion of facilities through the ensuing years included an additional factory at nearby Renton and another at Wichita in Kansas, but with these extensive facilities busy producing Boeing 707s, 727s and 737s a new factory had to be built to mass produce the huge 747s. The site chosen was close to the city of Everett, nearly 30 miles (48km) north of Seattle and alongside Snohomish County Airport, which is usually referred to by its earlier name of Paine Field. Preparation of the 780 acre (316 hectare) site began in June 1966 and the construction of the buildings started in the late summer of that year.

To assemble the world's largest airliners Boeing had to build the world's largest building (in terms of volume), a structure containing approximately 200 million cubic feet (5,6 million cubic metres) and covering about 43 acres (18 hectares). This main building was divided into three vast bays, each 1000 ft (305 m) long, 300 ft (92 m) wide and 115 ft (35 m) high. One bay housed the sub-assembly areas for the wings and sections of the fuselage, and the other two bays each housed a final assembly line with stations for four complete aircraft and an area at the start of the line for wing-to-centre section (wing stub) joining and wings-to-centre fuselage mating. The bays were linked and served by eleven 30-ton (27-tonne) capacity overhead cranes which are used to transfer the sub-assemblies through various stages of build-up and eventually carry the completed sub-assemblies to the start of one of the final assembly lines.

The first Boeing manufacturing personnel began work at the $200 million Everett factory in January 1967, and the buildings were occupied in stages throughout the year as each was completed. The main assembly building became activated in May 1967, and the actual assembly of components into sub-assemblies for the first 747 began in September of that year.

Although Boeing designers had considerable experience with big jet aircraft, like the B-52 bomber and 707, they still had problems with this project, their biggest yet. Their main problem was the unexpected increases in the weights of the structure and systems which caused the maximum take-off weight of the aircraft to go way above the planned 680,000 lb (308 450 kg). A severe weight-reduction programme was conducted in all areas and eventually the gross weight was held at 710,000 lb (322 055 kg). However, this increase meant that more power would be required from the engines if the 747 was to meet its promised performance specifications and therefore Pratt & Whitney was called on to condense the JT9D development programme and make available the more powerful JT9D-3 of 43,500 lb (19 730 kg) thrust for the first production aircraft.

One of the features of the 747 programme was that it had one of the largest sub-contracting arrangements in the history of commercial aircraft manufacturing up to that time. With no government funds for this programme, which was estimated to require an investment of $1 billion by the time the first 747s were delivered, Boeing arranged a work and cost/profit sharing agreement with some other American aircraft manufacturers. In this way, Northrop made the components for the main fuselage sections at

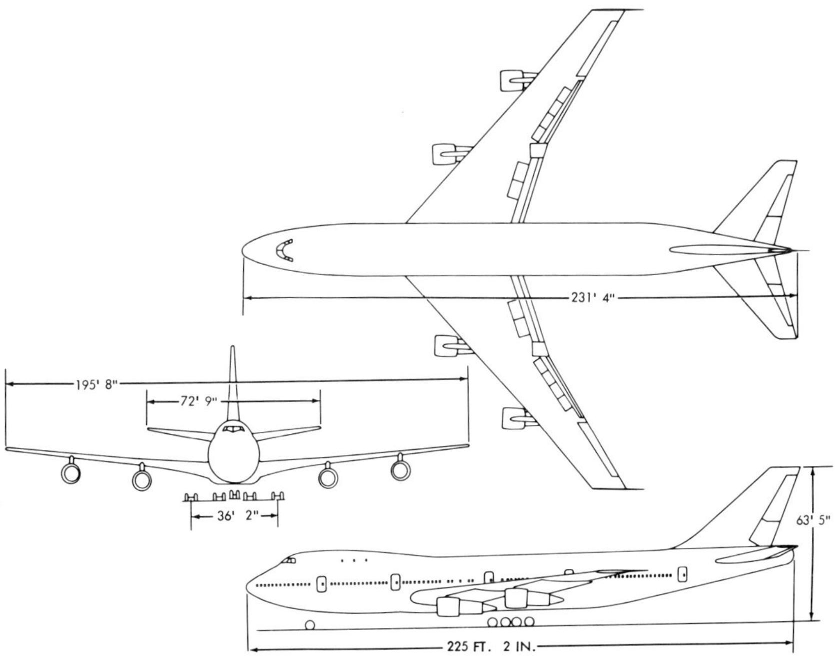

Hawthorne, California, and sent them by rail to Everett for assembly, a spur from the local railway line actually extending into the end of the main assembly building so that the components are unloaded inside it. Vought Systems Division of LTV (formerly Ling-Temco-Vought) made the rear fuselage, tailplane (horizontal stabiliser) and fin and rudder at Dallas, Texas; Rockwell International (formerly North American Rockwell) built the lower section of the centre fuselage and the fixed leading edges of the wings at Tulsa, Oklahoma; Fairchild Republic (formerly Fairchild Hiller) made the leading-edge and trailing-edge wing flaps, and the ailerons and spoilers, at Farmingdale, New York; Rhor Industries built the engine pods and pylons at Chula Vista, California; and Aeronca made the flap-track ('canoe') fairings at Middleton, Ohio, and its Aerocal Division made wing-box ribs at Torrance, California. In addition, the twin-wheel nose landing gear and the four-leg, 16-wheel main landing gear was supplied by Cleveland Pneumatic of Cleveland, Ohio, and the Pratt & Whitney engines came from East Hartford, Connecticut. (Later, engines also came from General Electric at Cincinnati, Ohio, and Rolls-Royce at Derby, England.)

These companies were the major sub-contractors at the start of the 747 programme, but there were also approximately 1500 primary suppliers and some 15,000 secondary suppliers located in most of the states of the USA and eight foreign countries. In fact, more than half of each 747 by weight and dollar value was sub-contracted to outside firms. These sub-contracted items were made to Boeing's engineering specifications and quality standards, and were delivered to Everett by rail, road or air for assembly into complete aircraft.

About 4½ million parts (including small items like fasteners) are required to make one 747, and, with many of the big components coming from all over the country, the major task is getting them all together at the right time at Everett, so the entire operation is monitored by computer. It takes approximately 21 months to build a 747 from scratch, but only the last two months of this time are spent of the final assembly line. Much of the system and component installation work is done at the sub-assembly stage so that major sub-assemblies are almost complete by the time they are brought together on the final assembly line, a technique developed by Boeing when mass-producing bombers in wartime.

Apart from the assembly of the major sub-assemblies from components made elsewhere, and the final assembly of the complete aircraft, Boeing's share of the 747 programme includes the manufacture of components for the main structural part of the wing (the wing box) and the nose section of the fuselage. Another new factory was built at Auburn (about 20 miles (32 km) south of Seattle) to serve as a machine shop and fabricating plant for the Boeing part of the programme. Among the components manufactured there are the huge panels which go to make up the top and bottom skins of the wing box. These panels are machined from solid billets of aluminium, the largest being over 100 ft (30 m) long, 5 ft (1,5 m) wide and 1 in. (2,54 cm) thick. Numerical-tape-controlled milling machines remove the unwanted metal, whittling away over two-thirds of it, to produce a tapered and shaped panel. These, together with other lengthy items like spars and stringers, are delivered to Everett on special road vehicles. Auburn also made many of the specialised machines, precision tools and assembly jigs for the programme, including the massive wing-assembly jigs for use at Everett. The structural componenets for the nose section of the 747s are made at Boeing's factory at Wichita, Kansas, and are delivered by rail to Everett.

The components for the nose section of the first 747, comprising frames, stringers and skin panels, arrived at Everett towards the end of 1967 and went into assembly jigs which had been made earlier at Wichita. These components were then riveted together to form the nose sub-assembly (referred to in the factory as Section 41). The components for the 20 ft (6 m) diameter main fuselage, made by Northrop, are assembled in jigs in a similar manner, but for ease of handling are built initially in 'small' sub-assemblies: Section 42, between the nose and the wing; Section 44, the centre section over the wing; Section 46, between the wing and the tail; and Section 48, the tail section. Before being taken by overhead crane to one of the final assembly lines, Sections 41 and 42 are bolted together to form the forward body, and Sections 46 and 48 are bolted together to form the aft body.

Left-hand and right-hand wing boxes are built up separately, from the machined panels, spars, ribs and stringers, in assembly jigs located in the sub-assembly bay of the main assembly building. When completed, each of these is 120 ft (37 m) long, with a width of nearly 20 ft (6 m) and a thickness of 7 ft (2 m) at its root end, and weighs 28,000 lb (12 700 kg). After assembly, the wing boxes are removed from the jigs by overhead crane for transfer to a clean, seal and paint shop, which is an extension of the main assembly

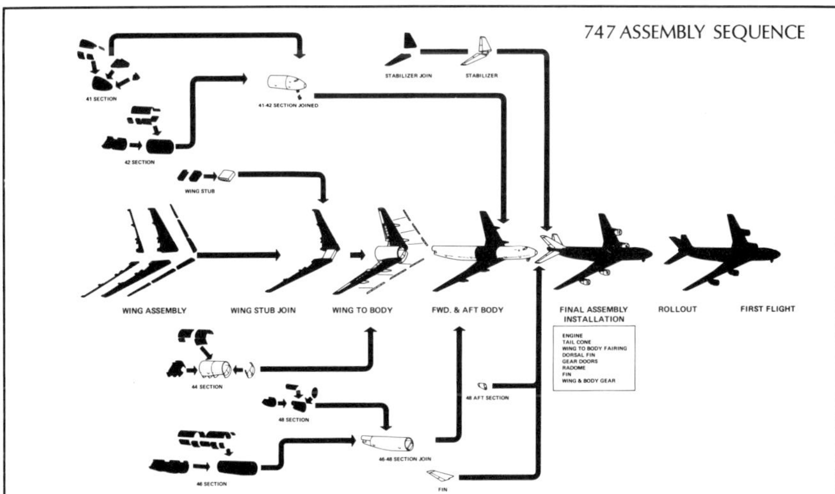

building. Here, the interior of the wing boxes are washed out and sealed to form the integral fuel tanks; there are three tanks in each wing box which, together with a tank formed in the centre section (wing stub), provided early aircraft with a total capacity of 47,210 US gal (178 709 l) of fuel. The exterior of the wing boxes, which are machined surfaces, are also painted here to protect them from corrosion. The wing boxes are then returned to the sub-assembly bay to have the leading-edge and trailing-edge fixed structure added before being transferred to the start of one of the final assembly lines where the left-hand and right-hand wings are joined to the centre section (wing stub) to form a complete wing assembly. The four pylons, which will carry the engines, are fitted to the leading edges of the wings at this stage.

At the next stage, the first of the fuselage (or body) sub-assemblies (Section 44) is lowered on to the wing and bolted in position. Also at this stage, the leading-edge flaps, spoilers (air brakes) and ailerons are fitted to the wings.

A 747 really begins to take on a recognisable form at the next station along the final assembly line, where the forward and aft body sub-assemblies (Sections 41 and 42, and Sections 46 and 48, respectively) are brought in to be joined to the front and rear of the centre body. From here onwards the sheer size of everything becomes really apparent, with only the Boeing personnel remaining normal size.

The start of the final assembly line, where left- and right-hand wings are joined to the wing stub and mated with the centre body. *(Boeing)*

The forward and aft body sub-assemblies being lowered into position where they will be bolted to the centre body. *(Boeing)*

The main structure is completed when the tailplane and elevators (horizontal stabiliser) and the fin and rudder are fitted. The tailplane is of the variable-incidence type (with its angle adjustable for trimming the aircraft's pitch) and it has a span only 15 in. (38 cm) less than the wing span of the Boeing 247. The 747s are not painted until after assembly and roll-out but the rudder has to be painted before this because it must be close to its final weight when it is balanced before being fitted to the fin. The triple-slotted trailing-edge flaps are now fitted to the wings, followed by the eight big glass-fibre 'canoe' fairings to cover the flap operating mechanisms.

Also fitted at this stage is the two-wheel nose landing gear and the unique four-leg main landing gear, so that from now on the aircraft can be moved on its own wheels. The inboard legs of the main landing gear are mounted in the fuselage and the outboard legs are mounted in the wings, and all four legs are fitted with a four-wheel bogie (truck) to spread the weight of the aircraft. The inboard bogies are steerable to prevent tyre 'scrubbing' on sharp turns.

Although the aircraft now looks almost complete there is a lot of equipment to install inside and the remaining parts to be fitted to the outside so it is now moved to the first of three 'fitting out' stations on the final assembly line. Here, the electrical, hydraulic and cabin air conditioning and pressurisation systems are completed; the under-floor cargo holds are fitted with handling systems for the cargo and baggage containers; and the passenger cabin is provided with galleys, toilets, wall and ceiling panels, and the 1001 other items to prepare it for human habitation, although the airlines often fit their own

The original 747 flight deck with accommodation for a crew of three: Captain (left), first officer and flight engineer (right). *(Boeing)*

carpets and seats after the aircraft has been delivered. Externally there are the four main engines to install, each weighing nearly 4 tons (3,6 tonnes), and the auxiliary power unit (APU), a 1100 hp gas turbine, in the rear of the fuselage, which supplies electrical power while the aircraft is on the ground as well as an air supply of cabin air conditioning and for starting the main engines. There are also the finishing touches to be made to the airframe, including the weather radar and its radome in the nose, the tail cone over the APU, and the landing gear doors. Some big items to be fitted at this stage are the wing-to-body fairings, which are 80 ft (24 m) long and made in sections from glass-fibre honeycombe material, and the wing tips, which are 14 ft (4,25 m) long, 2 ft (0,6 m) wide and 16 in. (40,6 cm) thick, and are made from aluminium/glass-fibre honeycomb sandwich so that they weigh only 38 lb (17 kg) each.

The flight deck is also completed at this stage, with its flying controls, control panels, instruments and avionics equipment. The flight deck on the 747 is surprisingly small for such a large aircraft but it was designed for a crew of three (captain, first officer and flight engineer), the navigator carried aboard earlier long-range jet airliners having been displaced by the inertial navigation system (INS). Adapted from a navigation system developed for the Apollo moon flights and nuclear-powered submarines, the INS is completely independent of ground aids and is highly accurate. By means of push-buttons, the pilots can insert into the equipment the latitude and longitude of the flight's terminal points and up to eight way-points (for en-route course changes). The INS is linked to the autopilot, and in flight the pilots monitor a

A general view of the final assembly line showing three aircraft in the 'fitting out' stations for installation of equipment and systems. *(Boeing)*

display showing present position, ground speed, heading, distance and time to the next way-point or the destination, and other navigational data. Two INS sets are fitted as standard and a third set can be fitted as a stand-by which can take over should one or both of the primary sets ever fail. (With the coming of the 747-400 the flight crew will be reduced to two, the flight engineer's systems panel being replaced by cathode ray tubes (CRTs) located in front of the two pilots. Further details are given later in the Variants section.)

On the 747, the primary flying controls consist of an inboard and outboard aileron on each side, a two-section elevator on each side of a variable-incidence tailplane, and a two-section rudder, all of which are power actuated from four hydraulic systems so arranged that each of the three attitude axes (roll, pitch and yaw) is powered by all four systems. These systems also provide hydraulic pressure for landing gear and wing flap actuation, spoiler deployment, wheel brake operation, and nose gear and body gear steering. The electrical system has a similar reserve of power, with four generators driven by the main engines in flight or two generators on the auxiliary power unit (APU) providing power when the aircraft is on the ground.

An unusual item of equipment which could be fitted to early 747s as an option was a satellite communications (SATCOM) aerial, located beneath a small fairing at the rear of the upper-deck 'hump' on the top of the fuselage, which could be used to relay radio messages via satellites. (Although the fairing can be seen in photographs of early 747s, the system did not go into general use and the fairings were eventually removed although a very much larger version can be seen on a few later aircraft and a new system is to be introduced for 747-400s, as described later in the Variants section.) Otherwise the 747s were equipped with all the latest avionics and instrumentation as befits a modern airliner, and the automatic flight control system provided for automatic landings to Category II as a basic and Category IIIA as an option.

When the aircraft is completed, the doors at the end of the final assembly line are opened and the great moment of the roll-out occurs. But the aircraft's first flight is still some way off because once outside there are tests to be made on the systems, including cabin pressurisation. Then the brand new, but bare, 747 is towed over a 60 ft (18 m) wide bridge (spanning a highway) to another part of the site alongside the airport where the paint hangar and pre-flight area are located.

Painting an aircraft the size of a 747 is no small undertaking and a special building was constructed for this purpose, fully equipped with track-mounted spray-gun platforms and overhead heaters to provide controlled drying conditions. The quantity of paint required for one 747 can be quite staggering, especially if the aircraft has a 'white top'. For example, a Pan American 747 in its original colour scheme required a total of 76 gallons (288 l) - 68 gal (257 l) of white, 7 gal (26 l) of blue for the cheat line and symbol on the tail, and 1 gal (3,8 l) of black for the titling (plus 1 pint (0,5 l) of red for the stripes in the US flag on the top of the fin).

Having received its glamour treatment, the aircraft is towed to the flight line where its tanks are filled with fuel; fuelling is through two valves located beneath the leading edge of each wing, between the engines, which allow fuel to be pumped aboard at a rate of 2000 gal (7570 l) per minute. Then come the engine tests and further system checks, and finally a visit to the compass-swinging bay where the aircraft is parked on an air-bearing turntable and rotated slowly by a small tractor while the aircraft's compass system is calibrated.

Now the aircraft is ready for its test flights, first by the Boeing test crew and then by the crew who will accept the aircraft on behalf of the airline.

For the ceremonial roll-out of 747 No. 1 on 30 September 1968, Boeing cheated a little by painting the aircraft earlier and returning it to the end of the final assembly line so that invited guests and the world's press did not see a bare aircraft emerging from the main assembly building on that great day but, instead, the world's largest airliner in all its glory, with a white top, red cheat line and fin flash, and blue "Boeing 747" titling, with the appropriate registration N7470. And painted on each side of the nose were the badges of the 27 airlines who had ordered between them 158 of the aircraft. In order of appearance, these airlines were: Pan American (25), Lufthansa (6), Japan Air Lines (6), BOAC (11), TWA (12), Air France (4), Continental Air Lines (3), American Airlines (10), Northwest Orient Airlines (15), United Air Lines (18), Alitalia (4), World Airways (3), Aer Lingus (2), National Airlines (2), KLM (3), Air India (4), Eastern Airlines (4), Delta Air Lines (3), Qantas (4), Swissair (2), Scandinavian Airlines System (2), Braniff International Airways

Inside the paint hangar where the 747s receive their glamour treatment from painters on track-mounted spray-gun platforms. *(Boeing)*

(2), El Al (2), Air Canada (3), South African Airways (3), Iberia (3), and Sabena (2).

The roll-out of 747 No. 1 was actually a day ahead of schedule, as planned at the start of the programme, but the preparations required for its first flight (including the installation of all the test instrumentation and automatic flight recorder equipment, as well as the usual engine and systems checks) took rather longer than anticipated so that the planned first-flight date of 17 December 1968 (the 65th Anniversary of the Wright Brothers' first flight) slipped a little. This was unfortunate from an historical point of view because of the significance of the date but such a happening is not unknown in the aircraft manufacturing world and only Boeing's pride was hurt when the new Queen of the Sky was a little late for her debut.

After the usual high-speed taxi runs along the runway, 747 No. 1 took to the air for the first time from Snohomish County Airport/Paine Field on 9 February 1969 in the hands of Jack Waddell, Boeing's senior experimental test pilot, with Brien Wygle, assistant director of flight operations, as co-pilot, and Jess Wallick, as flight engineer. The flight lasted over an hour but was cut short because of a slight problem with the trailing-edge flaps, and the landing gear was not retracted. However, the second flight was trouble-free and the landing gear was retracted so that the aircraft flew in its proper 'cleaned-up' state for the first time to show off its sleek lines. After a few more flights to get to know the handling characteristics of the huge aircraft, No. 1 was flown to Boeing Field, Seattle, the home of Boeing's flight test centre.

Then followed a year of intensive flight testing, with four other 747s joining No. 1 at Boeing Field. No. 2, rolled out on 28 February 1969, was the first to be painted in an airline's colours, the much photographed and appropriately registered N747PA *Clipper America* for Pan American, or rather Pan Am because the world-famous airline introduced its abbreviated title on this aircraft (to be strictly accurate, N747PA and other Pan Am 747s rolled out during this period had a "Jet Clipper" prefix to their names, like the airline's Boeing 707s, but the "Jet" part of the prefix was soon dropped). No. 4, N731PA for Pan Am, was next to be rolled out, on 23 April 1969, but carried "Boeing 747" titles and became the first 747 to be seen abroad when it appeared at the Paris Air Show on 3 June 1969 after flying the 5160 miles (8304 km) from Seattle non-stop in just over 9 hours – a few days earlier it had made a 10 hour endurance test by flying Seattle - New York - Seattle non-stop to check its specific range. At the Paris Air Show it was parked alongside Concorde No. 1, the first of the Anglo-French supersonic airliners, which gave visitors to the show food for thought as to which way air travel was heading.

The flight-test quintet was completed by No. 5, N93101 for TWA, which was rolled out on 8 May 1969, and No. 3, N732PA for Pan Am, which was late in appearing, on 16 May 1969, because it was specially fitted with a 32 ft (9,75 m) long aluminium boom on its nose for gust measuring and was equipped with special instrumentation to measure flight loads during excessive manoeuvres as part of the structure verification programme.

The official roll-out ceremony for 747 No. 1 on 30 September 1968, with the aircraft decorated with the badges of 27 customer airlines. *(Boeing)*

Also built during this period were two 747s that would never fly but would play a vital role in the non-flying part of the structure verification programme. This part of the programme consisted of static testing, to determine the strength of the aircraft's structure, and fatigue testing to check the fatigue life of the structure.

For the year-long static test, a structurally-complete airframe was located in an extension of the main assembly building at Everett in March 1969 and every part that would be subjected to loads in flight had simulated flight loads applied to it by hydraulic jacks, with the results being measured by strain gauges. Initially, these were proof load tests to satisfy the Federal Aviation Administration (FAA) that the 747 was safe for commercial service, and were a necessary part of the certification programme. After these were successfully completed, the tests were continued from where the proof tests left off to find the ultimate load. The 747 had been designed to have a structural strength at least 50% above proof-test level and therefore loads one and a half times greater than in the proof tests were applied, with similarly successful results. Finally came the test to destruction, which would determine the total strength of the aircraft and indicate the growth potential of the basic design, forming the basis for future increases in the maximum take-off weight to enable more payload to be carried or more fuel for greater range. The almighty bang that ended the static test came in February 1970 when, with its tail sawn off and its wing tips deflected upward 26 ft (7,92 m), so that it looked more like a butterfly than a Boeing airliner, the 747's wing was strained beyond endurance and structural failure occurred – at 116% of the design ultimate load of the aircraft.

The two-year fatigue test was also started in 1969 when another structurally complete airframe was installed in a steel framework on a 3 ft (0,9 m) thick concrete apron outside the main assembly building adjacent to the static test section. The aim of this programme was to duplicate the stresses experienced in day-to-day airline flying to make certain that no undetected metal fatigue would be encountered in the service life of the aircraft. The programme took the airframe through the equivalent of 20,000 airline flights, representing 60,000 flying hours or a 20-year life. With sophisticated test equipment, each 'flight' made by the fatigue-test airframe – comprising taxying, take-off, climb (with cabin pressurisation), cruise, descent (with cabin de-pressurisation, landing and taxying – could be achieved in about 10 minutes. Instead of being in a water tank, to prevent an explosive failure should any part of the pressurised cabin fail under test, the fuselage was practically filled with plastic granules, with passages left to provide access for inspection of the structure. This lengthy programme continued long after the first 747s entered service in January 1970, with the fatigue-test airframe accumulating 'flying hours' well ahead of any 747 in service, and was successfully concluded in September 1971. After this, the fatigue-test airframe was subjected to a programme of fail-safe testing, where primary structure was intentionally cracked or sawn through in 28 critical places, putting the equivalent of 12,000 additional hours in airline flights on the structure to make sure it would continue to operate safely even after being damaged. Changes found necessary from the results of these tests were incorporated in new production aircraft.

Apart from the flight and structure tests, the FAA also required other tests to be conducted on the 747, including proof that the emergency evacuation procedure would enable 500 passengers to escape from the aircraft in the event of an emergency. For this purpose, the 747 has 10 double-width doors (five on each side of the main deck), plus (on early aircraft a single door on the right-hand side of the upper deck, all equipped with inflatable slides. For the purpose of the evacuation tests, all the windows of the 747 were covered, only emergency (battery) lighting was used in the passenger cabin, and only half of the main doors were used. The 'passengers', volunteers of all ages, some of whom had never flown, were given the usual pre-flight description of the emergency equipment and exits by a normal cabin staff of 13 stewardesses who, when the order was given to evacuate the aircraft, directed the passengers to the available exits. Several of these tests were made, using different people each time, and the results proved that 500 people could be evacuated from a 747 in 90 seconds.

The 747 was certificated for commercial service on 30 December 1969. During the 10-month Boeing and FAA flight test programme the five 747s which had taken part had logged more than 1400 flying hours. Four of these aircraft were returned to Everett for refurbishing prior to delivery to their

The flight-test quintet at Boeing Field in 1969, with 747 No. 3 in the foreground equipped with a gust-measuring boom. *(Boeing)*

respective airlines (Pan Am or TWA), while 747 No. 1 remained in flight test status with Boeing ready to test new equipment as part of the development programme for the 747.

Service

Big changes have occurred in the airline world since the first Boeing 747 was rolled out of the factory in 1968. At that time, offering as it did twice the capacity of the existing Boeing 707s and Douglas DC-8s, it appeared suitable only for the most popular routes such as trans-Atlantic, trans-Pacific and the major US domestic trunks, but through the years air traffic has grown to such an extent that on some routes the 747 is now only just big enough even with extra seating installed.

The First Year

In 1970, the trans-Atlantic was the Blue Ribbon route in need of long-haul aircraft with additional capacity and it was therefore on the New York -London route that Pan Am launched its first 747 commercial service on 22 January. During the year that followed, Pan Am took delivery of 25 747s, introducing them on other trans-Atlantic services including New York to Amsterdam, Barcelona, Brussels, Frankfurt, Lisbon, Paris and Rome, plus Chicago to London and Frankfurt, Washington and Boston to London, and the polar route from Los Angeles and San Francisco to London and Paris. In addition, as more aircraft were delivered they were introduced on trans-Pacific services from Los Angeles and San Francisco to Honolulu, Tokyo and Hong Kong, and the service from New York to San Juan, Puerto Rico.

The second airline to start 747 services was TWA who got in a 'first' by introducing the aircraft initially on the coast-to-coast route between Los Angeles and New York in February 1970. The airline operated its first trans-Atlantic 747 service in March from New York to London. By the end of the first year, TWA had 14 747s and services had been extended to Paris, Rome and Madrid.

American Airlines also started its 747 services on the coast-to-coast New York to Los Angeles route and managed to make an early start, in March 1970, by leasing two aircraft from Pan Am. The first of the airline's own 747s were delivered in mid-1970, and by the end of the first year there were 10 in service.

The first foreign airline to start 747 services was Lufthansa, who introduced its aircraft on the Frankfurt - New York route in April 1970. These were joined over the Atlantic in June by Air France 747s on the Paris - New York route and Alitalia 747s on the Rome-New York route.

Following Pan Am's lead with trans-Pacific 747 services between Los Angeles and Honolulu in April 1970, Continental followed on the same route in June. Japan Air Lines also started its 747 operations over the Pacific in June, initially on the Tokyo-Honolulu route and extending this shortly afterwards to Los Angeles.

Northwest Orient started 747 operation on its Minneapolis/St Paul - New York route but in July 1970 began a daily service on the New York - Chicago -Seattle - Tokyo route. The following month 747s took over the Minneapolis/St Paul - San Francisco - Honolulu - Tokyo route, which was extended to Taipei (Taiwan) and Hong Kong in September. By the end of the 747's first year of service the airline had 10 747s in service.

The final airline to introduce 747s over the Pacific in the summer of 1970 was United, who made a start on the San Francisco - Honolulu route and later extended services to US domestic routes, including coast-to-coast. United had nine 747s in service by the end of the first year.

Two other US domestic operators started 747 operations in October 1970; National on its Miami - New York and Miami - Los Angeles routes, and Delta on its Atlanta - Dallas - Los Angeles route.

To round off the 747's introductory year, Iberia started services on its Madrid - New York route in December 1970, Eastern leased three of Pan Am's 747s during that winter and introduced them on its New York - San Juan, and New York and Chicago - Miami, routes in January 1971, and Braniff started a daily service on its Dallas/Fort Worth - Honolulu route on 15 January 1971 with 747 No. 100, the original Big Orange but advertised at that time as "747 Braniff Place, the Most Exclusive Address in the Sky".

Although Aer Lingus, BOAC, KLM and Sabena took delivery of some of their 747s during the year they did not start operating them until after the 747's first year of service was over.

Production of the 747 had been building up during the second half of 1969 and, although a problem with the installation of the Pratt & Whitney JT9D engines resulted in some aircraft being rolled out of the factory without engines, once the supply of modified engines started arriving at Everett the backlog of completed aircraft awaiting engines was soon cleared. And with production reaching its peak rate in March 1970, when a 747 was being rolled out every three working days, the deliveries to airlines reached impressive figures in double-quick time, so that by the end of the 747's first year of commercial service over 100 747s had been delivered to 18 airlines.

Teething troubles are not uncommon during the introductory phase of a new airliner, especially one powered by a new type of engine. The JT9D engines were troublesome during that first year of 747 operations but the problems were soon diagnosed and modifications introduced. There were also problems with the airframe, especially with some of the new equipment in the passenger cabin, but again modification action reduced the problems in later production aircraft and earlier aircraft were modified to the new standard.

For all its early faults, the 747 lost no time in becoming established on the major long-haul air routes of the world and, in the process, made a giant leap for air transport. In January 1971, Boeing was able to announce that in the first year 747s had carried 6 million passengers, had flown 72 million revenue miles and 15½ billion passenger miles, and the number of arrivals/ departures averaged 2900 a week.

The 1st class section in zone A and part of zone B of an early Alitalia 747, with the spiral staircase to the upstairs lounge in the centre. *(Alitalia)*

Passenger Accommodation

Although the 747 had been described as a 500-seater, the aircraft which entered service in 1970 had seating for only 350 or so passengers in a two-class arrangement of 1st and economy (or coach on US domestic routes). Even this was twice the number carried on existing long-haul jet airliners but the aircraft's passenger cabin was totally different from the 'open plan' style of most earlier jet airliners. The 185 ft (56,4 m) long cabin had a flat ceiling over 8 ft (2,4 m) high spanning the 20 ft (6,1 m) width between near-vertical walls. A clear area was required at each of the 10 doors, for emergency evacuation purposes, and these conveniently divided the cabin into five zones, lettered A to E from the nose. The breakdown of the interior into separate compartments was completed by locating galleys and groups of toilets in the centre of the cabin at each door location.

A unique feature of the 747 is that, because the flight deck is located on a level above the main deck, the passenger cabin extends right into the nose of the aircraft. This is the quietest part of the cabin and was therefore selected by scheduled airlines for the 1st-class compartment. Up to 24 passengers can be seated in zone A, which has double seats along each side at 40 in. (101,6 cm) pitch, and the spiral staircase to the upper deck is located in the centre of the cabin at the rear of the zone. A galley for serving 1st-class passenger meals is usually located immediately behind the spiral staircase so that cabin dividers can be fitted at this point to make zone A a separate 1st-class compartment, or the compartment can be extended to include part or the whole of zone B with the cabin dividers at the second door location. The Pan Am and TWA 747s, for example, had a further 34 1st-class passengers in zone B, making a total of 58.

Economy-class passengers in zones C, D and E had seating arrangements during that introductory year which were far more spacious than they had ever had on the earlier jet airliners. With nine-abreast seating (arranged 3 x 4 x 2) with two aisles, there was space to accommodate seats which were 2 in. (5 cm) wider and had wider armrests than those used previously. And the two wide aisles provided passengers with an easier access to the toilets, especially during one of the numerous trolley delivery services, such as drinks, meals on wheels or duty-free goods. There never seem to be enough toilets on an aircraft, especially at 'wakey-wakey' time after an over-night long-haul flight but at least on the 747s they were more numerous, the total depending on the airline but generally between 12 and 14, so that queues for them were not so long.

The three economy-class zones on TWA 747s had seating for 284 passengers, with 92 in zone C, 78 in zone D and 114 in zone E. To simplify seat-finding during boarding all the zones were colour-coded – gold for 1st class (zones A and B) and blue, red and green for zones C, D and E, respectively, and the passengers were given a boarding pass which was of the appropriate colour as well as bearing the seat row number and actual seat number.

Serving meals to so many passengers could have been a major problem but, by locating six or so galleys at strategic points throughout the cabin and having two aisles for the trolleys (or carts as some airlines call them) the cabin service was generally better. The number of cabin staff varied between airlines and routes but was generally around 15, who performed their duties under the watchful eye of a cabin services manager or someone with similar rank but different title, like Air France's chef de cabine.

The zoned passenger cabin of the 747 could have been designed especially for in-flight entertainment, with the rear walls of the dividing galleys and toilet groups serving as ideal locations for film screens, which are twice the size of those in earlier aircraft. Each zone is equipped with its own screen and in TWA 747s (and later those of some other airlines) a choice of film (or movie) was available, one for general audiences (suitable for children) being shown in some zones and a 'mature movie' in other zones, the selection being made at check-in time. The soundtrack is heard through headphones so that passengers not wishing to watch the film can read or doze undisturbed; the headphones can also be used to receive a variety of music and audio entertainment programmes, a selector switch (with a reading-light switch and a cabin-service call button) being located in the armrest of each seat. Although film shows are not appreciated by all passengers, when they are interspersed with meals they can help to relieve the boredom of over-ocean flying for the majority of passengers especially when flight times of 8 to 10 hours are involved. Zoning of the passenger cabin also simplifies the separation of non-smokers from smokers, and most airlines introduced separate zones for these with seats being selected to suit at check-in time.

Another unique feature of the 747 is its upper-deck compartment behind the flight deck which, during the 747's introductory year, was used by most airlines as a lounge for 1st-class passengers. Up to 16 passengers could be accommodated up there during flight and, being equipped with a bar, it proved to be as popular as the downstairs lounge in the earlier Stratocruisers. Some interior designers were allowed to apply their talents in this compartment, devising a decor to suit either the nationality of the airline, like Japan Air Lines' Teahouse of the Sky, or a particular atmosphere, such as Braniff's International Lounge, which the airline described as being 'like an intimate club overlooking the world'.

Baggage was another subject given much thought in the design of the 747. Overhead lockers (or stowage bins) fitted throughout the cabin accommodate a lot of the carry-on baggage of passengers, thereby reducing the usual congestion around their feet, especially in the economy-class zones. A container system was designed for the bigger checked-in baggage, the containers being packed with baggage in the terminal building and taken out to the aircraft to be loaded into the under-floor holds, avoiding the handling of hundreds of individual items which could have been very time consuming. The large doors of the under-floor holds are opened and closed electrically, and the holds are equipped with container handling systems to simplify loading and unloading. When space permitted, spare containers of mail or cargo could be carried, and last-minute items of baggage or batches of small packages could be loaded into a small compartment at the rear of the aircraft.

One of the economy class zones in an early TWA 747, equipped at the time with nine-abreast seating.(TWA)

The internally-extended upper-deck lounge in a CP Air 747 with early Canadian railroad decor. *(CP Air)*

High-Density Seating

Condor Flugdienst, the charter subsidiary of Lufthansa, became the first charter operator with a 747, which it introduced into service in May 1971. It was also the first aircraft with 10-abreast seating on the main deck, providing a high-density all-economy configuration for 470 passengers, including eight in the upper-deck compartment, which was the maximum permitted at the time for take-off and landing but later modifications increased this number.

Internally-extended Upper Deck

The first change to the external appearance of the 747 occurred in June 1971 when the first 200B for Qantas was rolled out with an internally-extended upper-deck compartment fitted with 10 windows on each side instead of the usual three. The external dimensions of the 'hump' remained the same but an internal re-arrangement extended the length of this compartment by 6 ft (1,82 m) to 25 ft (7,62 m) and increased the permitted accommodation for take-off and landing from eight to 16 passengers, and in flight from 16 to as many as 25 passengers. On the Qantas aircraft the compartment was fitted out as a Captain Cook Lounge (with appropriate nautical decor) for 1st-class passengers, but the modification was the first stage towards changing this compartment from an in-flight lounge for 1st-class passengers to one having saleable seats and, in some cases, a change of class from 1st to economy. Some later aircraft continued to have the smaller compartment, to match earlier aircraft in an airline's fleet, but most aircraft had the internal extension even if they did not have the additional windows fitted (or, if provision was made for the windows, they were blanked). This accounts for the variations in the external appearance of the 747s built in the early 1970s; some earlier aircraft were later returned to Boeing for modification and therefore also have the internally-extended compartment with the additional windows.

Lower-deck Galley

Another interesting feature on the first Qantas 200B was the location of an economy-class galley on the 'lower deck', occupying part of the rear under-floor hold, with lifts (or elevators) for carts and personnel linking it with a service centre on the main deck. This arrangement left more space for passengers on the main deck but the optional galley location was not favoured by many airlines because of the loss of cargo space.

The Spacious Age

It was during the years from 1971 to 1973 that the real Spacious Age for modern air travellers occurred. The 747 had been designed to be oversize at the start of commercial services and to be the correct size for the market after a few years of service, but this planning was based on a steady growth in air traffic. Unfortunately, there was a slow-down in the rate of growth during these years because of the world economic situation and this resulted in 'over-capacity' becoming the 'in' phrase of the time for airlines. However, the air travellers benefitted from this because airlines removed some of the

The popular piano/stand-up bar in the coach-class lounge in zone E of an American Airlines' 747 of the early 1970s. *(American)*

surplus seats and some equipped the 747 main decks with small lounges in both 1st and economy (or coach) zones, and offered these in their advertising as an inducement to would-be customers. As an example, in the 747 Luxury Liners of American Airlines a lounge, complete with stand-up bar, occupied the full cabin width at the rear of zone E, and the finishing touch was added later with the introduction of a piano, which proved to be very popular; in 1st class a table for four could be booked for dinner or card playing, etc. Pan Am also introduced its well-known dining room service on the main deck before transferring it to the upper-deck compartment.

Continental Airlines' 747 Proud Birds of the Pacific (a rare species, which became extinct in January 1974) had the lowest seating capacity of them all with a total of 290 passengers (reduced from 339). These were arranged in an unusual (for the time) three-class configuration – 1st, coach and economy. The 57 1st-class passengers were in zones A and B, and had the use in flight of an upstairs Diamond Head Lounge; the 145 coach passengers were in zones C and D, both equipped with four-seat mini-lounges; and the 88 economy passengers were in zone E, at the rear of which was an eight-seat Ponape Lounge for both coach and economy passengers. Coach passengers had a normal meal service, whereas economy passengers, who paid $10 less for their flights between Los Angeles and Honolulu, could purchase a sandwich meal and a small bottle of wine for $1.50.

High-density 747SR

Going to the other extreme in capacity, Japan Air Lines introduced its first 747SR (Short Range) on the airline's domestic trunk routes in October 1973 with a high-density seating arrangement for 498 passengers (an all-time high for the period). With an all-economy configuration, there were 482 seated 10-abreast at 33 in. (83,82 cm) pitch on the main deck and 16 in the upper-deck compartment (the latter seats, having more space, were assigned by the airline to preferred customers, VIPs and frequent travellers). Flight times were short because the distances between the major Japanese cities were only between 250 and 550 miles (402 and 885 km) but they were very busy routes and on the inter-island Tokyo to Sapporo route the airline was scheduling up to 10 daily 747 round-trip flights at peak times of the year.

Increasing Seating Capacity

The winter of 1973/4 was the time of the first OPEC-inspired oil price crisis, with its associated period of inflation, fuel shortage and economic gloom. This resulted in cut-backs to air services generally, the withdrawal of some 747s from service (to be placed into storage or put up for sale), and getting the maximum use out of the remaining aircraft. It was at this time that the extra space of the Spacious Age began to disappear, with the withdrawal of lounges from the main decks of 747s, first from the economy/coach zones and then from 1st Class, to allow more seats to be installed.

The 32-seat upper-deck compartment became available as an option on aircraft built from July 1974 onwards, provided that an additional door was fitted on the left-hand side of the upper deck and that both this and the existing right-hand door were equipped with a special inflatable slide (or chute) to serve as emergency exits. These slides were approved by the FAA together with other changes to the emergency equipment, including the introduction of combined inflatable slides and life rafts on the main deck which are stowed on the inside of the entrance doors and replaced the separate slides and inflatable life rafts previously carried (the life rafts in earlier aircraft were stowed in the ceiling of the passenger cabin). As with previous changes to the upper deck, many early aircraft were modified to have the extra door and so allow an increase in seating capacity.

Advance-purchase excursion (Apex) fares were introduced by IATA airlines on the North Atlantic route in April 1975. These were the scheduled airlines' answer to the advance-booking charters (ABC) being provided by air charter operators and offered passengers a cheaper flight provided that they booked it at least 60 days in advance and confined the stay at their destination to between 14 and 45 days. These lower fares, together with the inclusive-tour excursions (ITX) covering package holidays, proved very popular and started another change in 747 passenger cabins because, to achieve the same revenue from these low-yield fares, many scheduled airlines introduced 10-abreast seating (arranged 3 x 4 x 3). As with the introduction of tourist/economy class originally, this was a matter of comfort versus cost and passengers got the cheaper flights for a reduction in comfort, because to fit 10 seats across the cabin meant using narrower seats and reducing the width of the aisles.

This new fare structure brought forth an unfortunate situation where a businessman/businesswoman who had paid the full economy-class fare could be sitting among passengers who had paid considerably less for their ticket and yet had the same reduced-level of comfort and the same cabin service. This situation was rectified in the late 1970s and early 1980s by the introduction of an in-between class, generally called business or executive class but with most airlines giving it a fancy title of their own in an effort to attract the higher-yield fares. These passengers who had paid the full economy-class fare were treated to a reduced-density seating arrangement in their own section of the cabin and given an improved cabin service. In fact, the advertising for this class was so effective that some 1st-class passengers were attracted down to it (or more likely the companies paying for their tickets considered it adequate for senior personnel) with a result that 1st class had to be further improved by the introduction of fully-reclining sleeper seats (sometimes called sleeperettes to attract them back. Here again the 747 was ideally suited to the new arrangement with its zoned seating being adaptable to almost any whim of an airline. Currently, 1st class passengers generally occupy zone A, business class passengers zone B and sometimes also zone C, and economy class the remaining zones, with saleable seats in the upper-deck compartment being used as an extension of one of these classes.

A number of variations can be found that differ from this general arrangement and these increased with the introduction of the 747-300 and its stretched upper deck (SUD) in 1983. This was like mounting a small airliner

The rear half of the stretched upper-deck compartment on a Qantas 747-300, looking aft from the central doors; seating is provided for 38 business class passengers. *(Qantas)*

on top of the main one and could provide self-contained accommodation (with its own toilets and galley) for 26 1st-class sleeper seats, 42 business class at four abreast, 69 economy class at six abreast or a knee-bruising 96 high-density economy-class seats (without galley). In these aircraft the spiral staircase at the front is replaced by a straight staircase at the rear so that the compartment can be used as an extension of economy class on the main deck or used as a separate compartment for one of the other classes.

The external appearance of the 747 changed considerably with the upper-deck compartment stretched by over 23 ft (7 m) and the addition of up to 10 more windows on each side; the emergency-exit doors also had to be larger and re-positioned to the centre of the compartment. The increase in seating capacity available on aircraft with the stretched upper deck (the 300s plus some 200Bs modified to this standard) resulted in higher seating totals but generally on all-passenger aircraft being operated in a three-class configuration by scheduled airlines the figure is between 410 and 440 which is about the same as those reached in all-passenger 100s and 200Bs before the reduced-density seating of business class brought them down to the current 350 to 390.

Record-breaking Capacities

An exception to this norm is Japan Air Lines who introduced 300SRs on its busy domestic routes at the beginning of 1988 with a record-breaking seating capacity (all economy) of 563 which broke even its own previous record of 550

(11 abreast at 33 in. (84 cm) pitch) achieved with 100SRs from the early 1980s. Such very high-density seating might be tolerable for short flights by small-build Japanese (with the possible exception of Sumo wrestlers) but could prove rather uncomfortable on longer flights by broader-beam Americans and Europeans.

The 747 gets a mention in the Guinness Book of Records as 'the highest capacity jet airliner in the world, with a capacity of from 385 to more than 500 passengers'. Also mentioned is 'the greatest passenger load on a commercial airliner, of 674', which goes to the credit of the 747. The actual aircraft was the Qantas 200B VH-EBB *City of Melbourne* which carried the record load from Darwin to Sydney on 29 December 1974 during the evacuation of Darwin following the devastation caused by Cyclone Tracy. The 674 passengers comprised 306 adults, 328 children and 40 babies, and, as the aircraft was equipped with only 369 seats, every able-bodied adult was asked to nurse a child or baby, other children were placed two to a seat and some babies were placed on the floor between passengers' legs. The flight was one of several operated by Qantas 747s in association with smaller aircraft of the Australian domestic airlines.

Record-breaking Distances

The Guinness Book of Records also credits the 747 with 'the longest scheduled non-stop flight' which it gives as Sydney - San Francisco by a Pan Am 747SP with a distance of over 7475 miles (12 030 km) taking 13 hr 25 min.

Record Breaker 1. Qantas 200B VH-EBB City of Melbourne which holds the record for carrying the 'greatest passenger load' of 674. *(Qantas)*

The Pan Am Pacific division and the airline's 747SPs were taken over by United Airlines in February 1986 who now operate the route via Los Angeles, but Qantas operates the route non-stop with its 747SPs. Both Qantas and United Airlines operate 747SPs non-stop on the Los Angeles - Sydney route which, with a distance of 7487 miles (12 050 km), is slightly longer and is therefore the current record holder.

Early standard 747s had a range with normal airline reserves of around 5500 miles (8850 km) which was adequate for trans-polar services between Europe and the US west coast, the longest distances required in the early 1970s. However, when the smaller-capacity 747SP (Special Performance) entered service in 1976 its extra range was used to introduce non-stop flights between selected cities, such as New York and Tokyo (6737 miles, 10 842 km), New York and Teheran (6120 miles, 9849 km), and San Francisco and Hong Kong (6900 miles, 11 104 km), as well as some of over 7000 miles (11 265 km) like Los Angeles - Hong Kong and the Sydney services from Los Angeles and San Francisco.

Since then, improved engines with reduced fuel consumption have provided standard 747s with increased range so that they can now operate regular non-stop flights of over 6000 miles (9656 km), while longer flights, such as Singapore Airlines' London - Singapore service of 6746 miles (10 856 km), can be operated non-stop eastbound but still requires an en-route refuelling stop westbound. This airline, with others, has ordered the 747-400, which Boeing claims will have a range of over 8000 miles (12 875 km), so that many more non-stop long-distance flights should be possible from 1989.

Passenger reaction to very-long-distance, non-stop flying is reported to be good, with most preferring to complete the journey as quickly as possible instead of taking a few hours more on a one-stop or two-stop service. This is particularly so for businessmen/businesswomen who consider the time saved en-route can be used to better advantage at the destination recovering from any jet lag. And for those who can sleep on board an aircraft, there is a longer period undisturbed by en-route landings and take-offs. However, there can be problems caused by spending long periods in a cabin with a pressure set to that existing at 8000 ft (2438 m), and to overcome dehydration passengers on all flights of 10 hours or more are encouraged to take soft drinks frequently. Lack of exercise can also cause problems for some people, especially as passengers nowadays are recommended to remain seated with their seat belts loosely fastened, instead of walking up and down the aisles, in case of sudden in-flight turbulence.

The longest flight by a commercial jet airliner is given in the Guinness Book of Records as 17 hr 22½ min. This was made by the South African Airways 747SP ZS-SPA *Matroosberg* on 23-24 March 1976 when it was on its delivery flight from Seattle, Washington, to Cape Town, South Africa, a distance of 10,290 miles (16 560 km).

VIP Interiors

Not all 747s built are for airline use, some exceptions being those equipped

Record Breaker 2. South African Airways 747SP ZS-SPA Matroosberg set a record in 1976 by flying a distance of 10,290 miles (16 560 km). *(South African)*

with VIP interiors for use by kings, rulers or presidents of wealthy nations. The first of these was a 747SP delivered to the Saudi Arabian government in September 1979 for the personal use of the late King Khaled and the royal family. The King had been fitted with a heart pacemaker by a Cleveland, Ohio hospital and a section of this long-range aircraft was fitted out as a flying hospital to enable the King to be flown from Saudi Arabia to America in the event of problems, the on-board equipment being reported to include telemetry communications with the hospital. The aircraft, appropriately registered HZ-HMl, was also used by the King and his entourage when visiting foreign countries, including a state visit to Britain in June 1981. At the time it was the biggest and most expensive personal aircraft in the world but when the present King Fahd succeeded to the throne in 1982 he ordered an even bigger and more expensive 747-300, HZ-HM1A, and the 747SP was relegated to second place as HZ-HM1B.

Although both aircraft have a colour scheme similar to the Saudi Arabian airline Saudia, when the King's 300 made its appearance in 1986 it was easily distinguishable from the airline's 300s by a satellite communications dish aerial beneath a large fairing behind the usual stretched upper deck. Little was known about the aircraft's interior until the King used it for a state visit to Britain in March 1987 when somehow newspaper reporters managed to obtain some details. Apart from being described as a flying palace with chandeliers, gold fittings, plush upholstery and several bathrooms, it apparently has living and working space arranged on three decks with connection between them by lifts (elevators). The spacious main deck is said to contain two staterooms, two dining rooms, a conference room and a fully-equipped medical centre, plus, of course, servants' quarters. Three doors are provided on each side of the main deck but access is usually through what would normally be the forward under-floor hold, which is equipped with retractable airstairs having an elevator platform attached on which the King is raised or lowered.

Other Arab states which have bought 747s for use by their royal flights are the United Arab Emirates, who purchased an ex-TWA 747SP (A6-SMR) in 1985 and are currently awaiting delivery of a new 747SP which has spent the past year having its special interior fitted, and Oman who purchased an ex-Braniff 747SP (A40-SO) in 1984. The Omani aircraft spent about three years being converted for its VIP role and is another that is easily distinguishable by a satellite communications dish aerial beneath a large fairing behind the upper-deck compartment.

A satellite communications aerial is likely to be fitted to the two US Air Force 200Bs which are currently being fitted out, for delivery in November 1988 and May 1989, for use by the US President and his staff. Replacing the existing VC-137s (Boeing 707s), the VC-25As (as they will be known) are due to have a complete state-of-the-art communications centre as well as work and rest areas for the President and his staff and a fully-equipped medical facility. The aircraft are not likely to have quite the plush upholstery and gold fittings of King Fahd's 747 but one report states that they will have a spacious bedroom, with vanity units, toilet and bath, in the nose for the President and his wife, and further back will be the President's office, conference room, lounge and staff quarters. Like the VC-137s, the aircraft are likely to be referred to as Air Force One and Air Force Two (although 'Air Force One' is only the radio callsign when the President is on board and 'Air Force Two' is the Vice President's callsign) and are due to be operated by the 89th Military Airlift Wing at Andrews Air Force Base near Washington, D.C.

Military Duties

There are already four 747-200Bs in service with the US Air Force but these are known as E-4Bs (E for electronic missions) and serve as Advanced Airborne Command Posts, which would control air, land and sea forces in the event of a national emergency. The main deck is equipped (from nose to tail) with living and sleeping quarters for the President or the most senior officers on board (with washroom and toilet), a conference room, a briefing room, an operations room with data displays, a communications area and a staff rest area with washrooms and toilets. The under-floor holds are full of communications and data-processing equipment and, because the aircraft can remain airborne for 72 hours with in-flight refuelling, the upper-deck compartment has accommodation for the spare flight crew and crew rest area. The E-4Bs took over from EC-135s (Boeing 707s) and originally were equipped with communications equipment from the earlier aircraft but through the years they have been extensively modified and are now equipped with a satellite communications dish aerial beneath a large fairing behind the upper-deck compartment. The steerable dish is used to direct or receive super high frequency (SHF) radio signals between the aircraft and satellites for world-wide communications, and other radio equipment provides frequencies spread across ultra high frequency (UHF), very high frequency (VHF), high frequency (HF), low frequency (LF) and very low frequency (VLF). The last mentioned is used to pass information to and from submerged submarines and requires two 5-mile (8 km) long copper-wire aerials which are reeled out from the rear of the aircraft and, when fully extended, droop about 4000 ft (1219 m) below the aircraft, so, like the war-time trailing aerials, it is to be hoped that the operator remembers to reel them in before the aircraft comes in to land. Four doors are fitted on each side of the aircraft's main deck but access is usually via a retractable airstair in what would usually be the forward under-floor hold (called the lower lobe in this instance) with stairs up to the main deck.

Incidents and Accidents

Considering the number of 747s in service, there have been comparatively few major incidents and serious accidents since the aircraft entered service in 1970 but, of course, on the rare occasion when one of these large aircraft crashes the casualty figures can be very high.

Hi-jacking was a major problem in the early 1970s and the first 747 to be subjected to it was Pan Am's N735PA *Clipper Young America* on a flight from New York to San Juan, Puerto Rico, on 2 August 1970, which was forced to fly to Havana, Cuba. A more serious hi-jacking occurred of 6 September 1970 when Pan Am's N752PA *Clipper Fortune* on a flight from Amsterdam to New York was re-routed to Cairo where it was blown up by Palestinian Arab

An E-4B of the US Air Force; the extra lump at the rear of the upper-deck compartment houses a satellite communications aerial. *(Boeing)*

guerrillas. Fortunately the passengers and crew were allowed to leave the aircraft first but it meant that the aircraft had a very short life of only four months during which it had logged 1125 hours. A similar fate was suffered by Japan Air Lines' JA8109 on 24 July 1973 but this time the Palestinian Arab guerrillas chose Benghazi as the place to blow it up.

After almost five years of service without a serious accident, the 747's first accident occurred on 20 November 1974 when Lufthansa's D-ABYB *Hessen* crashed while taking off from Nairobi because the leading-edge flaps had not been extended, killing 55 passengers and 4 crew, although 85 passengers and 13 crew survived.

The fourth 747 to be lost was Air France's N28888 which burnt out on the ground at Bombay on 12 June 1975 after the landing gear caught fire while the aircraft was taxying, but there were no casualties.

Two 747s were nearly written off in December 1975 in unrelated accidents but were saved by the efforts of a team of Boeing engineers. The first was a 100SF OD-AGC of Trans Mediterranean Airways (TMA) on a non-scheduled freight flight from Beirut to Athens on 3 December, which over-ran a wet runway on landing, resulting in severe damage to the fuselage, engines and landing gear. The second was a Japan Air Lines 200B, JA8122, which was blown off an ice-covered taxiway by strong cross-winds while preparing to leave Anchorage, Alaska, on a scheduled passenger flight from London to Tokyo on 16 December. The aircraft suffered rather more damage than the TMA aircraft because it slid backwards down a 50-ft (15-m) snow-covered embankment and came to rest straddling a gulley. There were no casualties in either accident.

An Imperial Iranian Air Force freighter, 5-283, crashed near Madrid on 9 May 1976 after, it is thought, a lightning strike ignited fuel vapour issuing from the wing vents; the aircraft was using the military JP4 fuel at the time. All 17 personnel on board were killed.

One of the worst possible air disasters occurred on 27 March 1977 when two 747s collided on the ground at Tenerife, Canary Islands. The aircraft concerned were KLM's PH-BUF *The Rhine* and Pan Am's N736PA *Clipper Victor*. Like so many accidents, this one was an unfortunate culmination of several factors, the first being that both aircraft would not normally have been at Tenerife but had been diverted there because of a terrorist bomb explosion at Las Palmas, Gran Canaria, their intended destination. Then followed a delay of about three hours to await the re-opening of Las Palmas airport, by which time the visibility at Tenerife was deteriorating. The KLM aircraft taxied along the main runway followed by the Pan Am aircraft which was requested to turn off on to a taxiway once clear of several other diverted aircraft which had been parked on the taxiway. In poor visibility, and following confusing radio messages, the KLM aircraft started its take-off run before the Pan Am aircraft had cleared the runway with a result that the two aircraft collided and 583 people died (234 passengers and 14 crew on the KLM aircraft and 326 passengers and 9 crew on the Pan Am aircraft). Incredibly, 52 passengers and 9 crew escaped from the Pan Am aircraft.

The eighth 747 to be lost was Air India's VT-EBD *Emperor Ashoka* which, on a night take-off from Bombay airport on 1 January 1978, suffered the failure of an attitude director indicator which caused pilot disorientation, resulting in the aircraft crashing into the Arabian Sea, killing all 190 passengers and 23 crew.

In January 1980, on the tenth anniversary of the 747's first commercial service, Boeing announced that 420 747s had been delivered and were in service with 57 operators, flying to over 150 cities world-wide. Nearly 123,000 passengers were flying in 747s every day and the total number of passengers carried was over 266 million.

Korean Airlines' HL7445 landed short of the runway at Seoul in poor visibility on 18 November 1980, resulting in the aircraft catching fire and 8 passengers and 6 crew losing their lives; 190 passengers and 8 crew were evacuated safely.

A 747 became what the Guinness Book of Records described as 'the world's heaviest glider' when British Airways' G-BDXH *City of Edinburgh* suffered a total engine failure after flying into a cloud of volcanic ash from Mt Galunggung, Indonesia, on 24 June 1982. The aircraft was cruising at 37,000 ft (11 278m) while flying from Kuala Lumpur to Perth, Australia, on a night that, according to Captain Eric Moody, the pilot in command, was 'blacker than a badger's backside', and it had glided down to 13,000 ft (3962 m) some 13 minutes later before the flight crew managed to get one engine re-started, followed by the other three. There were no casualties among the 247 passengers and 16 crew. Singapore Airlines' 9V-SQD suffered the loss of two engines for a similar reason on 14 July 1982 but managed to land safely at Jakarta.

Yet another close thing occurred on 11 August 1982 when a bomb exploded in the rear of Pan Am's N754PA *Clipper Ocean Rover* as it was approaching Honolulu, killing one passenger and injuring five. The flight crew performed an emergency descent from 26,000 ft (7925 m) to 10,000 ft (3048 m) and landed the aircraft safely.

Another Pan Am 747, N738PA *Clipper Belle of the Sea,* skidded off the runway while landing at Karachi on 4 August 1983 and was later considered to be damaged beyond economical repair. there were no casualties.

Still surrounded in mystery are the circumstances by which Korean Airlines' HL7442 came to be shot down by Russian fighter aircraft when it flew into Russian airspace near Sakhalin Island on 1 September 1983. What is certain is that it crashed into the Sea of Japan killing 246 passengers and 23 crew.

The 12th 747 to be lost was Avianca's HK-2910X which was too low on a night approach to Madrid airport on 27 November 1983, resulting in the death of 161 passengers and 20 crew, although 11 passengers survived.

In January 1985, on the 15th anniversary of the 747's first commercial service, Boeing announced that 606 747s had been delivered and were in service with 70 operators. The world-wide 747 fleet had carried 550 million passengers more than 8000 million miles in more than 16 million revenue hours of service, more than any other commercial aircraft in production.

There was an unusually high number of serious airliner accidents in 1985 and the 747 also had its worst year with the loss of four aircraft, two of which resulted in the deaths of 849 people.

The year started with proof of the structural strength of the 747 when, on 19 February, China Air Lines' 747SP N4522V had a No. 4 engine failure while cruising at 41,000 ft (12 497 m) and the aircraft stalled, rolled almost inverted, and dived 60 degrees nose-down 32,000 ft (9754 m) until the flight crew managed to regain control at 9000 ft (2743 m). The aircraft suffered severe tail damage but was able to make a safe landing at San Francisco. Surprisingly, of the 290 passengers and crew on board, only four passengers were injured.

The first 747-300 to be lost was UTA's F-GDUA which caught fire in a maintenance area at Charles de Gaule airport, Paris, on 16 March 1985 and was so severely damaged that it was later declared a write-off.

A bomb explosion caused by Sikh terrorists is now considered to be the reason why Air India's VT-EFO *Kanishka* blew up in mid-air over the Atlantic, south-west of Ireland, on 23 June 1985, killing all 307 passengers and 22 crew on board.

This terrible crash was followed on 12 August 1985 by the worst single-aircraft accident in civil aviation history when Japan Air Lines' 747SR JA8119 on a domestic flight from Tokyo to Osaka crashed into a mountain, killing 505 passengers and 15 crew out of the the 524 people on board. After an extensive investigation it was found that an incorrectly-repaired rear pressure bulkhead had ruptured and the sudden decompression had seriously damaged the aircraft's tail and disabled all flying controls.

The fourth 747 to be lost in 1985 was Air France's 200B Combi F-GCBC which veered off the runway while landing at Rio de Janeiro on 2 December after a reverser on one of the engines failed to operate. There were no casualties but the aircraft was so badly damaged that it was declared a write-off.

Palestinian Arab guerrillas struck at a 747 again on 4 September 1986. They stormed Pan Am's N656PA *Clipper Empress of the Seas* while passengers were boarding at Karachi and later, as Pakistani commandos were boarding the aircraft, opened fire indiscriminately with automatic weapons killing 18 people. The aircraft was damaged by the gunfire but was repaired and returned to service, with a new name *Clipper New Horizons*.

The 17th 747 to be lost was South African Airways' 200B Combi ZS-SAS *Helderberg* which crashed into the Indian Ocean near Mauritius on 28 November 1987 while on a flight from Taipei to Johannesburg via Mauritius after the captain had reported a fire on board. There were no survivors among the 140 passengers and 19 crew on the aircraft.

Pro-Iranian terrorists hi-jacked Kuwait Airways' 9K-ADB *Al Jaberiya* while on a flight from Bangkok to Kuwait on 5 April 1988, and forced it to fly first to Mashhad, Iran, then to Larnaca, Cyprus (where two hostages were killed), and finally to Algiers before the last of the hostages were released on 20 April.

Variants

Over 700 Boeing 747s have been produced during the 20 years which have passed since 747 No. 1 was rolled out of the factory at Everett on 30 September 1968. At first glance most of these appear to be the same, with the exception of the smaller 747SP (Special Performance) and the enlarged versions with a stretched upper deck (SUD), but a closer inspection will reveal the many changes that have been introduced during the years as a result of a continuing development programme. Apart from the major changes to provide variants for specific duties, such as the Freighter, Convertible (passenger or freighter), Short Range (SR), and Combi (combination passenger and freighter) there have been numerous other changes to the basic design, such as the introduction of Pratt & Whitney engines of increased power, and engines from other manufacturers (General Electric and Rolls-Royce), increases in the maximum take-off weight and fuel capacity, and (as described in the previous section) changes to the passenger accommodation to suit the ever-changing requirements of the airlines.

When the airlines first started ordering 747s in the mid-1960s the only model available was the basic version so no model numbers were allocated. Most of these airlines were already operating other types of Boeing jet airliners (707s or 727s) and the customer indentification number which had been used for these, to indicate changes from the basic configuration to meet individual airline requirements, was carried over to the 747 orders, so that Pan Am aircraft were referred to as the 747-21, TWA aircraft as the 747-31, BOAC aircraft as the 747-36, etc. Any new Boeing customers were identified in a similar manner; to avoid lengthy numbers, this original series ended at 99 and later customers (for the 707, 727, 737 and 747) were identified in the 'alpha-numeric' series A1 to A9, B1 to B9, etc.

Some Convertible (C) and Freighter (F) versions of the basic 747 were ordered in the mid-1960s and these were identified by a suffix letter after the customer's number, so that a 747C for World Airways was a 747-73C and a 747F for Pan Am was a 747-21F. These orders were later either cancelled or changed to passenger versions because the empty weight of the basic aircraft had increased above that planned and this reduced the aircraft's weight-lifting ability in the freight-carrying role while the maximum take-off weight was restricted to 710,000 lb (322 056 kg).

In June 1968, before the first 747 had been completed, Boeing announced the availability of the 747B, a developed version with an increased maximum take-off weight of 775,000 lb (351 540 kg) with improved payload/range performance. This improvement made the Freighter a viable proposition again so the C and F versions were offered at this increased weight.

Before the first 747 deliveries were made in December 1969, Boeing introduced the current 'hundred series' model numbering system to identify the different take-off weights and any future major changes, in a similar fashion to the system used on other Boeing jet airliners. The basic version of the 747 then became the 747-100, with a Pan Am aircraft being identified as the 747-121, etc., and the 747B became the 747-200B (or 747-200C or 747-200F), with a Northwest Orient aircraft being identified as the 747-251B, etc.

Individual aircraft are identified by a construction number which remains with the aircraft throughout its life, regardless of changes of ownership or country of registration (and, therefore, changes of its registration markings). When 707s, 727s, 737s, 747s, 757s and 767s are ordered from Boeing each aircraft is allocated a five-figure construction number from a common series. These numbers then provide the means of identifying individual 747s before and after construction but they do not follow in strict numerical order, because of the other airliner types in between, and of those that are used for 747s the aircraft are not necessarily constructed in ascending order and are also subject to cancellation before construction. Throughout this book, therefore, a line number is used to identify individual 747s, because these numbers are allocated to an aircraft only when its major components are brought together for final assembly, and they have been issued to 747s in strict numerical order from 747 No. 1 onwards. The line numbers also give an indication of the age of the aircraft. A production list at the end of this book serves as a cross-reference between line numbers and construction numbers.

747-100 and 747-100B Passenger

The initial production version of the 747 was the 747-100 and this remained in production alongside other variants until 1978. As mentioned earlier, there was an unexpected increase in the weights of the structure and systems which caused the maximum take-off weight to increase from the planned 680,000 lb (308 448 kg) to the eventual 710,000 lb (322 056 kg) for the first production aircraft. This in turn led to a requirement for more powerful engines to enable the aircraft to meet its promised performance specifications and Pratt & Whitney JT9D-3 engines of 43,500 lb (19 732 kg) thrust were fitted to these aircraft.

During the flight test programme a problem arose with the installation of the engines which caused a loss of power and an increase in fuel consumption during cruising flight, and until a solution was found only the five aircraft in the programme had engines, the remaining 20 or so aircraft built during 1969 being rolled out without them. Eventually the problem was overcome and the 747 received its FAA certification on 30 December 1969, but some aircraft were delivered with unmodified engines to enable airlines, such as Pan Am and TWA, to start crew training and perform inaugural services. The fully modified JT9D-3A engines became available for later aircraft off the assembly line which in March 1970 reached its peak production rate of seven 747s per month.

Braniff's original Big Orange 747-100 which for many years led the field in the number of flying hours logged. *(Braniff)*

Pan Am's early aircraft were returned one by one to Boeing from November 1970 for a refurbishing programme 'to clean up the nitty gritty technical problems that developed in the first year's operations'. Major work included fitting the aircraft with JT9D-3AW engines, which had water injection to increase take-off thrust to 45,000 lb (20 412 kg), and increasing the maximum take-off weight to 735,000 lb (333 396 kg), adding another 460 miles (740 km) to the aircraft's range or increasing the payload by 15%. Other work included modifications to the landing gear, wing flaps, fuel system, doors and passenger-cabin entertainment system. When they emerged, the aircraft were designated (by Pan Am, not Boeing) the 747-100A. These modifications were also embodied on other 747-100s but without the change of designation.

The original 747-100s had a fuel capacity of 47,210 US gallons (178 709 l) and were restricted to Pratt & Whitney engines, the later aircraft having JT9D-7s of 45,500 lb (20 639kg) thrust, JT9D-7Ws with water injection and a take-off thrust of 47,900 lb (21 727 kg) or JT9D-7As of 46,950 lb (21 297 kg) thrust as optional engines.

In 1978 the 747-100B replaced the 747-100 and incorporated a strengthened structure and landing gear, to allow higher maximum take-off weights up to 750,000 lb (340 200 kg), and modifications to permit the installation of more powerful Pratt & Whitney engines and optional General Electric CF6-50 or Rolls-Royce RB211-524 engines. Iran Air took delivery of the first 747-100B (line No. 381, EP-IAM) with JT9D-7F engines of 48,000 lb (21 773 kg) thrust in August 1979 and Saudia took delivery of eight in 1981/2 powered by Rolls-

Royce RB211-524C engines of 51,000 lb (23 134 kg) thrust, but no orders have been received for this basic type since then although it remains available (and forms the basis for the Short Range (SR) variant described later).

Some of the earlier 747-100s will soon be 20 years old but in the airline world an aircraft's life is judged by its utilization, measured by the number of flight cycles (take-offs and landings), which is the major factor in short-haul operations, or the number of flying hours. The 747 with the most flying hours to its credit (known as the high-time aircraft) was for many years No. 100, Braniff's N601BN Big Orange. It set a good pace from the time it entered service in January 1971, operating a daily Dallas - Honolulu round-trip and averaging 14 hours in the air each day, and was the first 747 to pass the 10-million mile mark in March 1975. By March 1978 the aircraft had become the first 747 to log 35,000 flying hours and was transferred to the airline's new Dallas - London route which was also operated daily, requiring the aircraft to step-up its daily airborne time to nearly 18 hours. By the time Braniff ceased operations in May 1982, N601BN had logged 55,000 flying hours, having been airborne for more than half of its total life, and was transferred to another operator to continue adding to the impressive total.

According to Boeing's latest figures, more than 60 747s have logged over 60,000 flying hours and the high-time aircraft is an unidentified Pan Am 747 which had logged 71,435 flying hours by September 1987.

747-200B Passenger

Although identical in appearance to the 747-100, the 747-200B had a strengthened structure and landing gear to allow operation at an increased maximum take-off weight of 775,000 lb (351 540 kg), enabling the aircraft to carry an increased payload or an increased fuel load of 51,430 US gal (194 683 l). The initial production aircraft were powered by JT9D-3AW engines, which had a take-off thrust of 45,000 lb (20 412 kg) with water injection, but later aircraft were powered by the JT9D-7 which produced 45,500 lb (20 639 kg) thrust, dry. The first 747-200B was No. 88, N611US for Northwest Orient, which made its first flight on 11 October 1970 and established a world record for commercial aircraft on 12 November 1970 when, during its flight test programme, it took off at a gross weight of 820,700 lb (372 270 kg). FAA certification was completed on 23 December and the first 747-200B service was operated by KLM in February 1971.

The 747-200B went on to become the most numerous (so far) of the 747 variants and through the years the maximum take-off weight was increased as more power became available from later Pratt & Whitney engines and also General Electric and Rolls-Royce engines.

An initial increase in maximum take-off weight to 785,000 lb (356 076 kg) became available with JT9D-7AW engines which were rated at 46,950 lb (21 297 kg) thrust, dry, or 48,750 lb (22 113 kg) thrust with water injection. These engines were certificated for use after being tested on 747 No. 212, 4X-AXC for El Al, which became the 200th 747 to be delivered in April 1973.

On 26 June 1973, 747 No. 1 took to the air for the first time after being re-engined with General Electric CF6-50D engines of 51,000 lb (23 134 kg) thrust. At the time Boeing considered introducing the model number 747-300 to distinguish this variant from Pratt & Whitney powered aircraft but the idea was subsequently dropped and the choice of engine treated as an option. The first production 747 to be fitted with General Electric engines was No. 232, the third E-4A (200B), 40787, for the US Air Force which was powered by CF6-50E engines (or F103-GE-100, as the US Air Force call them) which had a take-off thrust of 52,500 lb (23 814 kg). This aircraft was delivered in October 1974.

A Qantas 747-200B, No. 260 VH-EBJ, delivered in May 1975, was the first to be powered by Pratt & Whitney JT9D-7FW engines, which were rated at 48,000 lb (21 773 kg) thrust, dry, or 50,000 lb (22 680 kg) thrust with water injection. This increase in power enabled a further increase in maximum take-off weight to be made, to 800,000 lb (362 880 kg). The aircraft was also equipped with optional 800 US gal (3028 l) extended-range fuel tanks in the outer wings which, together with some small changes in the existing tanks, increased the total fuel capacity to 53,160 US gal (201 232 l). This fuel load weighed over 355,000 lb (161 028 kg), which was greater than the maximum take-off weight of a Boeing 707.

The first civil operator to order 747s powered by General Electric engines was KLM, who took delivery of its first 200B Combi (No. 271, PH-BUH) equipped with CF6-50E engines of 52,500 lb (23 814 kg) thrust in October 1975; this also had the increased maximum take-off weight of 800,000 lb (362 880 kg).

The next stage in the development of the JT9D engine was a major re-design, resulting in the JT9D-70A of 53,000 lb (24 040 kg) thrust. This was an odd-ball in the Pratt & Whitney range because it had a long-chord fan cowling instead of the previously-used short-cord one; this was called a 'common nacelle' because it was the same as that used for the JT9D engines in the DC-10-40 and Airbus A300. The engines made their first appearance on a Seaboard World Airlines' 747 Freighter delivered in April 1976 but otherwise were used on only a few 200B Combis and a 200B for Aerolineas Argentinas (No. 349, LV-MLO), the airlines generally preferring the lighter short-chord fan cowling which became available at this rating in the JT9D-7Q engine later. The additional power of the JT9D-70A enabled the maximum take-off weight to be increased to 820,000 lb (371 952 kg).

Rolls Royce engines made their first appearance on a 747 on a British Airways' 200B, No. 292, G-BDXA, in the form of the RB211-524B of 50,000 lb (22 680 kg) thrust. During the certification programme for this airframe/engine combination, aimed at a maximum take-off weight of 820,000 lb (371 952 kg), the aircraft set a new world record on 1 November 1976 by taking off at a gross weight of 840,500 lb (381 250 kg).

A further increase in fuel capacity became available during 1977 as an option for 200B, 200C and 200F variants, taking the total to 53,985 US gal (204 355 l) for aircraft powered by JT9D-7A and JT9D-7F and RB211-524B engines, or 53,611 US gal (202 939 l) for aircraft powered by JT9D-70A and

CF6-50E engines, with the maximum take-off weight remaining within the range from 775,000 to 820,000 lb (351 540 to 371 952 kg).

The Pratt & Whitney JT9D-7Q of 53,000 lb (24 040 kg) thrust underwent its certification flight testing on 747-200B No. 354, N622US for Northwest Orient. In the process it got a mention in the Guinness Book of Records for 'the highest gross take-off weight of any aircraft' of 379·9 tons (386 tonnes) -851,000 lb (386 000 kg) - on 23 May 1979. By the time FAA flight certification was received in September 1979 a total of 19 airlines had ordered 71 747s powered by these engines and the improved performance of the aircraft they powered prompted Singapore Airlines to call theirs Super Bs.

In January 1980, while the 747 was celebrating the 10th anniversary of its entry into airline service, Boeing announced an optional increase in the aircraft's maximum take-off weight to 833,000 lb (377 850 kg), subject to small structural changes and the use of uprated engines. The first airline to operate a 747 at the new weight was due to be Qantas with aircraft powered by Rolls-Royce RB211-524D4 engines rated at 53,000 lb (24 040 kg) thrust. At the time of ordering, Qantas stated that, with a maximum complement of 436 passengers and 25,350 lb (11 500 kg) of cargo, the new 200B would have a maximum range of about 6275 miles (10 100 km); the airline's existing 747s with Pratt & Whitney JT9D-7F engines and a maximum take-off weight of 805,000 lb (365 148 kg), with the same payload, had a range of 5295 miles (8250 km).

The first 747 to be delivered at the new maximum take-off weight of 833,000 lb (377 850 kg) was actually a 200F Freighter for Cargolux, powered by JT9D-7Q engines of 53,000 lb (24 040 kg) thrust, in October 1980, with the Qantas 200B following in 1981.

By now the range of maximum take-off weights for 200Bs, with a choice of engines of adequate power from all three manufacturers, was sufficient to meet the needs of most airlines. Further advances in engine technology continued to improve their efficiency and reduce their fuel comsumption, which was of interest to airlines planning extended-range operations, but any increases in power was of more use in the heavier 300 and 400 variants unless the engines were to be operated de-rated to extend their life. Pratt & Whitney announced another stage in the development of the JT9D engine with the JT9D-7R series, the JT9D-7R4G of 54,000 lb (24 500 kg) thrust and the JT9D-7R4H of 56,000 lb (25 400 kg) thrust being the most powerful. General Electric introduced a new range with the CF6-80 series, with the CF6-80B of 54,000 lb (24 500 kg) thrust and CF6-80C of 56,000 lb (25 400 kg) thrust at the top end of the range. And Rolls-Royce continued to develop the RB211-524 series towards 56,000 lb (25 400 kg).

Boeing currently offers the 200B with a range of maximum take-off weights from the original 775,000 lb (351 540 kg) to 833,000 lb (377 850 kg) and a wide range of engine options, including the Pratt & Whitney JT9D-7R4G, the General Electric CF6-50E and CF6-80C, and the Rolls-Royce RB211-524B, C and D, providing thrust ratings from 46,500 to 56,500 lb (21 100 to 25 600kg).

The bare-shell interior of a 200F Freighter with cargo pallets and containers filling the left-hand track of the twin-track compartment. *(Lufthansa)*

100SF and 200F Freighters

As mentioned previously, the 747-200F Freighter had to wait for the increased maximum take-off weight of 775,000 lb (351 540 kg) to become available, and the first of this variant was No. 168, D-ABYE for Lufthansa, which was rolled out in October 1971; it was powered by Pratt & Whitney JT9D-7W engines with a take-off rating of 45,500 lb (20 639 kg) thrust, dry, or 47,900 lb (21 727 kg) thrust with water injection. Although basically a 200B, this variant was easily recognisable from the outside because it had no windows and only two of the usual 10 doors, located front and rear on the left-hand side. However, the major feature of the aircraft was the nose door, the whole of the nose in front of the flight deck opening upward under electrical power to allow straight-in loading and unloading of cargo in all shapes and sizes. The interior of the main deck compartment was a bare shell surrounding an unobstructed nose-to-tail hold with over 17,000 cubic feet (481 cubic metres) of 8 ft (2,4 m) high cargo volume, three times the volume of a Boeing 707 Freighter. The main-deck floor was strengthened to take heavier localised loads and equipped with a mechanised cargo-handling system, consisting of electrically-powered rollers located along the centre line of each of two parallel tracks which extended almost the full length of the compartment. The 747 was designed from the outset with the ability to accommodate 8 ft (2,4 m) high by 8 ft (2,4 m) wide containers in two rows down the main length of the compartment and these containers could have lengths in multiples of 10 ft (3 m) up to a maximum of 40 ft (12 m). Up to six 40 ft (12 m) long containers (plus a few smaller ones) could be carried in one load.

Normal loads for air freighters are small containers and cargo loaded on pallets, but the nose-loading 200F can also accommodate loads of unusual size and length. Drilling pipes and casing or other ducting in lengths up to 180 ft (55 m) and with diameters up to 8 ft (2,4 m) can be carried, and as many as 73 Volkswagens were once loaded aboard the Lufthansa aircraft, including 14 in the front and rear under-floor cargo holds which are also suitable for containerised or palletised cargo.

Boeing claimed that two men, a loadmaster at the nose and a loader in the interior of the aircraft, could complete the unloading or loading of a 200F in 30 minutes. The loadmaster has a control panel to operate the various sections of the cargo-handling system. Because the fuselage tapers at the nose, only a single track is fitted in the entrance and the containers or pallets are directed from here on to either the left-hand or right-hand track by steerable powered-roller units. Using local control panels provided along each side of the main-deck compartment, the loader controls the movement of the container or pallet to its stowed position. A scissor-lift platform is usually used to raise the containers or pallets from ground level to main-deck height.

This first 200F could carry a maximum payload of 260,000 lb (118 000 kg) nearly 2900 miles (4667 km), or a reduced payload of 200,000 lb (90 720 kg) nearly 4000 miles (6437 km), which was well beyond trans-Atlantic range. The normal flight crew was three but the upper-deck compartment could be used to accommodate additional crew members, for relief purposes, and was equipped with a toilet and small galley. Because there was no spiral staircase fitted in this variant to provide access from the main deck, a retractable ladder was installed for this purpose. The usual crew door was also fitted on the right-hand side of the upper deck behind the flight deck.

There was no great rush for orders for this variant and, in fact, for the next two years the Lufthansa Freighter was the only one in service. Then, in 1974, the air cargo market began to turn to bigger aircraft and the American cargo carrier Seaboard World Airlines took delivery of the first of its Freighters for use on its trans-Atlantic services. This aircraft, No. 242, N701SW, was similar to the Lufthansa 200F but in addition to the nose door it also had the optional side cargo door (SCD), which is an 11 ft (3,35 m) wide by 10 ft (3 m) high upward-opening door on the left-hand side of the fuselage behind the wing. Because of the flight deck/upper-deck compartment floor, loads entering the main-deck compartment through the nose opening are limited to just over 8 ft (2,4 m) high but once past the 'hump' the height of the compartment increases and the SCD provides access to this area, enabling items as high as 10 ft (3 m) to be accepted. Additional controls and handling equipment are fitted at this door position to simplify loading and unloading, and the transfer of containers or pallets to and from the main-deck tracks.

Containers with lengths of up to 20 ft (6,1 m) can be loaded through the SCD opening, allowing a certain amount of load changing at either end of the main-deck compartment at intermediate stops along a route. The Seaboard World Freighters were given the general name of *Containership*, and on the airline's trans-Atlantic cargo services emphasis was placed on the use of 'intermodal' containers, each 8 ft by 8 ft by 20 ft (2,4 m by 2,4 m by 6,1 m), which were suitable for transfer from one mode of transport to another (air/road/rail/sea) so that the container contents did not have to be removed from one type of container and repacked into another at points of transfer.

The first 200F for Seaboard World was initially delivered with a maximum take-off weight of 785,000 lb (356 000 kg) because it was powered by Pratt & Whitney JT9D-7W engines, of 47,900 lb (21 727 kg) thrust with water injection, but when the JT9D-70A engines of 53,000 lb (24 040 kg) thrust became available in 1975 it was returned to the factory for conversion to these more powerful engines so that its maximum take-off weight could be increased to 820,000 lb (371 952 kg). This matched the airline's second aircraft, No. 266, N702SW, which was delivered to this standard in April 1976. Apart from the SCD, the Seaboard World Freighters also differed from the Lufthansa 200F in having windows in the upper-deck compartment, and an extra emergency exit door on the left-hand side behind the flight deck, features that were to prove useful a few years later when the airline started carrying passengers up there on its trans-Atlantic cargo services between New York and Frankfurt.

Air France and Japan Air Lines also took delivery of their first 200Fs in 1974 and these too had both the nose door and side cargo door.

Another variant equipped with a side cargo door is the 747-100SF, which is the designation for a 747-100 passenger aircraft which has been converted into

The first of Air France's 200F Freighters with its nose and side cargo doors open, and in the original colour scheme. *(Air France)*

a freighter by the addition of a SCD. This variant resulted from the oil price crisis in 1974 when some 747-100 passenger aircraft were withdrawn from service and put up for sale. The Flying Tiger Line (at that time an American domestic and trans-Pacific cargo carrier) started the fashion when it bought two 747-100s of American Airlines, which had been sold back to Boeing, who converted the aircraft by stripping out the passenger interior, strengthening the main deck, covering the windows, sealing all doors except No. 1 and 5 on the left-hand side, equipping the interior with a cargo-handling system and installing a side cargo door. The last mentioned operation was best not watched by a squeamish owner of the aircraft because it involved Boeing engineers with portable electric saws cutting a large hole in the fuselage of a very expensive aircraft. This conversion job took two to three months and while the aircraft were being worked on Pratt & Whitney were converting the engines from JT9D-3A to JT9D-7A standard. When the aircraft were delivered in August and September 1974 they were cleared for an increased maximum take-off weight of 733,000 lb (332 490 kg) which enabled them to carry a payload of 222,000 lb (100 700 kg) on domestic routes and 215,000 lb (97 500 kg) on international routes. Flying Tigers paid \$22½ million for each aircraft, which was about \$10 million less than the cost of a new 747-200F at the time.

Flying Tigers later purchased four more 747-100SFs from Boeing (one ex-American and three ex-Delta) and American Airlines followed suit by having four of its remaining 747-100s converted to 100SFs. Both operators were concentrating on the use of 10 ft (3 m) long containers and palletised loads so that the container-length restriction of the SCD was not a problem, and the smaller payload of the 100SF was adequate for their operations.

During the following three years Pan Am had three of its 747-100s converted to 100SFs, and Japan Air Lines had one converted, and the Imperial Iranian Air Force, which had bought up 12 surplus 100s (nine of TWA and three of Continental), had 10 of these converted to transports with SCDs. At least two of the IIAF aircraft were further modified into flight-refuelling tankers with a retractable boom beneath their tails, the flight trials for which having been carried out earlier by 747 No. 1 in the hope of getting a US Air Force order for tanker aircraft.

The most unusual conversion of a 747-100 passenger aircraft appeared in February 1977 when a 747 took off with space shuttle Orbiter *Enterprise* on its back at the start of a test programme to enable the Orbiter to be released from high altitude to check its handling and landing characteristics. The aircraft was an ex-American Airlines 747-100 owned by the National Aeronautics and Space Administration (N905NA) and modified by Boeing to have a strengthened fuselage with support pylons for the attachment of the Orbiter and large end-plate fins on the tips of the tailplane, which were necessary to restore directional stability lost with the Orbiter mounted in front of the 747's tail. The combined weight of the two aircraft at take-off was 584,000 lb (264 900 kg) and the 747 was powered by Pratt & Whitney JT9D-7H engines (JT9D-3As modified to produce 46,950 lb (21 296 kg) thrust) to improve

National Aeronautics & Space Administration's modified 747-100 with space shuttle Orbiter Enterprise on its back. *(Military Aircraft Photographs)*

performance. The 747 was later used to ferry Orbiters from their usual landing airfield in California back to the launch site in Florida.

By the time that the 500th 747 had been rolled out in November 1980, 42 200F Freighters had been delivered, the later ones benefitting from the development of the 200B passenger aircraft (described earlier) in having more powerful engines and increased maximum take-off weights for improved payloads or extra range. Among those 42 200Fs were some powered by General Electric and Rolls-Royce engines and No. 482, LX-ECV for Cargolux, the first to be delivered at the latest maximum take-off weight of 833,000 lb (377 800 kg), powered by Pratt & Whitney JT9D-7Q engines of 53,000 lb (24 040 kg) thrust.

Since then, 17 more 200Fs have been delivered and, like the 200B, this variant is currently offered with a range of maximum take-off weights from 775,000 to 833,000 lb (351 540 to 377 800 kg) and with the same wide range of engines.

747-200C Convertible Passenger/Freighter

Although becoming available at the same time as the 200F Freighter, once the maximum take-off weight of the 200 series had been increased to 775,000 lb (351 540 kg), the first 747-200C Convertible - No. 209, N747WA for World Airways - was not rolled out until February 1973. At first glance it looked like a 747-200B passenger aircraft, because it had the doors and windows along the main and upper decks, but it also had the upward-opening nose door and strengthened floor of the 747-200F Freighter, and the interior could be converted to suit either passenger-carrying or freighter roles. Because of the nose door, the 200C differed externally from the 200B in having only 86 windows along each side of the main deck (including one in each door) instead of 88, two windows being missing from each side of the nose where the nose door joined the main fuselage.

The conversion of a 200C from one role to another is no easy task and requires considerably more work than the type of conversion possible with the specially-equipped quick-change (QC) versions of the Boeing 727 and 737 which can be converted in an hour so that they can carry passengers during the day and cargo at night for maximum utilization. The time required to convert a 200C is often measured in days rather than hours but it is still an economical proposition if it means that an airline can perform both types of operation with one aircraft instead of needing two aircraft, one for each role. A typical operator of 200Cs is El Al who converts its aircraft twice a year because it has a peak in passenger traffic during summer months and a peak in cargo traffic in winter months when it assists in the export of Israeli agricultural products. World Airways also started operations with its 200Cs that way, the aircraft being used initially for trans-Atlantic passenger charter flights during the summer of 1973 and were then transferred to military cargo charters for the US Air Force the following winter.

Conversion from an all-passenger to an all-cargo configuration involves first the removal of the passenger kit, which includes seats, carpets, upper-deck staircase, toilets, galleys, partitions, overhead stowage bins and drop ceilings. Then comes the installation of the cargo-handling kit, which includes the twin tracks of rollers, guides and loading controls, plus the ladder to the upper deck, as fitted in the 200F. The Boeing estimate for the minimum time required to complete the conversion was 24 hours, using a crew of 35 men working in shifts. This was put to the test, in a typical 'rush job' for a charter company, when in mid-May 1974 (at the start of the passenger-carrying season) there was an immediate need in Japan for 100 large pieces of oil-drilling equipment which were in Pittsburg, USA. World Airways was given the contract and a 200C was positioned to the airline's maintenance base at Oakland, California, on 12 May, where 35 men working in shifts against the clock managed to complete the conversion in 20 hours. The aircraft was then flown to Pittsburg to pick up the load, which included two 46 ft (14 m) long pipe assemblies each weighing 33,000 lb (14 970 kg), a crown assembly which was 20 ft (6 m) long by just under 10 ft (3 m) wide and weighed 28,000 lb (12 700 kg), and eight pieces of equipment each 40 ft (12,2 m) long. No special loading equipment was available so each item was first placed on a flat-bed truck which was then hoisted by two cranes to the 16 ft (4,88 m) sill height of the aircraft's main deck. The longer items were strapped to several pallets, to simplify the task of handling them once aboard the aircraft, and required the use of a third crane at the remote end when loading; the crown assembly cleared the nose-door opening by less than 2½ in. (6,35 cm). The total payload for the flight was 160,000 lb (72 575 kg).

The cargo-handling crew flew with the load to supervise the unloading in Japan and, during the $8\frac{1}{2}$ hour non-stop return flight from Tokyo to Oakland, began the reverse conversion back to the all-passenger configuration by dismantling the cargo-handling equipment and removing the power drive units. In this way, when the reverse conversion was completed at Oakland, it took the 35 men (again working shifts) only 27 hours, instead of the minimum time estimated by Boeing of 36 hours, and the aircraft was back in passenger service on 18 May.

These first 200Cs had a maximum take-off weight of 775,000 lb (351 540 kg) with power provided by Pratt & Whitney JT9D-7AW engines producing 48,750 lb (22 113 kg) thrust with water injection. As with the 200F, later aircraft benefitted from the development of the 200B passenger aircraft (described earlier) in having more powerful engines and increased maximum take-off weights for improved payloads or extra range. Further operational flexibility came with the introduction of the side cargo door (SCD) - described earlier under 100SF and 200F Freighters - and the first 200C to be so equipped was No. 287, YI-AGN for Iraqi Airways, which was rolled out in May 1976. The Iraqi aircraft was also unusual in having an on-board loader which, stowed in zone A and deployed through the nose-door opening, could be used to load containers or pallets into zones D and E through the SCD opening or simply load and accommodate one 20 ft (6 m) container, or two 10 ft (3 m) containers or three pallets in zone A. The equipment could be powered by the aircraft's auxiliary power unit, enabling the aircraft to be

Martinair's 200C Convertible in winter service as a Freighter; in summer it is converted to operate trans-Atlantic passenger charters. *(Martinair)*

completely self-contained at airports not equipped for cargo handling.

So far only 12 200Cs have been delivered (with one more on order) but this variant is still available and, like the 200B, is offered with a range of maximum take-off weights from 775,000 to 833,000 lb (351 540 to 377 850 kg) and with the same wide range of engines.

747-100SR and 747-100B (SR) (Short Range) Passenger

Only the Japanese, with their high-density, mainly inter-island, short-haul domestic routes, found an application for the 747-100SR, which is a high-capacity airliner for routes as short as 200 miles (322 km). The first 100SR -No. 221, JA8117 for Japan Air Lines - was rolled out in August 1973 and was basically a 747-100 in which the structure and landing gear had been strengthened to permit it to make 52,000 landings in 20 years; which means that it could average six to seven take-off/landing cycles per day compared with the three per day average for the standard long-range 747s. However, the normal 747-100 fuel capacity of 47,210 US gal (178 709 1) was retained so that these aircraft could be used on long-range operations if required. The maximum take-off weight of this variant could therefore vary from 520,000 lb (235 872 kg) for short-range flights to 735,000 lb (333 396 kg) for long-range flights.

When the 747-100SRs entered service with Japan Air Lines they had seating for 498 passengers, which was an all-time high for the period, but, as described in the previous section, the airline has gone on to break that record. Externally there is no way of distinguishing a 747-100SR from a 747-100, and the JAL aircraft were powered by JT9D-7A engines, the same as those that powered the airline's later standard 747s, but on short-range operations these engines can be operated at the reduced power of 43,500 lb (19 732 kg) thrust for longer life.

As described earlier under 747-100 and 747-100B Passenger, the 747-100 was replaced by the 747-100B in 1978 and the 747SR then became a short-range option of the new variant, retaining the same reduced maximum take-off weight for short-range operations. All Nippon Airways started its fleet of 747SRs at this time - with No. 346, JA8133 - and chose the less powerful General Electric CF6-45A engines of 46,500 lb (21 092 kg) thrust to power them.

Japan Air Lines has gone on to have the 100B(SR) with a stretched upper deck (·SUD) and more recently 300SRs (described later) with increased seating capacity but the normal 100B(SR) is still available.

747-100 Combi and 747-200B Combi, Combined Passenger/Freighter

Providing greater operational flexibility than the 747-200C Convertible, described earlier, the Combi - Combined Passenger/Freighter - became the most popular variant after the standard 200B passenger aircraft during the late 1970s and early 1980s.

The oil-price crisis during the 1973/4 winter forced airlines to get the maximum use out of their existing aircraft and one idea that materialised at

The 200B Combi, which can carry a variety of payloads from all-passenger to a mix of passengers and cargo in zones D and E. *(Lufthansa)*

the time was to convert passenger-carrying 747s into combined passenger/freighter aircraft by fitting a large cargo door on the left-hand side of the main deck just behind the wing. The first aircraft to have this side cargo door (SCD) modification were the two 747-100s of Sabena, which were returned to the factory at the beginning of 1974.

A side cargo door enabled six pallets of cargo, or containers of similar size, to be carried at the rear of the main deck (zone E) and reduced the passenger accommodation from a total of 365 (32 1st class and 333 economy class) to 242 (28 1st class and 214 economy class, but with 1st class passengers still having the use of a lounge on the upper deck). The upward-opening SCD was 11 ft (3,35 m) wide by 10 ft (3 m) high and the floor of zone E was strengthened and equipped with cargo handling equipment, including a ball-transfer unit in the entrance and roller tracks to facilitate positioning of the pallets once they were aboard.

Although, in Sabena's case, the passenger/freighter combination proved useful during the two economically-difficult years that followed the modification of the aircraft, it created a problem during summer months when there was a need to operate all-passenger flights as additional services on scheduled routes and as charters. This meant a time-consuming conversion job and, to overcome this problem, Sabena's engineering department developed a Quick-Change procedure for the 747's zone E based on the procedures used in the airline's Boeing 727QCs and 737QCs. With this procedure, the cargo-handling equipment is left in position on the floor and 12 rows of mainly 10-abreast seats, mounted on eight pallets (complete with carpets and power connections) are loaded aboard and locked in position. This raises the floor in zone E by about 8 in. (20,3 cm) but the step is eliminated by using carpeted ramps. With this procedure, the rear galley (of reduced size), rear toilets, cabin trim and drop ceiling remain in place when the zone is used for cargo, to reduce the amount of change required, and it only remains to fit the overhead stowage bins to complete the conversion. Using this quick-change procedure, Sabena claimed that the conversion of zone E from one mode to another could be done by six men in 75 minutes.

The first 747 to be built as a 747-200B Combi was No. 250, C-GAGA for Air Canada, which also became the 250th 747 to be delivered, in March 1975. This variant is basically a 747-200B with an optional side cargo door and strengthened floor (with cargo handling equipment) to accommodate cargo pallets in both zones D and E on the main deck. The arrangement suits airlines with seasonal fluctuations in passenger and cargo traffic demands, and a typical application could have the aircraft with an all-passenger configuration during summer months, with passengers plus cargo in zone E (six pallets) during spring and autumn, and with passengers plus cargo in both zones D and E (12 pallets or five 20 ft (6,1 m) containers and two 10 ft (3 m) containers) during winter. Other applications include the use of the aircraft in a combined passenger/freighter configuration all-year round on routes where neither passenger traffic nor cargo loads could support a separate service; this application is good for both because it provides wide-body airliner comfort for passengers and regular container shipments for cargo agents. With cargo in zone E, a 200B Combi has about the same capacity as one wide-body tri-jet (DC-10 or Lockheed L-1011) passenger aircraft and one Boeing 707 or DC-8 freighter combined.

A divider wall, which separates the cargo in the rear from the normal passenger cabin in the front, can have the same decor as the remainder of the cabin so that passengers entering the aircraft through the usual doorways at the front will probably not realise that there is a cargo compartment behind them. Loading and unloading of both cargo and passengers can be performed simultaneously so that no extra time is required for turn-rounds at intermediate stops.

Typical conversion times quoted by Boeing, when employing an experienced 16-man crew and confining the conversion to an 8 ft (2,44 m) ceiling, are 8 hours for all-passenger to six pallets in zone E, or 14 hours for all-passenger to 12 pallets in zones D and E, or 6 hours to extend the cargo compartment from zone E to zones D and E. The reverse conversions take slightly longer and are 8 hours to reduce the cargo compartment from zones D and E to zone E, 18 hours for 12 pallets in zones D and E to all-passenger, and 10 hours for six pallets in zone E to all-passenger.

Passenger accommodation in the 200B Combi can be arranged to suit an individual airline's requirements within the limits of the zones available. Typical mixed-class totals in the late 1970s, with 28 1st class passengers and 10-abreast seating in economy zones for each layout, were 439 all-passenger, 303 with cargo in zone E, and 225 with cargo in zones D and E. In all three layouts, the 1st class passengers occupied zone A, and the upper-deck compartment was given over to 32 economy-class passengers (seated six abreast with a central aisle).

As with all variants in the 200 series, later 200B Combis benefitted from the development of the 200B passenger aircraft (described earlier) in having more powerful engines, from a choice of three manufacturers, and increased maximum take-off weights for improved payloads or extra range.

Recently several airlines have taken delivery of Combi versions of the 747-300 and others have ordered Combi versions of the 747-400 (both described later), but the 200B Combi is still available and, like the 200B passenger aircraft, is currently offered with a range of maximum take-off weights from 775,000 to 833,000 lb (351 540 to 377 850 kg) and with the same wide range of engines.

747SP (Special Performance) Passenger

With a fuselage 48 ft (14,63 m) shorter than all existing 747s, the first 747SP (Special Performance) - No. 265, N530PA for Pan Am - was easily recognisable when it was rolled out in May 1975.

The first details of the 747SP were given in August 1973 when Boeing announced that it was proceeding with a new variant which would have a shorter fuselage and carry about 100 fewer passengers but would have a range of nearly 6900 miles (11 104 km), would climb quicker to cruising altitudes which would be up to 6000 ft (1829 m) higher and would cruise faster, at M = 0·85, with a 20% reduction in fuel consumption. Once again, Pan Am led the way with an order for 10 in September 1973.

Basically the 747SP was a 747-100 with a shortened fuselage, but the removal of 48 ft 5 in. (14,8 m) of the fuselage required other changes and the opportunity was taken to reduce weight wherever possible. Even shortening the fuselage was not a simple matter of removing a single section because portions had to be taken from both ahead of and behind the wing. To retain the same upper-deck compartment, it was necessary to modify the centre section of the fuselage, and a new rear fuselage section was required to provide a more abrupt reduction in fuselage width and lower the tail for aerodynamic reasons. To compensate for the shorter fuselage, the tip of the fin was extended 5 ft (1,52 m) and a double-hinged rudder was fitted in place of the single-hinged original. Because of the lowering of the tail, the increase in the fin height results in an overall height increase of only 2 ft (0,6 m) and a difference in overall length of 47 ft (14,33 m). The span of the tailplane was increased by 10 ft (3 m) by adding to the tips so that the main part of the tailplane and the elevators remained the same.

The wing box and centre section of the 747SP's wing were similar to those of the 747-100 except that it was possible to save weight by reducing the gauge of the components because of the lower loads; the optional outer tanks were fitted as standard to allow the fuel capacity to be increased from 47,661 to 49,231 US gal (180 416 to 186 359 l) when required. The trailing edges of the wings were completely new because, in place of the triple-slotted flaps, the 747SP had simplified single-slotted flaps which resulted in a considerable weight saving, and a reduction in drag because of the deletion of the big 'canoe' fairings covering the actuating mechanism of the original version. The basic engine for the 747SP was the 46,950 lb (21 297 kg) thrust Pratt & Whitney JT9D-7A but the engine attachments were modified to permit the installation of engines from other manufacturers. A maximum take-off weight of 660,000 lb (299 376 kg) was standard for the early 747SPs, with an optional 690,000 lb (312 984 kg) for an increased fuel load.

Although the changes appeared quite drastic, the 747SP still used major parts of the standard 747-100 structure, or similar structure that could be built on the same jigs, and overall Boeing claimed a 90% commonality of components and parts likely to require changing by an airline.

The shortening of the fuselage, and the resultant reduction in the number of passengers carried, reduced the number of emergency exits required, and therefore the 747SP had only four doors on each side of the main deck. The positioning of these doors changed the interior of the aircraft somewhat, with the cabin now having only four zones, a similar size zone A, a shorter zone B, a larger zone C and a similar size but tapering zone D. Boeing took the opportunity when launching the 747SP of introducing some interior changes and additional options, which then became available for customers of standard 747s. One of the problems with the existing transverse galleys was that they were often used by passengers passing from one aisle to another, which caused some irritation to cabin staff during busy meal times, so to overcome this Boeing introduced a 16 ft (4,88 m) longitudinal galley on the right-hand side of zone B, which could serve both 1st class and economy class areas, and an aft galley at the rear of zone D. These galleys provided private working areas for the cabin staff but reduced passenger amenities by displacing six window seats in zone B and four or six toilets in zone D.

Further improvements were made to the upper-deck compartment by introducing illuminated and contoured ceilings, increased sound-proofing and separate air-conditioning controls. The 16 1st class (four abreast) or 32 economy class (six abreast) seating was already available as an option on standard 747s, provided the additional left-hand door was fitted, but now an optional aft galley was available up there to cater for those passengers, supplies for it being provided by elevator (lift) from the longitudinal galley on the main deck. For airlines having less concern for these passengers, or cabin-staff fatigue, the galley could be replaced by even more seats, making a total of 45, provided that a straight staircase was fitted in place of the spiral one to improve emergency evacuation.

The first four 747SPs were used in a seven-month flight test programme during 1975/6 and the fourth - No. 273, N533PA for Pan Am - also accumulated 140 hours on a month-long, 72,000 mile (115 870 km), world-wide demonstration tour visiting 18 countries. Flown by Boeing crews headed by senior experimental test pilot Jack Waddell and carrying Boeing personnel and representatives from various interested airlines picked up along the route, the aircraft first positioned from Boeing Field, Seattle, to New York, from where it set a record by flying 7015 miles (11 289 km) non-stop to Tokyo in 13 hours 33 minutes. From there the tour continued to Taiwan, Singapore, Afghanistan (where Kabul airport is 5871 ft (1789 m) above sea level), India and Australia. From Sydney, the aircraft made another long non-stop flight, this time 7143 miles (11 495 km) across the Pacific to Santiago, Chile, in 12 hr 14 min. While in South America, the 747SP visited La Paz (which has the world's highest commercial airport at 13,354 ft (4070 m) above sea level), Ecuador and Mexico. The airport at Mexico City is 7340 ft (2237 m) above sea level and the aircraft took off from there at a weight of 631,000 lb (286 222 kg) in a temperature of 75_2F (24_2C) for its longest non-stop flight of the tour, 7205 miles (11 595 km) across the Atlantic to Belgrade, Yugoslavia, which it reached in 12 hr 56 min. From there it flew on to Africa, via Greece, and visited Lusaka (Zambia), Nairobi (Kenya) and Abidjan (Ivory Coast) before returning across the Atlantic to Kingston (Jamaica) and Seattle.

For this demonstration tour the aircraft had been in a Boeing colour scheme and registered N40135 so when it returned it was re-painted in Pan Am colours ready to become the first 747SP to be delivered, as N533PA *Clipper Freedom*, on 5 March 1976.

In May 1976, N533PA was re-named *Clipper Liberty Bell* to continue its globe-trotting activities by making it "Around the World in 46 Hours". This special trip, arranged by Pan Am and carrying fare-paying passengers plus personnel from the airline and manufacturers, flew eastward from New York across the Atlantic and on to Delhi (for refuelling), then to Tokyo (for another refuelling), and finally across the Pacific back to New York. The flying time

The first 747SP to be delivered was Pan Am's N533PA Clipper Freedom, later re-named Liberty Bell and later still New Horizons. *(Boeing)*

The roll-out ceremony for the 500th 747 (a 200B Combi for SAS) in November 1980. The first 747SP for Qantas is behind it. *(Boeing)*

for the 22,864 mile (36 795 km) trip totalled 39 hr 26 min. and the elapsed time, New York to New York (including a 2 hour stop at Delhi and a 4 hour stop at Tokyo) was 46 hr 26 min.

To mark its 50th Anniversary in October 1977, Pan Am re-named N533PA *Clipper New Horizons* and took it on another round-the-world trip, this time flying 165 fare-paying passengers over both the North and South Poles. Starting from San Francisco, it flew over the North Pole to London, then continued to Cape Town, and finally flew over the South Pole to Auckland before returning to San Francisco. The elapsed time for this 26,706 mile (42 978 km) trip was 54 hr 7 min. (including the three refuelling stops) breaking the previous record of 62 hr 27 min. set up in November 1965 by a specially-modified Boeing 707 of Flying Tigers.

Another record-breaking round-the-world trip was made in January 1988, this time by a 747SP of United Airlines, who took over the Pan Am 747SP fleet in 1986. Named *Friendship One*, the aircraft (N147UA) took off from Boeing Field, Seattle, and, like the first Pan Am flight in 1976, headed eastward, this time to Athens (for refuelling) and then on to Taipei (for another refuelling) before continuing round to Seattle. The elapsed time for this trip was 36 hr 54 min. The 100 passengers on board were supporters of the Friendship Foundation, set up to help children in need, and paid $5000 each for the trip.

The 747SP did not prove as popular as Boeing had hoped and a lull in orders following the delivery of the 44th 747SP - No. 567, YI-ALM for the Iraqi Government - in August 1982 made it appear to be the end of the line, until the

United Arab Emirates took delivery of one in 1987 for use on VIP duties, an increasingly popular role for this variant. Boeing currently offers the 747SP with maximum take-off weights from 630,000 to 700,000 lb (285 768 to 317 520 kg) and with the current wide range of engines, the more powerful of which are de-rated to suit the smaller aircraft.

The 500th 747

The incredible total of 500 mighty 747s was reached on 19 November 1980, when a 747-200B Combi for Scandinavian Airlines System (SAS) - OY-KHB, later re-registered N4501Q - was rolled out of Boeing's Everett factory.

All the variants produced up to that time were well represented in that 500, the total comprising:

169	747-100/100B Passenger (including 747 No. 1, 24 converted to 100SF Freighters, 2 converted to 100 Combis, and 1 converted to a space-shuttle Orbiter carrier)
173	747-200B Passenger
42	747-200F Freighter
9	747-200C Convertible Passenger/Freighter
20	747SR (Short Range) Passenger
52	747-200B Combi, Combined Passenger/Freighter
35	747SP (Special Performance) Passenger

These aircraft had been built for 62 different customers representing 42 countries.

747-300 Passenger & 747-300 Combi, Combined Passenger/Freighter

Seven years elapsed before another variant appeared to follow the reduced-size 747SP. During these years Boeing devoted considerable time planning 747s of increased size, including some with sections (plugs) added to the fuselage to increase its length by 25 ft (7,62 m), but eventually an intermediate step-up in capacity was made by extending only the upper-deck compartment by 23 ft (7 m). This Stretched Upper Deck (SUD), as it became known, was initially offered as an option on 747-100B, 747SR, 200B and 200B Combi models but later became a variant in its own right, the 747-300.

Basically a 747-200B, the 747-300 benefitted from all the early development of that variant and became available at a time when the maximum take-off weight had reached 833,000 lb (377 849 kg), using engines developing around 53,000 lb (24 040 kg) thrust, with considerably reduced fuel consumption. The 300 was available as an all-passenger aircraft or as a Combi (combined passenger/freighter), and the first of this variant was a 300 Combi for Swissair - No. 570, HB-IGC - which was rolled out in September 1982.

For only a comparatively slight increase in structure weight, the stretched upper deck compartment, with its 20 windows on each side, could be used to accommodate 69 economy-class passengers, with their own galley and toilets. Such a large compartment could also be used with other arrangements, especially in a three-class aircraft, it being suitable for a self-contained 1st-class section with 26 sleeper seats, or a 42-seat business-class section. The

Singapore Airline's first 747-300 on a test flight before being given its Big Top sub-titles and registration 9V-SKA. *(Boeing)*

increase in the number of passengers upstairs required a change in the emergency evacuation procedures, so a large, upward-opening door was provided each side, both equipped with a much larger, two-lane, 49 ft (15 m) long inflatable slide. Access to the stretched upper deck was via a straight staircase from door No. 2 on the main deck to the rear of the compartment.

The stretched upper deck was also available as a kit for modifying existing 200Bs, and KLM had its 10 General Electric powered 200Bs and 200B Combis converted by Boeing, followed by UTA, who had the conversion done to its two 200B Combis. For UTA, this made it possible to move some economy-class passengers upstairs and allow more space for cargo pallets in zone D.

The 600th 747 to be built was a 747-300 Combi for KLM - N4551N *Sir Geoffrey de Havilland* - which was rolled out in July 1984, and the 600th 747 to be delivered was the first 747-300 for Qantas - No. 602, VH-EBT *City of Canberra* - with seating for 418 passengers (30 1st class, 38 business class in the stretched upper deck compartment, and 350 economy class). At that time, Boeing expected the 300 variant to become the production standard passenger 747 but it did not become that popular and some 200Bs and 200B Combis have continued to appear on the assembly line for established customers.

Another 747 weight-lifting record was created on 19 July 1987 when a 300 for Thai Airways International took off at a gross weight of 871,000 lb (395 086 kg) during certification trials. The aircraft - No. 681, HS-TGD *Suchada* - was the first 747 to be powered by General Electric CF6-80C2 engines which produce 57,900 lb (26 263 kg) thrust.

The first 747-400 (N661US for Northwest) had its ceremonial roll-out in January 1988 in a Boeing colour scheme and displaying the badges of 18 future operators. *(Boeing)*

747-400 Passenger & 747-400 Combi, Combined Passenger/Freighter

The most exciting 747 variant to appear since the 747SP is the 747-400, 118 of which were on order even before the first aircraft had been rolled out.

The 18 operators who had placed these early orders (with their engine selection, where specified) were:

Air France	16	General Electric CF6-80C2
Air New Zealand	1	Rolls-Royce RB211-524G
British Airways	16	Rolls-Royce RB211-524G
CAAC (China)	3	Pratt & Whitney PW4256
Cathay Pacific Airways	2	Rolls-Royce RB211-524G
China Airlines	5	Pratt & Whitney PW4256
Japan Air Lines	5	General Electric CF6-80C2
Japanese Government	2	
KLM	6	General Electric CF6-80C2
Korean Air	3	Pratt & Whitney PW4256
Lufthansa	10	General Electric CF6-80C2
Malaysia Airlines	2	General Electric CF6-80C2
Northwest Airlines	10	Pratt & Whitney PW4256
Qantas	4	Rolls-Royce RB211-524G
Singapore Airlines	14	Pratt & Whitney PW4256
Thai Airways International	2	General Electric CF6-80C2
United Airlines	15	Pratt & Whitney PW4256
UTA	2	General Electric CF6-80C2

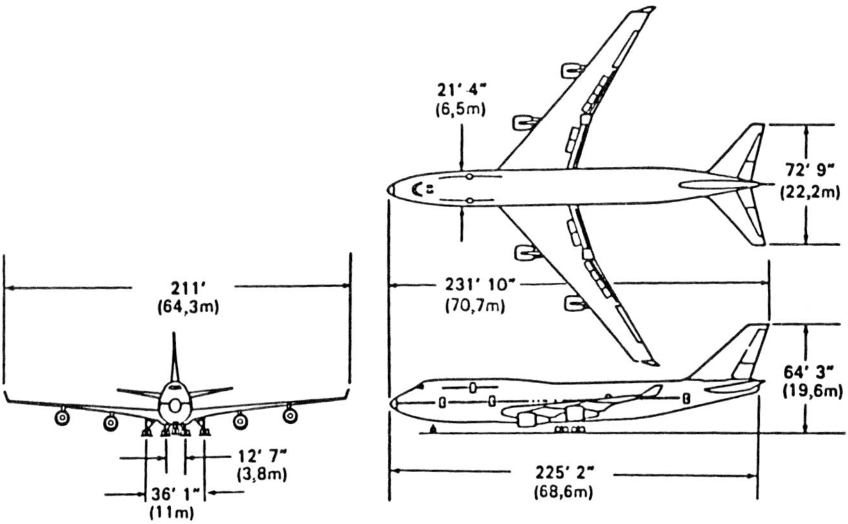

A mock-up of the 747-400's winglet, the black skin being of graphite-epoxy composite material. *(Boeing)*

The first of this important new variant was No. 696, N661US for Northwest Airlines, which was given an official roll-out ceremony on 26 January 1988, painted in Boeing colours and registered N401PW. Powered by Pratt & Whitney PW4256 engines it will be used in a flight test programme prior to certification expected towards the end of 1988. It was joined in April by the first 400 powered by General Electric CF6-80C2 engines - No. 700, D-ABVB for Lufthansa - and in June by the first 400 powered by Rolls-Royce RB211-524G engines - No. 705, VR-HOO for Cathay Pacific Airways.

Although having the general appearance of a 747-300, with its stretched upper deck (SUD), the 747-400 is easily recognisable externally by the large winglets on its wing tips, after the fashion set by some biz-jets, and is a much more advanced aircraft. The fuselage is basically the same as that of a 300 but the wing is completely new, incorporating aerodynamic improvements to reduce fuel consumption and increase range. It has had 6 ft (1,83 m) added to each of the wing tips, which have 6 ft (1,83 m) high winglets attached to provide an even greater wing span, without causing airport space problems, and also to provide a fuel-consumption improvement of about 3%. Higher strength aluminium alloys are used for the skins, stringers and lower-spar chords of the wing, to achieve a weight saving of 5000 lb (2268 kg), and the winglets are constructed from graphite-epoxy composite material and aluminium to save 60 lb (27 kg) per aircraft compared with an all-aluminium structure. The winglets are angled upward and slightly outward so that the total wing span is now 211 ft (64,3 m).

The wing-to-fuselage fairing has been re-contoured to reduce drag, and additional efficiency is achieved with re-designed nacelles and pylons (struts) for the advanced engines from all three manufacturers: the General Electric CF6-80C2 of 57,900 lb (26 263 kg) thrust; the Pratt & Whitney PW4256 of 56,750 lb (25 742 kg) thrust; and the Rolls-Royce RB211-524G of 58,000 lb (26 309 kg) thrust.

Advanced materials have also allowed considerable weight reductions elsewhere. For example, the metal flooring in the passenger cabin has been replaced with light, tough, graphite composite floor panels. Carbon brakes will also be available, which offer an estimated weight saving on a 747-400 with its 16 main landing gear wheels of 1800 lb (817 kg).

Boeing claims that the range of the 747-400 will be 8200 miles (13 196 km), which is 920 to 1150 miles (1480 to 1850 km) more than the 747-300, and that the aircraft will consume 11 to 15% less fuel than the 300; Boeing expects an improved performance of up to 25% over earlier 747s currently in service. The additional range will make possible non-stop services, with typical full-passenger, three-class payloads, on such routes as London - Tokyo, New York - Seoul, Singapore - London and Los Angeles -Sydney. For airlines requiring more range, there will be an optional 3300 US gal (12 492 l) fuel tank in the tailplane (horizontal stabiliser) to add a further 400 miles (645 km) to the range and increase the total fuel capacity to 57,285 US gal (216 846 l). The normal maximum take-off weight will be 850,000 lb (385 560 kg), with an optional 870,000 lb (394 632 kg) for an improved payload or increased range.

Another major change in the 747-400 is in the design of the flight deck. The original analogue flight deck with electro-mechanical instruments and a crew of three (two pilots and a flight engineer) has been transformed into a fully digital, two-crew (two pilots only) flight deck with cathode ray tube (CRT) -big glass screen - displays. Six 8 in. by 8 in. (20 cm by 20 cm) cathode ray tubes are used to display aircraft flight control, navigation, engine and systems information and crew alerting functions. In front of each pilot are two CRTs side by side, the left-hand one being the primary flight display (PFD) and the right-hand one the navigation display (ND) which can also be selected to present four-colour weather radar pictures. Also on the main panel between the two pilots are two CRTs mounted one above the other which are called the engine indication and crew alerting system (EICAS). The top one displays engine data (rpm, temperatures and pressures) and fuel state, plus landing gear and flap positions, and the bottom one is used to present secondary engine data, aircraft system diagrams and 'trouble shooting' information.

The basic equipment in the new flight deck has already been proved on the Boeing 757 and 767, and Boeing states that the CRTs allow more information to be displayed with a reduction in the number of conventional instruments; in fact, the number of flight-deck lights, gauges and switches has been reduced from 971 on the earlier 747s to 365 on the 747-400. Automatic and manual switching is provided in the event of an individual CRT failure. Flight crews

A mock-up of the 747-400's two-crew flight deck with its six cathode ray tube displays. (Boeing)

will also be able to obtain an update on the aircraft's mechanical condition while at cruising altitude, information that was previously available only to maintenance staff while the aircraft was on the ground.

Boeing claims that the work load on the 747-400's flight deck is designed to be one-half to one-third that of the earlier 747s. However, there will still be the problem of crew fatigue on the very long-range flights some airlines are planning for their aircraft and it is likely that two flight crews will be carried; a flight-crew rest area, with a double-tier bunk, can be installed immediately behind the flight deck for the resting crew.

Fatigue can also affect the cabin staff on these very long-range flights and, to alleviate this problem, a new cabin-staff rest area has been designed which can be located in a 'loft', the unused over-head space at the rear of the passenger cabin above the drop ceiling of the rear toilets. Typically, this can be equipped with four double-tier bunks and two seats, providing isolation from the passenger cabin for off-duty staff while preserving all the usual seating for the paying customers.

The interior of the passenger cabin in the 747-400 has been re-designed 'to improve passenger convenience and interior appeal'. Ceiling and sidewall panels have been re-contoured with new, lighter-weight materials that are

A view inside the mock-up of the 1st class section in the 747-400's passenger cabin showing the new sidewall and ceiling panels and improved lighting. *(Boeing)*

said, with new lighting, to lend an open, airy look. The overhead lockers (or bins) for the stowage of carry-on baggage have been made considerably bigger and now have upward-opening doors instead of downward-dropping lower portions, which tended to shed the contents on to the heads of unsuspecting passengers beneath.

New materials used in the passenger cabin to meet Boeing's goals for fireworthiness include replacing epoxy/glass with phenolic glass or carbon construction for partitions (class dividers), doors, coat closets, galleys, toilet walls and other interior surfaces. A change from polycarbonate to a new thermo-plastic blend is claimed to reduce smoke and toxicity levels in the event of a fire, and the ceilings of the upper-deck compartment will be made of improved polyester and phenolic sheet moulding materials instead of polyester.

Additional flexibility of the interior arrangement will permit airlines to re-locate partitions (class dividers) and galleys and toilet modules quickly to suit a particular route. Extra locations for galleys and toilets will be available and these 'quick-change' features will allow major re-arrangement within 48 hours; seats and class dividers can be changed overnight.

Some of the additional flexibility of the interior arrangement will depend on the attitude of the Federal Aviation Administration (FAA), and the aviation authorities of other countries, towards the deletion of the over-wing door No. 3 on each side of the cabin, which is claimed to save weight and cost, and allow extra seats to be fitted. Considerable discussion on the subject arose in the mid-1980s when some non-American airlines (including British Airways, Cathay Pacific Airways, KLM and Korean Air) decided to seal these doors on their existing 200Bs and 300s, and take delivery of new aircraft without them. Fortunately, most 747 operators have retained the No. 3 doors and some have specified that they are fitted to their 747-400s. The 747 has always had a more than adequate number of emergency exits and Boeing claims that the 90-second evacuation time can still be met even with only half of the eight remaining doors in use, but, on the other hand, the deletion of the No. 3 doors increases considerably the distance to an exit door for some passengers. One amenity on 747-400s that could be of benefit to passengers, particularly businessmen/businesswomen, is an in-flight telephone system, where calls are relayed via communications satellites. In the early days of 747s provision was made for fitting a satellite communications (SATCOM) aerial beneath a small fairing behind the upper-deck compartment; this was intended mainly for passing air traffic control messages but was not adopted. This latest system is likely to be more popular, with calls being paid for by simply inserting a credit card which then releases a wall-mounted hand-set.

Besides the usual big-screen film shows, various other forms of in-flight entertainment have been tried in 747s through the years, including live entertainers, fashion shows, a casino area with one-armed bandits, and a system employing numerous television sets (video monitors) mounted throughout the cabin to show video films, advertisements, emergency demonstrations and even views of take-offs and landings from a camera on the nose landing gear. One of the latest ideas, which could be used on 747-400s, is seat-back television, where each passenger has a 3 in. by 3 in. (7,62 cm by 7,62 cm) screen on which can be selected six channels of video entertainment or information.

A Combi (combined passenger/freighter) version of the 747-400 will be available to airlines in 1989 which will have all the features of this new variant plus the advantages of a side cargo door (SCD) - described earlier under 747-200B Combi - to provide additional operational flexibility.

Engines

The high by-pass ratio turbo-fan engines which power Boeing 747s were developed from the by-pass engines and small turbo-fans fitted to later versions of the first generation of long-range jet airliners - Boeing 707s, DC-8s and VC10s. Those engines were able to provide more power with considerably reduced fuel consumption, thereby improving the economics of jet airliner operation.

Basically, the turbo-fan is a cross between a turbo-jet and a turbo-prop, with an enclosed fan at the front (replacing the propeller) producing a flow of air which is divided to provide a supercharged supply to a normal turbo-jet while the remainder of the air is ducted around the outside of the engine (i.e. by-passes it). The difference between the amount of air by-passing the core engine (as the turbo-jet part is called) and the amount flowing into it is known as the by-pass ratio; on early turbo-fans this figure was around 1·5:1.

The by-pass principle was conceived by Sir Frank Whittle in the early days of gas turbine aero-engines and was first put into practice by Britain's Metropolitan-Vickers with the Metrovik F.3 ducted-fan engine, which was a turbo-jet with a fan at the rear formed by having fan blades as extensions to one set of turbine blades. In this way, some of the energy in the high-velocity gas stream was converted, via the turbine/fan, into a larger but slower-moving air stream. Greater propulsive efficiency is achieved when the ratio of the engine's jet velocity to the aircraft's flight speed is kept as low as possible, and the turbo-fan was developed to provide a power-plant for aircraft with high subsonic speeds operating at high altitudes, whereas the turbo-jet is generally considered to be more suitable for supersonic aircraft and the turbo-prop (with its by-pass ratio of between 40:1 and 50:1) for lower subsonic speeds at lower altitudes.

General Electric (USA) converted its CJ-805 turbo-jet into an aft-fan engine, with a by-pass ratio of 1÷5:1, to provide a suitable engine for the Convair CV990 jet airliner in 1960; this conversion increased the thrust from 11,000 lb (4990 kg) to 16,000 lb (7258 kg), and reduced the specific fuel consumption, for only small increases in frontal area, length and weight. A different approach to the by-pass principle was used in the Rolls-Royce Conway of the same period, which was a two-shaft engine with an oversize seven-stage low-pressure compressor, the excess delivery air from which was ducted around the outside of the engine; initially the by-pass ratio was 0÷3:1 but this was later increased to 0÷6:1. The first engine to enter airline service with a fan at the front was the Pratt & Whitney JT3D, a modified version of the JT3 Turbo Wasp turbo-jet. The original JT3 was a two-shaft engine with a nine-stage low-pressure compressor driven by a two-stage l.p. turbine, and a seven-stage high-pressure compressor driven by a single-stage h.p. turbine, and produced 11,000 lb (4990 kg) of thrust. To provide the by-pass airflow in the JT3D version, a 53 in. (135 cm) diameter two-stage fan replaced the first three stages of the low-pressure compressor, and a third l.p. turbine stage was added to provide the necessary increase in shaft power to drive the fan. The by-pass ratio was 1÷4:1 and the fan airstream was discharged through a short-chord duct surrounding the front of the engine. The JT3D turbo-fan retained 90% of the parts of the original JT3 turbo-jet but gave 52% more take-off thrust with a 15% better specific fuel consumption.

General Electric (USA) was first to develop big turbo-fans with high by-pass ratios, in which the by-pass airflow produces about 70% of the thrust, and won the competition to power the US Air Force's Lockheed C-5A Galaxy transports with the TF-39 of 41,000 lb (18 598 kg) thrust, the first of the big-fan engines, later to be developed into the civil CF6. Pratt & Whitney (with its JTF-14, later the JT9D) and Rolls-Royce (with its RB178, later the RB211) were close behind and it was not long before all three manufacturers were able to offer 747 customers a choice of these engines which have fans with a diameter of about 8 ft (2,44 m), by-pass ratios of around 5:1 and current thrust ratings of up to 58,000 lb (26 300 kg), with 60,000 lb (27 216 kg) available in the near future.

The Pratt & Whitney JT9D-1 of 41,000 lb (18 598 kg) thrust was selected as the initial power-plant for the 747-100. However, with the unexpected

Shown testing the fifth engine position (for ferrying spare engines), 747 No. 1 is here powered by early JT9D engines with blow-in doors around the air intakes. *(Boeing)*

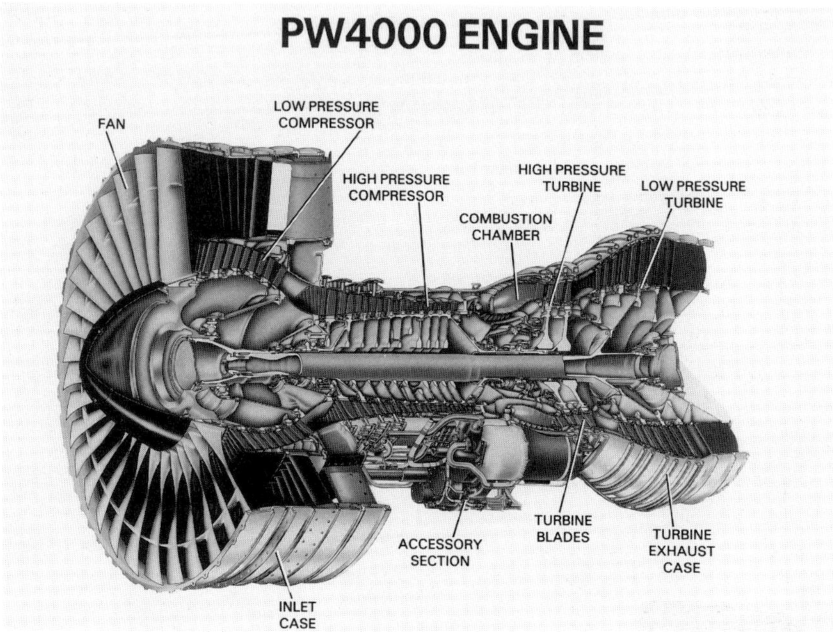

A cutaway view of the new Pratt & Whitney PW4256 engine, selected by some airlines to power their 747-400s. *(Pratt & Whitney*

increase in airframe and systems weight in 1968, this version was restricted to use in the flight test programme and the more powerful JT9D-3 of 43,500 lb (19 732 kg) thrust was made available for initial 747 deliveries. Early problems with this version were mainly overcome with the JT9D-3A which could produce 45,000 lb (20 412 kg) of thrust with water injection at take-off.

Basically, the early JT9D was a two-shaft (or two-spool) engine, with the fan and a three-stage low-pressure compressor driven by a three-stage l.p. turbine on one shaft, and an 11-stage high-pressure compressor driven by a two-stage h.p. turbine on the other shaft. Internal modifications to increase pressures and the use of improved materials to increase operating temperatures led to a steady development of the JT9D series, providing more power with reduced fuel consumption for later 747s, thereby increasing their range or payload. First was the JT9D-7 of 45,500 lb (20 639 kg) thrust, or 47,900 lb (21 727 kg) wet (i.e. with water injection), then in 1973 the -7A of 46,950 lb (21 297 kg) thrust dry or 48,750 lb (22 113 kg) wet, in 1975 the -7F of 48,000 lb (21 773 kg) thrust dry or 50,000 lb (22 680 kg) wet, and in 1979 the -7J of 50,000 lb (22 680 kg) thrust dry.

To provide for future power increases, the JT9D underwent a major re-design to produce the 53,000 lb (24 040 kg) thrust -70A in 1976. The fan diameter was increased by 1 in. (2,54 cm), a fourth low-pressure compressor stage was added and a modified combustion system fitted. This version also had a change in external appearance, having a long-chord fan cowling in place of the familiar short-chord one; the only previous major external change had been the deletion of the 'blow-in' doors around the air intake to reduce noise. The long-chord cowling was called a 'common-nacelle' because it was the same as that used for the JT9D engines in the Airbus A300 and DC-10-40 but was not chosen by many 747 airlines, the majority preferring the -7Q - the same basic engine with a lighter short-chord cowling - which, in 1980, permitted an optional increase in the 747's maximum take-off weight to 833,000 lb (377 850 kg).

Pratt & Whitney then introduced a complete range of big fan engines developed from the -70 designated JT9D-7R4 with thrust ratings from 44,000 lb (19 958 kg) to 56,000 lb (25 400 kg) to suit all wide-bodied airliners from the big twins to the 747. The JT9D-7R4G2 was the basic engine for the 747 which, by incorporating a modified fan and improved materials and manufacturing techniques for the turbine blades, has a thrust of 54,000 lb (24 495 kg). These more powerful engines have been chosen by all the airlines which have selected Pratt & Whitney engines for their 747-300s and for some later aircraft in the 200 series.

With its engine designations becoming rather involved, it was fortunate that Pratt & Whitney had introduced a new system of designations by the time the company launched its latest range of big fan engines. Again with thrust ratings to suit all wide-bodied airliners from the Airbus A300/A310 and Boeing 767 to the 747, the PW4000 is an entirely new design based on

General Electric CF6-50 engines were fitted to 747 No. 1 for certification trials on the airframe/engine combination. *(Boeing)*

General Electric's engine for the 747-400 is the CF6-80C2, one of which is shown here being prepared for a test run. *(General Electric)*

experience with the JT9D series and incorporating the advanced technology developed for the smaller PW2037 engines which power some Boeing 757s. The 747 engine in this range is the PW4256 - the 4 indicating the engine type, the 2 being the aircraft type, and the 56 being the thrust rating x 1000 lb - and is intended to provide the increased power required by the 747-4000, with an initial thrust of 56,750 lb (25 742 kg).

Basically, the PW4256 is a two-spool engine, with a 93 in. (236 cm) diameter fan (with titanium blades) and a four-stage low-pressure compressor driven by a four-stage l.p. turbine on one shaft, and an 11-stage high-pressure compressor driven by a two-stage h.p. turbine. Pratt & Whitney claim a 7% reduction in fuel consumption for these engines, compared with the JT9D-7R4 range of engines, and considerably reduced maintenance costs resulting from improved manufacturing techniques and an incredible 54% reduction in the number of parts. This parts reduction was achieved by increasing the efficiency of aerodynamic components (resulting in 23% fewer blades and guide vanes) and combining a number of parts into single large components, thus eliminating numerous fasteners. Thrust ratings up to 65,000 lb (29 484 kg) are considered possible from this range to meet future requirements.

A second choice of engine manufacturer became available to 747 customers in 1974 with the General Electric (USA) CF6-50E of 52,500 lb (23 814 kg) thrust, after certification trials on this airframe/engine combination had been completed on 747 No. 1. This engine had been developed from the 40,000 lb (18 144 kg) thrust CF6-6 which had entered airline service in 1971 powering DC-10-10s. The CF6-50E is a two-spool engine which has a fan and three-stage low-pressure compressor (called a booster) driven by a four-stage l.p. turbine, and a 14-stage high-pressure compressor driven by a two-stage h.p. turbine. It is basically the same as the CF6-50C engines which power the early Airbus A300s and DC-10-30s, and is fitted with a similar nacelle with a long-chord fan cowling.

The CF6-45A engine is the same as the CF6-50E but is de-rated to produce a lower thrust of 46,500 lb (21 092 kg) which gives it a longer in-service life. It is used in some 747SRs and is also suitable for 747-100Bs and 747SPs where the additional power is not required.

A major re-design of the CF6-50 series resulted in the CF6-80 series which started with the CF6-80A for the big twins. Changes in the internal structure reduced the engine length by 27 in. (69cm) and, together with improved aerodynamics for the fan and compressors, resulted in a lighter and more fuel-efficient engine.

Further demands by industry for more power has led to the development of General Electic's latest engine, the 57,900 lb (26 263 kg) thrust CF6-80C2 which is the company's offering for the 747-400. In this version, the fan

The first Rolls-Royce powered 747, a 200B of British Airways, entered service in July 1977. *(Rolls-Royce)*

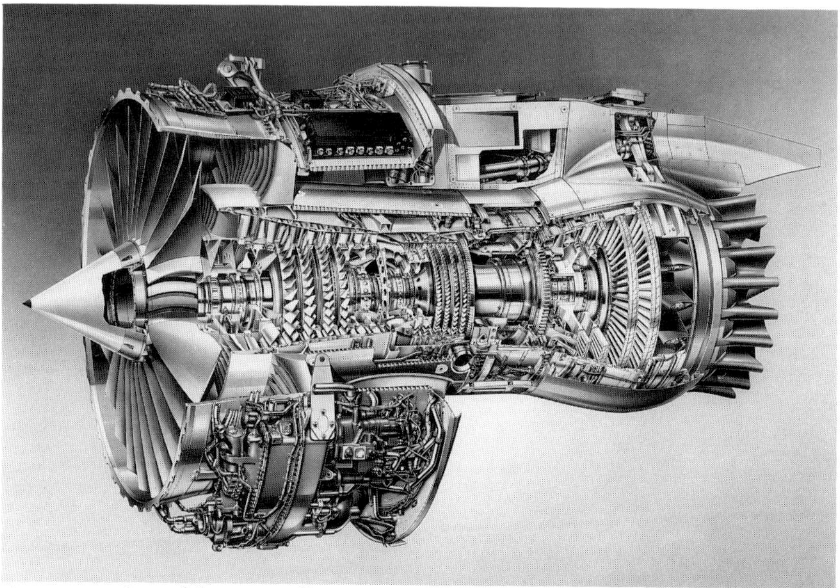

A cutaway view of the new Rolls-Royce RB211-524G engine which has been selected to power some 747-400s *(Rolls-Royce)*

diameter has been increased to 93 in. (236cm) and an additional stage has been added to the low-pressure compressor (booster) and to the l.p. turbine. General improvements have also been made to incorporate the latest technology and the new range of engines is considered capable of meeting future power requirements up to 65,000 lb (29 484 kg) thrust. The certification trials on the 747/CF6-80C2 combination were completed in 1987 on a 747-300 for Thai Airways International (HS-TGD).

Rolls-Royce RB211-524B engines of 50,000 lb (22 680 kg) thrust became available for 747 customers in 1977, with the certification trials for this airframe/engine combination being carried out on the first Rolls/Royce powered 747-200B for British Airways (G-BDXA). These engines were developed from the 42,000 lb (19 050 kg) thrust RB211-22 which entered airline service in 1972 powering the Lockheed L-1011 TriStar. The RB211 is unusual in that is is a three-shaft engine, and the -524 version has a fan driven by a three-stage low-pressure turbine on one shaft, a seven-stage intermediate-pressure compressor driven by a single-stage i.p. turbine on a second shaft, and a six-stage high-pressure compressor driven by a single-stage h.p. turbine on a third shaft. This arrangement results in a shorter engine, and its long-chord fan cowling extends to almost the full length of the engine.

By improving the cooling of the h.p. turbine blades, an increase in fuel flow was made possible, enabling the thrust to be increased to 51,500 lb (23 360 kg) in the RB211-524C. A further increase in thrust, to 53,000 lb (24 040 kg), and reduced fuel consumption, were achieved in the RB211-524D4 by modifying the fan and l.p. turbine.

Further development led to the 58,000 lb (26 310 kg) thrust RB211-524D4D but fortunately just as the engine designations were getting complicated Rolls-Royce re-designated this version as the RB211-524G. This is the engine offered for the 747-400 and is claimed to be 14% more fuel efficient and to offer 16% more power than the first RB211s fitted to 747s. The main change to this version is the 86 in. (218 cm) diameter fan with fewer, wide-chord blades and no snubbers, plus internal improvements and an integrated exhaust nozzle and mixer to reduce noise. The -524G is capable of thrust ratings up to 60,000 lb (27 216 kg) and from there Rolls-Royce is planning a version with a larger diameter fan to take the thrust ratings to 65,000 lb (29 484 kg) and beyond.

Thrust reversal is provided on all big-fan engines, the rear section of the fan cowling being slid rearwards to expose cascade vanes and the fan airstream deflected forward through these to provide reverse thrust for braking purposes during landing.

Operators

This section contains details and fleet lists of all airlines, air forces and governments who have operated Boeing 747s since 1970, with the exception of airlines who have had aircraft on short-term leases with only their titles applied.

Abbreviations

Cvtd	Converted	Ret.	Returned
Del.	Delivered	S.	Sold
L.	Leased	SCD	Side cargo door
NTU	Not taken up	SUD	Stretched upper deck
Orig.	Originally	WFU	Withdrawn from use
Reg.	Registration	W.O.	Written off

AER LINGUS (EI/EIN) — IRELAND (EIRE)

The shamrock has appeared on the tail of a 747 since the earliest days, with Aer Lingus starting trans-Atlantic services from Dublin and Shannon to New York in April 1971, and to Boston the following month. At first the aircraft had a white top and tail with a green shamrock but the airline had a complete change of colour scheme in the mid-1970s and the aircraft now have a green top and tail with a white shamrock.

Passenger accommodation originally totalled 366, with 24 1st class in zone A, called the Tara Room (after the ancient seat of the High Kings of Ireland) — plus the in-flight use of an upstairs lounge (the State Room) — and 342 economy (seated 9 abreast) in the other zones, named after the four historic provinces of Ireland; Ulster, Connaught (Connacht), Leinster and Munster. Aer Lingus was quick to introduce 10-abreast economy seating, when the total rose to 397 passengers, with 373 in economy. The introduction of business class in the 1980s changed the configuration again, to a total of 401, with 16 1st class (called Golden Shamrock, with sleeper seats), 46 business class (called super executive, 6-abreast at 39 in. (99cm) pitch) and 339 economy.

FLEET

Reg.	Line No.	Model	Delivery Date	Name	Remarks
EI-ASI	84	148	15/Dec/70	St Patrick/Padraig (Orig. St Colmcille)	
EI-ASJ	108	148	18/Mar/71	St Colmcille (Orig. St Patrick)	
EI-BED	44	130	05/Jan/79	St Kieran/Ciaran	Second-hand Ex Lufthansa D-ABYC

AEROLINEAS ARGENTINAS (AR/ARG) — ARGENTINA

Although Aerolineas Argentinas planned to start 747 operations in 1975 with an ex-Delta aircraft leased from Boeing, this was prevented by political problems and it was not until January 1977 that the first services were operated, with a new aircraft, from Buenos Aires to Frankfurt via Madrid and Rome or Rio de Janeiro and Paris. Through the years the 747 route network increased to include London (dropped with the Falkland Islands' conflict), Los Angeles, Mexico City, Miami, Montreal and New York. In addition, a most unusual route introduced in June 1980 was Buenos Aires to Auckland, New Zealand, over the South Pole.

FLEET

Reg.	Line No.	Model	Delivery Date	Remarks
LV-LRG	72	132	Not del.	Ex Delta N9896 To China A/L B-1868
LV-LZD	274	287B	16/Dec/76	Stored 1 year before del. Ret. to Boeing Jan/82 To Virgin Atlantic G-VIRG
LV-MLO	349	287B	13/Jan/79	L. to Fl. Tigers Jul/83
LV-MLP	403	287B	11/Oct/79	400th 747 delivered
LV-MLR	404	287B	26/Oct/79	
LV-OEP	487	287B	18/Nov/80	
LV-OOZ	532	287B	26/Aug/81	
LV-OPA	552	287B	23/Jan/82	
747SP				
LV-OHV	413	SP27	12/Sep/80	S/H. Ex Braniff N604BN

AIR AFRIQUE (RK) — IVORY COAST

One of the lone flyers, the two-tone green and white 747 Freighter of Air Afrique was operated from October 1980 until March 1984, generally on the Abidjan - Paris route, but was then leased out to other airlines and was eventually sold in 1985 when the airline had financial problems.

Various passenger 747s have been operated in recent years on short-term leases during Hadj periods but were identified only by the airline's titles.

FLEET

Reg.	Line No.	Model	Delivery Date	Name	Remarks
TU-TAP	472	2S4F	03/Oct/80	Lome	S. to Japan Leasing Sep/85 To Korean Air HL7474

AIR ALGERIE (AH) — ALGERIA

After starting 747 services between Algiers and Paris in December 1979 with a leased Aer Lingus aircraft in the Irish airline's colours, Air Algerie leased an

AIR ALGERIE (AH) (continued)

aircraft from World Airways the following year and this was painted in the airline's full red and white colours. This was in service for a year, and since then Air Algerie has had 747s only on short-term leases usually for the Hadj period.

In May 1983 two ex-Braniff 747s were re-painted in Air Algerie's new red, green and white colour scheme but the deal fell through and the aircraft were not delivered.

FLEET

Reg.	Line No.	Model	Delivery Date	Remarks
EI-BED	44	130	15/Oct/79	L. from Aer Lingus Ret. Apr/80
N747WR	209	273C	01/Apr/80	L. from World A/W (N747WA) Ret. Mar/81
N8284V	437	227B	Not del.	Ex Braniff N605BN To Northwest N633US
N8285V	465	227B	Not del.	Ex Braniff N1607B To Northwest N634US

AIR CANADA (AC/ACA) CANADA

The maple-leaf-bearing 747s of Air Canada were introduced on the Vancouver-Toronto route in April 1971, followed by Toronto-London services in the June and Montreal-Toronto-Paris-Frankfurt services in the July.

Passenger accommodation originally totalled 365, with 32 in 1st class who had the in-flight use of an upstairs Voyageur Lounge. Nowadays, the total is usually 390 with 18 1st class, 54 business class and 318 economy, with reduced economy seating in 200B Combis having mixed-traffic configurations, with cargo pallets in zones D and E.

FLEET

Reg.	Line No.	Model	Delivery Date	Remarks
C-FTOA	104	133	11/Feb/71	Orig. CF-TOA S. to Guinness Peat N749R & EI-BPH Jul/84
C-FTOB	121	133	18/Mar/71	Orig. CF-TOB S. to Guinness Peat EI-BRR May/85
C-FTOC	144	133	24/Jun/71	Orig. CF-TOC
C-FTOD	214	133	14/May/73	Orig. CF-TOD
C-FTOE	236	133	13/May/74	
C-GAGA	250	233B Combi	07/Mar/75	First 747-200B Combi 250th 747 built
C-GAGB	355	233B Combi	31/Jan/79	
C-GAGC	314	238B Combi	11/Jan/88	S/H. Ex Qantas VH-ECA

Air Canada
-233B Combi
C-GAGB (355)
(Phillipe Petit)

Air France
-228B Combi
F-BPVT (313)
(Christian Laugier)

Air Gabon
-2Q2B Combi
F-ODJG (324)
(Stephane Salandre)

Air Lanka
-238B
(ex Qantas)
4R-ULF (147)
(Christian Volpati)

Alitalia
-243B Combi
I-DEMF (499)
(Michael Steinlein)

Braniff Intl.
-SP27
N603BN (405)
(Boeing)

British Airways
-236F
G-KILO (480)
(Boeing)

Cathay Pacific
-267B
VR-HIC (493)
(George Ditchfield)

Continental
-238B
(ex Qantas)
N610PE (217)
(Maurice Bertrand)

Evergreen Intl.
-131SF
(ex TWA)
N472EV (98)
(Russell E. Lown)

Flying Tigers
-249F
N808FT (458)
(Chris Green)

Garuda
-2U3B
PK-GSF (562)
(Marcel Walther)

Gulf Air
-283B
(ex SAS)
LN-AET (114)
(Mogens Jacobsen)

Highland Express
-123
(ex American A/Ls)
N14939/G-HIHO (87)
(Michael Steinlein)

Iberia
-256B
EC-DIA (450)
(Boeing)

Japan Air Lines
-346
N212JL (588)
(Scott Meredith)

KLM
-206B
N1295E (474)
(A.J.M. Hofstra)

Koreanair
-2B5B
HL7464 (215)
(Marcel Walther)

Martinair
-21AC
PH-MCE (669)
(Ron Mak)

MEA/GPA
-133
(ex Air Canada)
EI-BPH (104)
(Christian Laugier)

Minerve
-283B
(ex SAS)
F-GHBM (114)
(Christian Laugier)

Nippon Cargo
-281F
JA8167 (604)
(Browcom files)

Oman Govt.
-SP27
(ex Braniff)
A40-SO (405)
(Richard Vandervord)

Pan American
-212B
(ex Singapore A/Ls)
N723PA (312)
(Antonio Branca)

Philippine A/Ls
-2F6B
N741PR (421)
(Marcel Walther)

Qantas
-SP38
VH-EAA (505)
(Rick Skoroszewski

Saudi Govt.
-3GI
HZ-HM1A (592)
(Browcom files)

South African A/Ws
-SP44
ZS-SPA (280)
(Marcel Walther)

Thai Intl.
-2D7B
HS-TGF (479)
(Browcom files)

United Airlines
-SP21
(ex Pan American)
N148UA (367)
(Brian J. Gore)

UTA
-3B3
F-GDUA (573)
(Browcom files)

Virgin Atlantic
-287B
(ex Aero Argentinas)
G-VIRG (274)
(Chris Green)

AIR FRANCE (AF/AFR) FRANCE

Air France 747s entered service on the Paris-New York route in June 1970 and have since extended their activities world-wide to include other destinations in North America, the Caribbean, South America, Africa and the Far East.

Early aircraft had the original dark blue and white Air France colour scheme but after passing through a light blue and white trial period the airline settled on a white fuselage with blue, white and red flashes up the tail and large blue titling, as introduced on the airline's Concordes in 1976.

Originally, accommodation was provided for 360 passengers, with 36 in 1st class who had the use in flight of a lounge/bar on the upper deck. When the 200B Combis were introduced in 1977 they carried 281 passengers, with 24 in 1st class and cargo in zone E. Various configurations are now used but typical for an all-passenger aircraft is 24 1st class, 54 business class (called Le Club) and 295 economy, and for a 200B Combi 16 1st class, 54 business class and 187 economy, plus cargo pallets in zone E.

FLEET

Reg.	Line No.	Model	Delivery Date	Remarks
Pratt & Whitney Powered Aircraft				
F-BPVA	19	128	20/Mar/70	
F-BPVB	22	128	25/Mar/70	
F-BPVC	39	128	12/May/70	
F-BPVD	53	128	14/Jul/70	
F-BPVE	105	128	16/Mar/71	
F-BPVF	174	128	04/Feb/72	
F-BPVG	176	128	02/Feb/72	
F-BPVH	177	128	01/Mar/72	
F-BPVJ	200	128	21/Feb/73	N28903 1973-82
F-BPVK	203	128	21/Feb/73	N28899 1973-82
F-BPVL	224	128	21/Mar/74	
F-BPVM	227	128	21/Dec/73	N63305 1973-82
F-BPVN	228	128	08/Feb/74	N28366 1974-82
F-BPVO	245	228F	04/Oct/74	N18815 1974-82
F-BPVP	252	128	13/Mar/75	
F-BPVQ	279	128	27/Feb/76	N40116 1976-83
N28888	201	128	20/Mar/73	W.O. Fire on ground Bombay 12/Jun/75
General Electric Powered Aircraft				
F-BPVR	295	228F	13/Oct/76	
F-BPVS	303	228B Combi	04/Apr/77	
F-BPVT	313	228B Combi	30/Sep/77	
F-BPVU	333	228B Combi	07/Aug/78	N1252E 1978-85
F-BPVV	334	228F	09/Aug/78	

AIR FRANCE (AF/AFR) (continued)

Reg.	Line No.	Model	Delivery Date	Name	Remarks
F-BPVX	364	228B Combi	28/Mar/79		
F-BPVY	370	228B	28/Apr/79		
F-BPVZ	398	228F	18/Sep/79		
F-GCBA	428	228B	29/Feb/80		
F-GCBC	485	228B Combi	17/Oct/80		W.O. Landing, Rio de Janeiro 02/Dec/85
F-GCBD	503	228B Combi	25/Mar/81		N1305E 1981-6
F-GCBH	656	228B Combi	16/Sep/86		
F-GCBI	661	228B Combi	29/Oct/86		
F-GCBJ	698	228B Combi	11/Mar/88		
F-GCBK		228F	Due Sep/88		
N1289E	463	228B Combi	03/Jul/80		F-GCBB n.t.u.
N4508E	535	228F	11/Sep/81		F-GCBE n.t.u.
N4506H	558	228B Combi	26/Mar/82		F-GCBF n.t.u.
N4544F	569	228F	01/Oct/82		F-GCBG n.t.u.

Second-hand Aircraft

Reg.	Line No.	Model	Delivery Date	Name	Remarks
F-GPAN	337	2B3F	28/Mar/86		Ex UTA

747-428 (General Electric CF6-80C2 Engines)

16 on order for delivery from 1991 to 1996

AIR GABON (GN/AGN) GABON, CENTRAL AFRICA

Another airline which operates a lone-flyer 747, Air Gabon started its services between Libreville and Paris (via Geneva, Marseilles or Nice) in June 1977 with a 747 leased from Middle East Airlines which was re-painted in the airline's full colours, having a green, yellow and blue cheat line with a green parrot on the tail. The following year Air Gabon took delivery of a new 200B Combi in the same colour scheme and this usually operates on the same routes but occasionally goes further afield when Air France uses it for one of its services.

FLEET

Reg.	Line No.	Model	Delivery Date	Name	Remarks
OD-AGJ	264	2B4B Combi	May/77	–	L. from MEA Ret. May/78
F-ODJG	324	2Q2B Combi	16/Jul/78	President Leon Mba	TR-LXK before del.

AIR-INDIA (AI/AIC) — INDIA

With each main-deck window painted with a red surround to represent a Rajasthani-style arch, the Air-India 747s well justify their description of a Palace in the Sky – their interiors are equally decorative. They entered service in May 1971 on the Bombay-London-New York route and later extended their network to include other European, Far Eastern and Australian destinations.

Originally, accommodation was provided for 346 passengers, with 58 in 1st class who had the use of an upstairs Maharajah Lounge in flight. With the introduction of business class, the configuration was changed to a total of 377, with 16 1st class (in slumberettes), 40 business class (18 in the upper-deck compartment) and 321 economy.

The names of the first eight aircraft originally had the prefix Emperor but this was later removed.

FLEET

Reg.	Line No.	Model	Delivery Date	Name	Remarks
VT-EBD	124	237B	22/Mar/71	Ashoka	W.O. Nr Bombay 01/Jan/78
VT-EBE	130	237B	20/Apr/71	Shahjehan	
VT-EBN	185	237B	28/Mar/72	Rajendra Chola	
VT-EBO	188	237B	01/Jun/72	Vikramaditya	
VT-EDU	277	237B	23/Dec/75	Akbar	
VT-EFJ	318	237B	03/Feb/78	Chandragupta	
VT-EFO	330	237B	30/Jun/78	Kanishka	W.O. Over Atlantic 23/Jun/85
VT-EFU	390	237B	14/Aug/79	Krishna Deva Raya	
VT-EGA	414	237B	21/Dec/79	Samudra Gupta	
VT-EGB	431	237B	20/Feb/80	Mahendra Varman	
VT-EGC	434	237B	04/Apr/80	Harsha Vardhana	
VT-EPW		337 Combi	Due Oct/88		
VT-EPX		337 Combi	Due Nov/88		
Second-hand and Leased Aircraft					
VT-ENQ	401	212B	22/May/87	Himalaya	Ex Singapore 9V-SQK
N471EV	209	273C	18/May/86		L. from Evergreen

AIR INTER (IT/ITF) — FRANCE

After numerous short-term leases of various 747s, including LX-LCV and LX-MCV of Cargolux and N204AE of Middle East Airlines (with stickers), during 1986 and 1987, Air Inter, the French domestic operator, has plans to become a more permanent operator by leasing a 747 from Air France from April 1988.

AIR JAMAICA (JM/AJM) — JAMAICA

Air Jamaica wet-leased an Aer Lingus 747 for a weekly service on the Frankfurt-London-Montego Bay-Kingston route from November 1982 to May 1984; various Aer Lingus aircraft were used with Air Jamaica titles on the nose. During the 1986/87 winter, EI-BED was leased for a daily service on the New York-Montego Bay-Kingston route, still in Aer Lingus colours but with Air Jamaica titles on the nose and logo on the tail, and from July 1987 Air Jamaica leased Tower Air's all-white N602FF for a similar service with Air Jamaica titles and tail logo displayed.

AIR LANKA (UL) — SRI LANKA

For a short time Air Lanka had two 747s in service, both in the full red and white colour scheme of the airline with its stylised peacock logo on their tails. Both were ex-Qantas aircraft and the first entered service on the Colombo-Dubai-Zurich-London route in June 1984, with other European, Middle East and Far East destinations being added later. The 747 proved too big for the airline and operations ended in June 1987.

FLEET

Reg.	Line No.	Model	Delivery Date	Name	Remarks
4R-ULF	147	238B	08/Jun/84	King Vijaya	Ex Qantas VH-EBA Ret. to Qantas Sep/86
4R-ULG	149	238B	23/Oct/85	King Tissa	Ex Qantas VH-EBB Ret. to Qantas Jul/87

AIR MADAGASCAR (MD/MDG) — MADAGASCAR

Another of the lone flyers, the 200B Combi of Air Madagascar entered service in March 1979 with a non-stop flight from Paris to Antananarivo. Normal services on the route include stops on the way at Nairobi, Djibouti and Zurich or Djibouti and Jeddah. The aircraft can also be seen elsewhere when used by Air France during its stop-overs in Paris. It is usually operated in a mixed-traffic configuration with cargo pallets in zone E and seats for 281 passengers, 24 in 1st class and 257 economy, 30 of whom are in the upper-deck compartment.

FLEET

Reg.	Line No.	Model	Delivery Date	Name
5R-MFT	353	2B2B Combi	26/Jan/79	Tolom piavotana

AIR MALAWI (QM) — MALAWI, CENTRAL AFRICA

For just one month in 1985, Air Malawi became the proud operator of a 747SP. Leased from South African Airways (ZS-SPB), it was actually used for the state visit to Britain of the President of Malawi, Dr Hastings Banda, but it was painted in the airline's colours for the occasion and was given a Malawi registration (7Q-YKL) and named Mulanje. It flew from Blantyre to London, via Amsterdam, arriving in London on 16 April and remaining there until the end of the three-week visit when it returned to Malawi and went back to South African Airways.

AIR MAURITIUS (MK/MAU) — MAURITIUS

The first of the Air Mauritius 747SPs entered service in November 1984 on the Mauritius-Paris-London and Mauritius-Rome-Zurich routes. When the second 747SP was introduced in April 1987 the route network included Bombay, Johannesburg and Singapore plus additional services to Paris (via Munich) and London (via Geneva). Accommodation was provided for 295 passengers, including 12 1st class (in sleeperettes) and 27 business (Super-Jet) class.

Two new Boeing 767s are due for delivery in the spring of 1988 which could possibly replace the leased 747SPs.

FLEET

Reg.	Line No.	Model	Delivery Date	Name	Remarks
3B-NAG	288	SP44	28/Oct/84	Chateau du Reduit	L. from South African ZS-SPC
3B-NAJ	280	SP44	Apr/87	Chateau Mon Plaisir	L. from South African ZS-SPA

AIR NATIONAL (AN) — U.S.A.

A short-lived 747 operator, Air National (of California) leased an Air Canada 747 to operate trans-Atlantic charters from May to November 1983; this had a red, white and blue cheat line with a flash of the same colours up the tail. In March 1984 the airline leased an ex-Swissair 747 for similar services but this aircraft retained its Swissair brown and black cheat line and had a tail flash of similar colours. The airline ceased operations in July 1984.

FLEET

Reg.	Line No.	Model	Delivery Date	Remarks
C-GAGA	250	233B Combi	13/May/83	L. from Air Canada Ret. Nov/83
LX-SAL	112	257B	02/Mar/84	Ex Swissair HB-IGA Ret. Aug/84

AIR NEW ZEALAND (TE/ANZ) — NEW ZEALAND

A Maori influence is obvious in the colour scheme and names of the Air New Zealand 747s which entered service in June 1981 serving various Australian cities and Singapore. Trans-Pacific services from Auckland to Los Angeles via Fiji, Hawaii or Tahiti started the following month with an extension to London in August 1982. A one-stop Auckland-London service, calling only at Los Angeles, was introduced in April 1983, making it possible to fly half way round the world in 26 hours; one-stop services in the reverse direction were started in November 1987.

Sheepskin covers are fitted to the 16 1st class seats and also to the 16 business class (called Pacific Class) seats which are in the upper-deck compartment; economy seating is provided for 388 passengers.

FLEET

Reg.	Line No.	Delivery Date	Name
747-219B			
ZK-NZV	523	22/May/81	Aotea (Long White Cloud)
ZK-NZW	527	09/Jun/81	Tainui (Big Sea)
ZK-NZX	528	21/Jun/81	Takitimu (Company of Chiefs)
ZK-NZY	563	22/Jun/82	Te Arawa (The Path of Time)
ZK-NZZ	568	25/Aug/82	Tokomaru (A Stone or Post Marking Authority)
747-419 (Rolls-Royce RB211-524G Engines)			
ZK-NZU		Due Jul/89	

AIR PACIFIC (FJ/FJI) — FIJI

Two of the most colourful 747s are those of Air Pacific which, after a white nose, have broad fuselage bands of yellow, orange and red before ending with a blue one which sweeps up the tail. The first aircraft (VH-EBK) was leased from Qantas in March 1985 and operated services from Nadi to Auckland, Brisbane, Christchurch, Melbourne and Sydney. In November 1987 this aircraft was transferred to part Air Pacific/part Qantas duties and a second Qantas 747 (VH-EBB) took over the full-time duties.

FLEET

Reg.	Line No.	Delivery Date	Name	Remarks
VH-EBB	149	Nov/87	Island of Viti Levu	L. from Qantas
VH-EBK	267	25/Mar/85	Orig. Island of Viti Levu	L. from Qantas

AIR SIAM (VG) — THAILAND

Using the original name for Thailand, Air Siam was an independent airline which operated an Aer Lingus 747 as a lone flyer from September 1973 on scheduled services on the Bangkok-Hong Kong-Tokyo-Honolulu route. It was painted in the airline's blue and white colour scheme, which a white bird-in-flight logo on the tail, and had accommodation for 387 passengers, eight of whom were 1st class located in the upper-deck compartment. When this lease expired, a KLM 747 (also in full Air Siam colours) was leased until the airline ceased operations in January 1977.

FLEET

Reg.	Line No.	Model	Delivery Date	Name	Remarks
HS-VGB	84	148	29/Sep/73	Doi Suthep	L. from Aer Lingus (EI-ASI) Ret. Apr/76
HS-VGG	156	206B	16/Apr/76	Doi Suthep	L. from KLM (PH-BUE) Ret. Jan/77

AIR ZAIRE (QC) — ZAIRE, CENTRAL AFRICA

Pan Am's 747 flagship N747PA *Clipper America* was leased by Air Zaire as a lone flyer in November 1973 to operate services on the Kinshasa – Brussels – Kinshasa and Kinshasa – Geneva – Brussels – Rome – Kinshasa routes. It was painted in the full Air Zaire colour scheme, which is based on the national colours of red, yellow and green with a gold winged-leopard on the tail, and was re-registered N747QC. The services continued until March 1975 when the aircraft was returned to Pan Am.

FLEET

Reg.	Line No.	Model	Delivery Date	Name	Remarks
N747QC	2	121	24/Nov/73	Mont Hoyo	L. from Pan Am (N747PA) Ret. Mar/75

ALIA (see ROYAL JORDANIAN)

ALITALIA (AZ/AZA) — ITALY

Alitalia's original fleet of five Pratt & Whitney powered 747s spent most of its time on trans-Atlantic routes, starting with Rome to New York in June 1970. These aircraft were replaced from 1980 with General Electric powered all-passenger and 200B Combi versions which have grown steadily in numbers over the years and now spread their activities world-wide.

In the early aircraft, passenger accommodation was for a total of 365, with 32 in 1st class who had the use of an in-flight upstairs lounge. The current

ALITALIA (AZ/AZA) (continued)

arrangement is for 12 1st class (called Top Class) in the upper-deck compartment, 28 business class in zone A on the main deck and either 392 (all-passenger) or 258 (Combi) economy passengers.

The current Alitalia colour scheme, with its broad green cheat line and stylised green and red A on the tail, was introduced just before the first 747s were delivered so there has been no change. Early aircraft were named after aviation and space pioneers but later aircraft have carried the names of Italian beauty spots.

FLEET

Reg.	Line No.	Model	Delivery Date	Name	Remarks
Original Pratt & Whitney Powered Aircraft					
I-DEMA	36	143	13/May/70	Neil Armstrong	S. to Boeing Nov/81 To Hawaii Ex N355AS & People Ex N603PE
I-DEME	56	143	01/Jul/70	Arturo Ferrarin	S. to Boeing Sep/81 To SAS & ONA N356AS & People Ex N606PE
I-DEMO	120	243B	30/Mar/71	Francesco de Pinedo	S. to Boeing Dec/81 To Cargolux N357AS & People Ex N604PE
I-DEMU	134	243B	07/May/71	Geo Chavez	S. to Boeing Nov/81 To ONA N358AS & Virgin G-VGIN
I-DEMB	190	243B	26/May/72	Carlo del Prete	S. to Boeing Dec/80 To Cargolux N359AS & People Ex N605PE
Later General Electric Powered Aircraft					
I-DEMC	492	243B Combi	26/Nov/80	Taormina	
I-DEMD	497	243B Combi	12/Dec/80	Cortina d'Ampezzo	
I-DEMF	499	243B Combi	22/Dec/80	Portofino	
I-DEMG	533	243B	05/Aug/81	Cervinia	
I-DEML	536	243B	16/Sep/81	Sorrento	
I-DEMN	542	243B	05/Nov/81	Porto Cervo	
I-DEMP	546	243B	03/Dec/81	Capri	
I-DEMR	545	243F	18/Dec/81	Stresa	
I-DEMS	575	243B	28/Feb/83	Monte Argentario	
I-DEMT	613	243B Combi	29/May/85	Monte Catini	
I-DEMV	618	243B	24/Jul/85	Sestriere	
I-DEMW	647	243B Combi	13/Jun/86	Spoleto	

ALL NIPPON AIRWAYS (NH/ANA) JAPAN

The 747SRs of All Nippon were introduced on high-density domestic routes out of Tokyo in January 1979 and were the first 747s to have seats for 500 passengers (10-abreast, all-economy, with 20 in the upper-deck compartment). Their colour scheme was light blue and white, with an unusual blue 'spine' along the top of the fuselage, and the airline's logo – Leonardo de Vinci's helicopter design, indicating the airline's origins as a helicopter operator – in a red disc on the tail. Recently the colour scheme has been changed to one of two-tone blue with ANA on the tail.

International services from Tokyo to Los Angeles and Washington D.C., using 200Bs, were started in July 1986 and extended to Sydney in October 1987.

FLEET

Reg.	Line No.	Model	Delivery Date
JA8133	346	181B/SR	21/Dec/78
JA8134	351	181B/SR	20/Dec/78
JA8135	360	181B/SR	28/Feb/79
JA8136	393	181B/SR	09/Oct/79
JA8137	395	181B/SR	05/Sep/79
JA8138	420	181B/SR	16/Jan/80
JA8139	422	181B/SR	15/Feb/80
JA8145	453	181B/SR	16/May/80
JA8146	456	181B/SR	16/Jun/80
JA8147	477	181B/SR	25/Nov/80
JA8148	481	181B/SR	25/Nov/80
JA8152	511	181B/SR	27/Feb/81
JA8153	516	181B/SR	28/May/81
JA8156	541	181B/SR	17/Dec/81
JA8157	544	181B/SR	17/Dec/81
JA8158	559	181B/SR	17/Jun/82
JA8159	572	181B/SR	12/Nov/82
JA8174	648	281B	25/Jun/86
JA8175	649	281B	02/Jul/86
JA8181	667	281B	22/Dec/86
JA8182	683	281B	13/Jul/87

AMERICAN AIRLINES (AA/AAL) U.S.A.

Two Pan Am aircraft were leased to start American Airline's 747 services on the New York-Los Angeles route in March 1970 but were soon replaced by the airline's own 16 Astroliners (later re-named 747 Luxury Liners) which were in service until the fuel-price crisis of early 1974 when some were sold and others converted to freighters. Some passenger aircraft remained and were used at the start of the Dallas-London service in May 1982 (taken over from Braniff) and some 100SF freighters were bought back but all the 747s had been sold by December 1984.

American became a 747 operator again in May 1987 when it introduced two ex-TWA 747SPs on its Dallas-Tokyo service. These are in the familiar American Airlines' colour scheme of an unpainted fuselage with a red, white and blue cheat line and red and blue As on the tail, which has remained unchanged throughout.

AMERICAN AIRLINES (AA/AAL) (continued)
FLEET

Reg.	Line No.	Model	Delivery Date	Remarks
747-123				
N9661	46	123	18/Jun/70	S. to Boeing Feb/74 To Fl. Tigers N800FT
		123SF	02/May/81	Bought back from Fl. Tigers S. to United Parcel N674UP Dec/84
N9662	57	123	16/Jul/70	S. to Boeing Feb/74 To Fl. Tigers N801FT Bought back from Fl. Tigers as 123SF N9676 Mar/81
N9663	59	123	30/Jul/70	S. to Citicorp Jun/84
N9664	65	123	27/Aug/70	S. to Citicorp Apr/84
N9665	69	123	18/Sep/70	S. to Citicorp May/84
N9666	77	123	02/Oct/70	S. to Citicorp Mar/84
N9667	79	123	08/Oct/70	S. to Citicorp May/84
N9668	86	123	29/Oct/70	S. to NASA N905NA Jul/74
N9669	87	123	27/Nov/70	S. to Citicorp May/84
N9670	90	123	29/Dec/70	S. to Pan Am May/84
N9671	115	123	26/Feb/71	S. to Boeing Jul/75 To F1. Tigers N802FT
		123SF	07/Jun/81	Bought back from Fl. Tigers S. to United Parcel N671UP Nov/84
N9672	119	123	16/Apr/71	Cvtd to 123SF Jun/76 S. to United Parcel N672UP Oct/84
N9673	125	123	20/Apr/71	Cvtd to 123SF Oct/76 S. to United Parcel N673UP Aug/84
N9674	133	123	12/May/71	S. to Pan Am Dec/83
N9675	136	123	25/May/71	Cvtd to 123SF Nov/74 S. to TMA OD-AGM May/76
		123SF	08/Jan/77	Bought back from TMA S. to United Parcel N675UP Sep/84
N9676	143	123	25/Jun/71	Cvtd to 123SF Oct/74 S. to TMA OD-AGC May/75
N9676	57	123SF	31/Mar/81	Orig. N9662 before sale Bought back from Fl. Tigers S. to United Parcel N676UP Dec/84
747SP (Second-hand Aircraft)				
N601AA	439	SP31	17/Jul/86	Ex TWA N57202
N602AA	441	SP31	16/Oct/86	Ex TWA N57203
Leased Aircraft				
N740PA	16	121	25/Feb/70	L. from Pan Am Ret. May/71
N743PA	24	121	29/Mar/70	L. from Pan Am Ret. Oct/70

AVIANCA (AV/AVA) COLOMBIA, SOUTH AMERICA

The outstanding red and white colour scheme of Avianca has appeared on various 747s, some of which have been leased (including freighters), since the airline started 747 services in December 1976 on the Bogota-Miami, Bogota-New York and Bogota-San Juan-Madrid-Paris-Frankfurt routes.

The current 200B Combi has accommodation for 278 passengers, with 36 in 1st class, plus cargo pallets, and is kept company by a second-hand 100SF freighter.

FLEET

Reg.	Line No.	Model	Delivery Date	Name	Remarks
HK-2000	58	124	03/Dec/76	Eldorado	Ex Continental N26862 Ret. to Boeing Jan/83
HK-2300	372	259B Combi	08/Jun/79	–	S. to Chemco May/83 L. back as HK-2980X
HK-2400X	64	124SF	21/Jul/81	–	L. from El Al (4X-AXZ) Ret. Jul/82
HK-2900	42	124SF	02/Jul/82	–	L. from World (N750WA) Purchased Jul/86
HK-2910X	311	283B Combi	03/Aug/82	–	L. from SAS (LN-RNA) W.O. Madrid 27/Nov/83
HK-2980X	372	259B Combi	30/May/83	Cartagena de Indias	L. from Chemco Orig. HK-2300
N9664	65	123	20/May/84	–	L. from Cicicorp Ret. Feb/87

BOEING COMPANY U.S.A.

The first 747 (N7470), always referred to as No. 1 rather than a prototype, has remained with Boeing since the initial flight test programme, serving as a development aircraft for new equipment and engine/airframe combinations. It was re-registered N1352B and named *City of Everett* in July 1970 but has since reverted to its original registration, N7470. When retired, it is likely to go into a planned Smithsonian museum at Washington (Dulles) Airport.

BRANIFF INTERNATIONAL AIRWAYS (BN) U.S.A.

Braniff's colourful Big Orange 747 N601BN entered service in January 1971 on the Dallas-Hawaii route and was a lone flyer until March 1978 when it was transferred to the Dallas-London route and was soon joined by other 747s in the bright orange colour scheme. The 747 route network was extended to other European cities, the Far East and South America but the expansion was too big and too fast with a result that new aircraft were cancelled, routes had to be suspended and eventually the airline had to cease operations in May 1982.

BRANIFF INTERNATIONAL AIRWAYS (BN) (continued)

FLEET

Reg.	Line No.	Model	Delivery Date	Remarks
N601BN	100	127	05/Jan/71	Ret. to leasing co. Jun/82 To Metro & Tower Air
N602BN	123	127	Not del.	Stored 1971/3 To Wardair CF-DJC
N602BN	375	227B	31/May/79	Stored 1982/3 To People Ex N602PE
N603BN	405	SP27	30/Oct/79	S. to Boeing Jan/81 To Oman Gvmt A40-SO
N604BN	413	SP27	23/Apr/80	S. to Aero. Argentinas LV-OHV Sep/80
N605BN	437	227B	Not del.	Stored 1980/4 To Air Algerie N8284V & Northwest N633US
N606BN	447	SP27	30/May/80	Stored 1982/3 To Pan Am N529PA
N1607B	465	227B	Not del.	Stored 1981/4 To Air Algerie N8285V & Northwest N634US
N1608B	473	SP27	Not del.	Stored 1980/2 To CAAC N1301E

Leased Aircraft

Reg.	Line No.	Model	Delivery Date	Remarks
N610BN	12	130	29/Nov/78	Ex Lufthansa D-ABYA Ret. to Itel Air Oct/81
N611BN	179	230B	05/May/79	Ex Lufthansa D-ABYG Ret. to Itel Air Mar/82
N749WA	237	273C	10/Apr/79	L. from World Ret. Jun/81
N9666	77	123	01/Mar/78	L. from American Not in full colours Ret. May/80

BRITISH AIRTOURS (KT) — BRITAIN

The charter subsidiary of British Airways leased a 747 from the parent company for most of 1984 to operate trans-Atlantic charters from London and Manchester. Similar charters were operated with an ex SAS aircraft until the airline was absorbed into Caledonian Airways.

FLEET

Reg.	Line No.	Model	Delivery Date	Name	Remarks
G-BDXL	506	236B	09/Feb/84	City of Winchester	L. from British A/W Ret. Oct/84
G-BMGS	167	283B	03/Mar/86	City of Swansea	L. from Air Invest (Ex SAS LN-AEO) Trs to British A/W Oct/87

BRITISH AIRWAYS (BA/BAW) — BRITAIN

The original 747s of British Airways have had three colour schemes, being delivered in the golden speedbird scheme of British Overseas Airways Corporation (BOAC), then changing to the quartered union jack and blue speedbird of British Airways from late 1973 and getting the current pearl-grey top, family crest and red speedwing from 1984. They entered service on the London-New York route in April 1971 with accommodation for 358 passengers, including 27 1st class who had the use in flight of an upstairs lounge.

The 747 fleet has grown considerably through the years and its route network has extended to other North American destinations, Africa, Australia and New Zealand, the Caribbean and the Far East. Passenger accommodation now totals 366, including 18 1st class and 70 business class (called Club) on the main deck plus 20 in the upper-deck compartment.

British Airways' take-over of British Caledonian may add more 747s.

FLEET

Reg.	Line No.	Delivery Date	Name (Prefix City of)	Remarks
747-136 (Pratt & Whitney Powered)				
G-AWNA	23	20/Apr/70	Peterborough (Orig. Sir Richard Grenville)	Del. in BOAC colours
G-AWNB	41	22/May/70	Newcastle	Del. in BOAC colours
G-AWNC	48	29/Jun/70	Belfast	Del. in BOAC colours
G-AWND	107	28/Feb/71	Leeds (Orig. Christopher Marlowe)	Del. in BOAC colours
G-AWNE	109	05/Mar/71	Southampton (Orig. Sir Francis Drake)	Del. in BOAC colours
G-AWNF	111	14/Mar/71	Westminster	Del. in BOAC colours
G-AWNG	150	08/Sep/71	London	Del. in BOAC colours
G-AWNH	169	23/Nov/71	Inverness (Orig. Sir Walter Raleigh)	Del. in BOAC colours
G-AWNI	172	07/Jan/72	–	Del. in BOAC colours S. to TWA N17125 Mar/81
G-AWNJ	183	21/Mar/72	Sheffield (Orig. John Donne)	Del. in BOAC colours
G-AWNK	184	24/Mar/72	William Shakespeare	Del. in BOAC colours S. to TWA N17126 Mar/81
G-AWNL	187	19/Apr/72	Nottingham (Orig. William Shakespeare)	Del. in BOAC colours
G-AWNM	210	03/May/73	Bristol	Del. in BOAC colours
G-AWNN	220	07/Nov/73	Leicester (Orig. Sebastian Cabot)	
G-AWNO	222	07/Dec/73	Durham (Orig. Sir Francis Bacon)	
G-AWNP	246	06/Nov/74	Portsmouth (Orig. Sir John Hawkins)	
G-BBPU	248	14/Mar/75	Dundee (Orig. Henry Hudson)	
G-BDPV	281	08/Apr/76	Aberdeen	

747-236B (Rolls-Royce Powered)

Reg.	Line No.	Model	Delivery Date	Name	Remarks
G-BDXA	292		27/Jul/77	Cardiff	First 747 with R-R engines
G-BDXB	302		16/Jun/77	Liverpool	
G-BDXC	305		22/Jun/77	Manchester	
G-BDXD	317		04/Apr/78	Plymouth	
G-BDXE	321		27/Mar/78	Glasgow	
G-BDXF	323		24/Apr/78	York	
G-BDXG	328		16/Jun/78	Oxford	
G-BDXH	365		27/Mar/79	Edinburgh	
G-BDXI	430		05/Mar/80	Cambridge	
G-BDXJ	440		02/May/80	Birmingham	
G-BDXK	495		30/Mar/83	Canterbury	Stored 1980/3
G-BDXL	502		Not del.	–	Stored 1981/2 S. to Malaysian 9M-MHI
G-BDXL	506		09/Feb/84	Winchester	Orig. allot. G-BDXM Stored 1981/4 Del. in Br. Airtours c/s
G-BDXN	526		Not del.	–	S. to Malaysian 9M-MHJ
G-BDXO	677		23/Apr/87	Bath	

747-236F (Rolls-Royce Powered)

Reg.	Line No.	Model	Delivery Date	Name	Remarks
G-KILO	480		30/Sep/80	British Trader	Orig. allot. G-BDXK First 200F with R-R engines S. to Cathay Pacific VR-HVY Mar/82

747-236B Combi (Rolls-Royce Powered)

Reg.	Line No.	Model	Delivery Date	Name	Remarks
G-BDXM	672		25/Feb/87	Derby	
G-BDXN	674		17/Mar/87	Stoke on Trent	
G-BDXP	697		24/Feb/88	Salisbury	

747-436 (Rolls-Royce RB211-524G Engines)

Reg.	Line No.	Model	Delivery Date	Name	Remarks
G-BNLA			Due Mar/89		
G-BNLB			Due /89		
G-BNLC			Due /89		
G-BNLD			Due /89		

Plus 12 more for delivery in 1990

Leased Aircraft

Reg.	Line No.	Model	Delivery Date	Name	Remarks
G-BDPZ	108		01/Apr/76	–	L. from Aer Lingus 148 EI-ASJ Ret. May/81
G-BLVE	262		09/May/85	Lincoln	L. from MEA 2B4B Combi OD-AGH/N202AE
G-BLVF	263		01/Nov/85	Lancaster	L. from MEA 2B4B Combi OD-AGI/N203AE
G-BMGS	167		Oct/87	Swansea	L. from Air Invest Ex SAS 283B LN-AEO Trs from Br. Airtours

BRITISH CALEDONIAN AIRWAYS (BR) — BRITAIN

The golden lion of British Caledonian Airways made a brief appearance on the tail of a 747 in October 1978 when the airline leased an Aer Lingus aircraft for three months to start its London-Houston service, but B. Cal's 747 operations proper started in May 1982 on the London (Gatwick)-Lagos route. After that the airline added a 747 to its fleet each time it started a new long-haul route, with New York in June 1985, Hong Kong in November 1986 and Tokyo in May 1987.

British Caledonian Airways was taken over by British Airways in December 1987, which is likely to mean the end of the golden lion colour scheme and possibly the sale of at least some of the 747s because they do not have the same engines as those of British Airways.

FLEET

Reg.	Line No.	Model	Delivery Date	Name	Remarks
G-BDPZ	108	148	28/Oct/78	–	L. from Aer Lingus (EI-ASJ) Ret. Feb/79
G-BJXN	179	230B	15/Apr/82	Mungo Park The Scottish Explorer	Ex Lufthansa D-ABYG & Braniff N611BN
G-CITB	514	2D3B	10/Sep/87	–	Ex Royal Jordanian JY-AFS
G-GLYN	326	211B	01/Oct/86	–	Ex Wardair C-GXRA
G-HUGE	297	2D3B Combi	18/Mar/85	Andrew Carnegie The Scottish American Philanthropist	Ex Alia JY-AFB
G-NIGB	368	211B	09/Mar/87	–	Ex Wardair C-GXRD

BRUNEI GOVERNMENT — BRUNEI

The Brunei Government was understood to have bought ex-TWA 747SP N57202 in July 1984 for use by the Brunei Royal Flight. During the following year it was reported to be having a VIP interior installed and eventually appeared at Frankfurt in May 1985 with a new colour scheme comprising a dark blue and gold cheat line which was continued as a flash up the tail. However, the aircraft was not delivered and, after spending a year in storage at Frankfurt, was sold to American Airlines as N601AA in July 1986.

BWIA INTERNATIONAL (BW) — TRINIDAD & TOBAGO

A Cargolux 747 (LX-LCV) was wet-leased for a short period from April 1987 by BWIA (the initials of the original British West Indian Airways) for trans-Atlantic services between Port of Spain and London and Frankfurt, in addition to the airline's usual TriStar flights. The aircraft was not painted in the BWIA colour scheme but had the titles BWIA International, Trinidad and Tobago Airways. This arrangement appeared to meet a seasonal peak in tourist traffic and could become a regular feature with different 747s being used.

CAAC (CA/CCA) PEOPLE'S REPUBLIC OF CHINA

Not to be confused with China Airlines of Taiwan, the Civil Aviation Administration of China (or CAAC for short) of mainland China started 747 operations with its 747SPs on the Beijing (Peking)-Paris route in April 1980, followed soon after by services to Tokyo, London via Frankfurt, and New York via San Francisco. Some 200B Combis have been added in recent years and the 747s have spread their wings to include routes to Australia, Canada and Hong Kong (which Chinese call Xianggang).

FLEET

Reg.	Line No.	Model	Delivery Date	Remarks
747SP				
B-2442	433	SPJ6	29/Feb/80	
B-2444	455	SPJ6	26/Jun/80	
B-2452	467	SPJ6	23/Sep/80	Orig. B-2446 & N1304E
N1301E	473	SP27	29/Dec/82	Second-hand. Ex Braniff N1608B
747-200B				
B-2446	591	2J6B Combi	20/Dec/83	
B-2448	628	2J6B Combi	10/Dec/85	
B-2450	670	2J6B Combi	28/Mar/87	
747-400 (Pratt & Whitney PW4256 Engines)				
B-		4J6	Due Mar/89	
B-		4J6	Due Mar/89	
Plus one more for delivery in 1990				
Leased Aircraft				
B-2440	134	243B	20/May/85	L. from Boeing N358AS Ex Alitalia I-DEMU Ret. Dec/85

CAMEROON AIRLINES (UY/UYC) CAMEROON, CENTRAL AFRICA

The lone flyer 200B Combi of Cameroon Airlines entered service on the Douala-Paris route in April 1981 and this is still the main route served. Since May 1985 one of the services has been extended to London each week and there is also a weekly service to Frankfurt via Geneva.

Cameroon's national colours of green, red and yellow are used for the cheat line on the aircraft, with a green bird-in-flight logo in a red circle on the tail.

FLEET

Reg.	Line No.	Model	Delivery Date	Name
TJ-CAB	508	2H7B Combi	26/Feb/81	Mont Cameroon

CARGO AIR LINES (C.A.L.) (CH/ICL) — ISRAEL

C.A.L. does not have any 747s of its own but wet leases freighters from other operators, usually El Al or Flying Tigers, which sometimes carry C.A.L. titles. The company is normally most active in winter months when there are big loads of fruit and vegetables to be flown from Isreal to various European countries.

CARGOLUX AIRLINES INTERNATIONAL (CV/CLX) — LUXEMBOURG

As its name implies, Cargolux was formed to operate cargo services from Luxembourg and operated its first 747 Freighter flight on the Luxembourg-Hong Kong route in February 1979. When the second Freighter was delivered the services were extended to other Far East destinations and the USA but recently the Freighters have been replaced with three ex-Transamerica 200Cs.

Cargolux has also leased and sub-leased out various passenger 747s during the past few years but this business is now likely to be performed by a recently-formed subsidiary called Lionair.

FLEET

Reg.	Line No.	Model	Delivery Date	Name (Prefix City of)	Remarks
LX-DCV	354	2R7F	31/Jan/79	Luxembourg	S. to Guinness Peat Sep/87 To Fl. Tigers N809FT
LX-ECV	482	2R7F	10/Oct/80	Esch-sur-Alzette	S. to Taiwan Gvmt for China A/L B-198 Feb/85
Leased Aircraft					
LX-ACV	416	271C	10/Oct/86		Ex Transamerica N741TV
LX-BCV	524	271C	01/Apr/86		Ex Transamerica N743TV
LX-ECV	438	271C	19/Jun/87		Ex Transamerica N742TV
LX-KCV	59	123	Jul/86		Ex American N9663 & Citicorp N14943 Ret. Jan/88 To United N153UA
LX-LCV	77	123	Jul/86		Ex American N9666 & Citicorp N14936 Ret. Oct/87 To United N156UA
LX-MCV	79	123	Jul/86		Ex American N9667 & Citicorp N14937 Ret. Oct/87 To United N157UA
LX-NCV	65	123	30/Jun/87		Ex American N9664 & Citicorp N14930 Ret. Sep/87 To United N154UA
LX-TAP	472	254F	May/85		Ex Air Afrique TU-TAP Ret. to Korean Apr/86 HL7474

Plus various 747s on short-term leases from 1982

CARIBBEAN AIRWAYS (IQ) BARBADOS, WEST INDIES

Caribbean Airways wet-leased a 747 from Cargolux in December 1986 for services on the Frankfurt-Brussels-London-Barbados route until March 1987.

The aircraft (LX-KCV) was still in Jet 24 colours, from a previous lease, with Caribbean Airways, 'The National Airline of Barbados, titles. The aircraft then operated charter flights for a few months.

CATHAY PACIFIC AIRWAYS (CX/CPX) HONG KONG

Cathay Pacific started 747 operations in August 1979 with services from Hong Kong to Melbourne and Sydney and to Seoul via Taipei (Taiwan) and Tokyo.

Services to London via Bahrain started in July 1980. Very long-range non-stop flights were first introduced on the Hong Kong-Vancouver route in May 1983 (11¼ hours outbound and 13¼ hours for the return) followed in the July by the first non-stop London-Hong Kong flight (12½ hours), operated weekly at the start; non-stop Hong Kong-London flights (13¾ hours) had to await improved engines which became available from May 1984. The first 747-300 joined the fleet in 1985 and the route network gradually increased to include San Francisco and other destinations in Europe and the Far East.

Current passenger accommodation in the 200Bs is for 412, with 35 1st class (including 14 in the upper-deck compartment), 40 business class (called Marco Polo) and 337 economy. In the 300s the total is 420, with 29 1st class, 86 business class and 305 economy, 69 of whom are in the upper-deck compartment.

FLEET

Reg.	Line No.	Model	Delivery Date	Remarks
VR-HIA	446	267B	24/Apr/80	
VR-HIB	466	267B	16/Jul/80	
VR-HIC	493	267B	19/Dec/80	
VR-HID	531	267B	25/Jun/81	
VR-HIE	566	267B	23/Jul/82	
VR-HIF	582	267B	23/May/83	
VR-HIH	596	267B	27/Apr/84	
VR-HII	615	367	13/Jun/85	
VR-HIJ	634	367	14/Feb/86	
VR-HIK	659	367	10/Oct/86	
VR-HKG	385	267B	20/Jul/79	
VR-HOL	671	367	12/Feb/87	
VR-HOM	690	367	18/Nov/87	
VR-HON		367	Due Jul/88	
VR-HVZ	687	267F	22/Sep/87	
747-400 (Rolls Royce RB211-524G Engines)				
VR-HOO	705	467	Due Apr/89	
VR-HOP		467	Due May/89	
Second-hand Aircraft				
VR-HVY	480	236F	15/Mar/82	Ex British A/W G-KILO

CHINA AIRLINES (CI/CAL) TAIWAN

Based on the island of Taiwan (formerly Formosa), China Airlines started 747 operations in June 1975 on the Taipei-Honolulu-Los Angeles route and introduced non-stop services to the USA (San Francisco) with its first 747SP in May 1977. A Taipei-Anchorage-New York route was added in March 1983, and in April 1984 one flight each week was extended to Amsterdam to link up with a Taipei-Bangkok-Dhahran-Amsterdam route to complete a 747 round-the-world service.

FLEET

Reg.	Line No.	Model	Delivery Date	Remarks
Standard Aircraft				
B-1864	322	209B Combi	20/Apr/78	
B-1866	386	209B	31/Jul/79	
B-1886	519	209B	17/Apr/81	
B-1888	556	209B	04/Mar/82	
B-1894	462	209F	24/Jul/80	Orig. allot. B-1885
747SP				
B-1862	304	SP09	06/Apr/77	
B-1880	445	SP09	30/Apr/80	Orig. allot. B-1861
N4508H	534	SP09	30/Sep/81	Orig. allot. B-1882
N4522V	564	SP09	29/Jun/82	
747-400 (Pratt & Whitney PW4256 Engines)				
B-		409	Due /89	
B-		409	Due /89	
Plus 3 more on order for 1990				
Second-hand Aircraft				
B-198	482	2R7F	26/Feb/85	Ex Cargolux LX-ECV
B-1860	94	132	16/May/75	Ex Delta N9898 S. to Guinness Peat EI-BOS Apr/84. To Pan Am N725PA
Leased Aircraft				
B-1868	72	132	15/Jun/76	L. from Boeing Ex Delta N9896 Ret. Apr/78. To Pan Am N902PA

CONDOR FLUGDIENST (DF) WEST GERMANY

Condor, the charter subsidiary of Lufthansa, became the first non-scheduled operator of a 747 when it introduced its first aircraft in May 1971 on inclusive-tour holiday flights from various West German cities to seaside resorts in Spain, Majorca and the Canary Islands. The aircraft had an all-economy layout for 470 passengers (the first 747 with 10-abreast seating) including eight in the upper-deck compartment (later increased to 32). When the second aircraft was delivered charter flights were extended to the Far East and the USA. Both aircraft were swapped for DC-10s in 1979, but until they arrived a 200B Combi was leased from Lufthansa for a year and was painted in the full Condor colours.

CONDOR FLUGDIENST (DF) (continued)

FLEET

Reg.	Line No.	Model	Delivery Date	Remarks
D-ABYF	128	230B	02/Apr/71	S. to Itel Air Jun/79 To Korean HL-7447
D-ABYH	186	230B	31/Mar/72	S. to Itel Air Feb/79 To Korean HL-7442
D-ABYR	352	230B Combi	11/Jan/79	L. from Lufthansa Ret. May/80

CONTINENTAL AIRLINES (CO/COA) U.S.A.

The golden tail of Continental Airlines has appeared on two fleets of 747s. The first was when the airline was in its original form and its four aircraft were used mainly on the Los Angeles-Honolulu route from June 1970. These 747s were known as the Proud Birds of the Pacific and were unusual in having the lowest seating capacity at the time with a total of 290 passengers arranged in an equally unusual three-class configuration; 57 1st class (with an upper-deck Diamond Head Lounge), 145 coach and 88 economy, who had a cheaper fare but no meals. The aircraft were withdrawn from service during the fuel crisis in January 1974 and were stored until sold.

Continental's second 747 fleet arrived complete with routes from People Express in February 1987 after Texas Air had taken over the airlines. Most aircraft have since received their golden tails but their seating capacity is somewhat higher at 434 passengers, including 16 1st class and 28 business class.

FLEET

Reg.	Line No.	Model	Delivery Date	Remarks
Original Aircraft (1970/4)				
N26861	42	124	18/May/70	S. to Iranian A/F 5-289 Sep/75 To World A/W N750WA
N26862	58	124	13/Jul/70	S. to Iranian A/F 5-290 Oct/75 To Avianca HK-2000
N26863	64	124	12/Aug/70	S. to Iranian A/F 5-291 Oct/75 To El Al 4X-AXZ
N26864	146	124	25/Jun/71	S. to Wardair C-FFUN Dec/74
People Express Aircraft				
N603PE	36	143	01/Feb/87	Ex Alitalia I-DEMA
N604PE	120	243B	01/Feb/87	Ex Alitalia I-DEMO
N605PE	190	243B	01/Feb/87	Ex Alitalia I-DEMB
N606PE	56	143	01/Feb/87	Ex Alitalia I-DEME
N607PE	162	238B	01/Feb/87	Ex Qantas VH-EBC
N608PE	171	238B	01/Feb/87	Ex Qantas VH-EBD
N609PE	195	238B	01/Feb/87	Ex Qantas VH-EBE
N610PE	217	238B	01/Feb/87	Ex Qantas VH-EBF

CORSE AIR INTERNATIONAL (CS/CRL) — FRANCE

Another French charter airline planning to introduce a 747 in 1988 is Corse Air, who hope to use it on trans-Atlantic flights, including a weekly Paris-Los Angeles service.

CP AIR (CP) — CANADA

A colourful quartet of 747s no longer around were the aircraft of CP Air (Canadian Pacific Airlines), the first of which entered service on the Vancouver-Tokyo-Hong Kong route in December 1973. At that time their seating was for 305 passengers, including 28 1st class who had the use of an upstairs lounge with early Canadian railroad decor. With their orange and red tops and tails, they later extended their activities to Honolulu, the polar route to Amsterdam and Rome, trans-Atlantic charters to other destinations including London, and the domestic route to Toronto. The 747s were swapped for DC-10s in 1986.

FLEET

Reg.	Line No.	Model	Delivery Date	Name (Prefix Empress of)	Remarks
C-FCRA	225	217B	15/Nov/73	Italy (Orig. Asia & Japan)	S. to Pakistan Int. Sep/86 AP-BCN
C-FCRB	226	217B	03/Dec/73	Japan (Orig. Canada)	S. to Pakistan Int. May/86 AP-BCM
C-FCRD	244	217B	05/Nov/74	Canada (Orig. Australia)	S. to Pakistan Int. Nov/86 AP-BCO
C-FCRE	247	217B	02/Dec/74	Australia (Orig. Italy)	S. to Pakistan Int. Dec/85 AP-BCL

DELTA AIR LINES (DL) — U.S.A.

An early 747 operator, Delta started services in October 1970 on the Atlanta-Dallas-Los Angeles route, later extending these to include other domestic trunk routes and, between 1973 and 1975, a Pan Am inter-change service on the Atlanta-Washington-London route. Delta ended 747 operations in March 1977.

FLEET

Reg.	Line No.	Model	Delivery Date	Remarks
N9896	72	132	02/Oct/70	S. to Boeing Sep/74 To China A/L B-1868
N9897	82	132	22/Oct/70	S. to Boeing Feb/77 To Flying Tigers N803FT
N9898	94	132	18/Nov/70	S. to Boeing Mar/75 To China A/L B-1860
N9899	155	132	30/Sep/71	S. to Boeing Mar/77 To Flying Tigers N804FT
N9900	159	132	11/Nov/71	S. to Boeing Apr/77 To Flying Tigers N805FT

DOMINICANA (DO) — DOMINICAN REPUPLIC

Very little was spent on the paintwork of an ex-American Airlines 747 (N9665) which Dominicana leased for a year from June 1985 to operate services from Santo Domingo to Madrid and New York. It already had its blue Citicorp cheat line and to this was added Dominicana titles plus a Dominicana logo on the outer engines; it was also given a name (Volando en Grande) and later a Dominican registration HI-472.

EASTERN AIR LINES (EA) — U.S.A.

Eastern ordered four 747s for delivery in 1970/1 but sold the assembly-line positions to TWA and leased Pan Am aircraft (in Eastern colours) for its New York-Miami and New York-San Juan routes from January 1971 to April 1972. In 1980, Eastern planned to buy two Qantas 747s for use on a Miami-London service and one was painted in Eastern colours but Pan Am got the route and the sale was cancelled.

All aircraft had a white top with the usual two-tone blue cheat line extending up the tail.

FLEET

Reg.	Line No.	Model	Delivery Date	Remarks
N371EA	171	238B	Not del.	Ex Qantas VH-EBD
N372EA	161	238B	Not del.	Ex Qantas VH-EBC
N731PA	4	121	03/Jan/71	L. from Pan Am for winters 1971 and 1971/2
N735PA	10	121	26/Nov/70	L. from Pan Am Ret. Apr/72
N737PA	13	121	01/Jan/71	L. from Pan Am Ret. May/72

EGYPTAIR (MS/EGY) — EGYPT

Having been a 747 lone-flyer operator since May 1983, with a different leased aircraft each year, Egyptair planned to have its own two 747-300s in June 1988. Originally, the main route operated was Cairo to Tokyo via Bangkok and Manila but in 1985 this was changed to New York via Paris. The colour scheme on the aircraft has not always been a complete Egyptair one, the cheat line in some cases remaining as that of the airline from whom it was leased instead of red and gold, but the Egyptair logo was always on the tail.

FLEET

Reg.	Line No.	Model	Delivery Date	Name	Remarks
SU-GAL		366	Due Jun/88		
SU-GAM		366	Due Jun/88		

EGYPTAIR (MS/EGY) (continued)

Leased Aircraft

Reg.	Line No.	Model	Delivery Date	Name	Remarks
I-DEMV	618	243B	03/Jul/86	Cleopatra	L. from Alitalia Ret. Jun/87
LX-SAL	112	257B	27/Feb/85		Ex Swissair HB-IGA Ret. Apr/85 To TWA N303TW
N204AE	264	2B4B Combi	07/May/85	Cleopatra	L. from MEA (OD-AGJ) Ret. Jul/86
N480GX	12	130	15/May/83	Cleopatra	Ex Lufthansa D-ABYA & Braniff N610BN Ret. May/84 To Transamerica N780T
N4501Q	500	283B Combi	03/Jun/87		L. from SAS Ret. Nov/87
SU-GAK	126	257B	15/May/84		Ex Swissair HB-IGB Ret. Feb/85 To TWA N304TW
9K-ADA	332	269B Combi	26/Nov/87		L. from Kuwait Ret. due Jun/88

EL AL — ISRAEL AIRLINES (LY/ELY) ISRAEL

When El Al started 747 services on the Tel Aviv-London-New York route in June 1971 its aircraft had, for the time, an unusual configuration of eight 1st class passengers in the upper-deck compartment and the whole of the main deck occupied by 393 economy passengers.

El Al now operates a mixed 747 fleet, comprising all-passenger aircraft, freighters, and convertibles which really live up to their name, being used for passenger carrying in summer months then converted to freighters in winter, Israel's peak season for agricultural produce.

FLEET

Reg.	Line No.	Model	Delivery Date	Remarks
4X-AXA	140	258B	26/May/71	
4X-AXB	164	258B	22/Nov/71	
4X-AXC	212	258B	18/Apr/73	200th 747 delivered
4X-AXD	272	258C	31/Dec/75	
4X-AXF	327	258C	16/Jun/78	
4X-AXG	362	258F	19/Mar/79	
4X-AXH	418	258B	21/Dec/79	

Second-hand Aircraft

Reg.	Line No.	Model	Delivery Date	Remarks
4X-AXQ	233	238B	16/Nov/87	Ex Qantas VH-EBG
4X-AXZ	64	124SF	21/Jun/77	Ex Continental N26863 & Iranian A/F 5-291/5-8112

EVERGREEN INTERNATIONAL AIRLINES (EZ/EIA) U.S.A.

Although Evergreen's two ex-World Airways 747s have been leased out since acquisition, the company does operate charter services in its own name so the aircraft could some day wear the Evergreen colours.

FLEET

Reg.	Line No.	Model	Delivery Date	Remarks
N471EV	209	273C	18/Mar/86	Ex World A/W N747WR L. to Air India Mar/86
N749WA	237	273C	15/May/87	Ex World A/W N749WA L. to Flying Tigers

FLYING TIGERS (FT/FTL) U.S.A.

The Flying Tiger Line started 747 Freighter operations in September 1974 on its New York-Anchorage-Tokyo-Taipei route. Trans-Atlantic Freighter services followed a merger with Seaboard World Airlines in 1980. Passenger charters are also operated, mainly for the US military.

Early 747s had blue tails carrying a white T on a red disc, although this was soon changed to the words Flying Tigers in large white letters, but recently the airline has changed its mind and has reverted to the original design. However, the red and blue 'cummerbund' around the mid-fuselage has remained the same throughout.

FLEET

Reg.	Line No.	Model	Delivery Date	Name	Remarks
N806FT	406	249F	31/Oct/79	Robert W. Prescott	
N807FT	408	249F	11/Dec/79	Thomas Haywood	
N808FT	458	249F	03/Jul/80	William E. Bartling	
N810FT	460	249F	12/Sep/80	Clifford G. Groh	
N815FT	476	245F	03/Oct/80	W. Henry Renninger	Ordered as Seaboard World N705SW
N816FT	478	245F	14/Oct/80	Henry L. Heguy	Ordered as Seaboard World N706SW
Second-hand Aircraft					
N800FT	46	123SF	28/Aug/74		Ex American N9661 S. to American May/81

FLYING TIGERS (FT/FTL) (continued)

Reg.	Line No.	Model	Delivery Date	Name	Remarks
N801FT	57	123SF	28/Sep/74		Ex American N9662 S. to American Mar/81 as N9676
N802FT	115	123SF	22/Jul/75		Ex American N9671 S. to American Sep/81
N803FT	82	132SF	11/Feb/77		Ex Delta N9897
N804FT	155	132SF	24/Mar/77		Ex Delta N9899
N805FT	159	132SF	06/May/77		Ex Delta N9900
N811FT	242	245F	01/Oct/80	Houston Rehrig	Ex Seaboard World N701SW
N812FT	266	245F	01/Oct/80		Ex Seaboard World N702SW
N813FT	394	245F	01/Oct/80		Ex Seaboard World N703SW
N814FT	396	245F	01/Oct/80		Ex Seaboard World N704SW
N817FT	110	121SF	24/Feb/83		Ex Pan Am N654PA
N818FT	131	121SF	24/Feb/83		Ex Pan Am N658PA
N819FT	70	121SF	24/Feb/83		Ex Pan Am N771PA
N820FT	143	123SF	24/Feb/83		Ex Pan Am N901PA

Leased Aircraft

Reg.	Line No.	Model	Delivery Date	Name	Remarks
EI-BPH	104	133	22/Sep/85		L. from Guinness Peat Ex Air Canada C-FTOA Passenger charters
LV-MLO	349	287B	04/Jul/83		L. from Aero. Argentinas Passenger charters
N747TA	218	212B	08/Dec/79		L. from Tiger Air Ex Singapore 9V-SIA Passenger charters Trs to Metro Feb/81
N748TA	219	212B	31/Jul/80		L. from Tiger Air Ex Singapore 9V-SIB Passenger charters Trs to Metro Feb/81
N749TA	240	212B	16/Sep/80		L. from Tiger Air Ex Singapore 9V-SQC Passenger charters Trs to Metro Feb/81
N747WR	209	273C	16/Mar/85		L. from National Ret. Mar/86
N748WA	211	273C	05/Mar/83		L. from National Ret. Apr/85
N749WA	237	273C	10/Oct/84		L. from Evergreen
N809FT	42	124SF	01/Jul/78		L. from World N750WA Ret. Jul/80
N809FT	354	2R7F	22/Sep/87		L. from Guinness Peat Ex Cargolux LX-DCV

Plus various other aircraft on short-term leases

GARUDA INDONESIA (GA/GIA) — INDONESIA

Currently being painted in a pleasing new colour scheme, the 747s of Garuda Indonesian Airways (or Garuda Indonesia, to give its revised title) were first used on flights between Jakarta and Jeddah for the 1980 Hadj season, with seating for a record total for long-haul flights at the time of 546 passengers. Scheduled services from Jakarta to Amsterdam, Frankfurt, London and Paris via Singapore, Bangkok and various intermediate stops were started in December 1980, with seating for a somewhat lower total of 446 passengers (28 in 1st class).

The aircraft were originally named after the major cities of Indonesia but the names are not included in the new colour scheme.

FLEET

Reg.	Line No.	Model	Delivery Date	Name (Prefix City of)
PK-GSA	452	2U3B	02/Jul/80	Jakarta
PK-GSB	459	2U3B	30/Jul/80	Bandung
PK-GSC	461	2U3B	11/Aug/80	Medan
PK-GSD	468	2U3B	26/Aug/80	Surabaya
PK-GSE	561	2U3B	05/May/82	Yogyakarta
PK-GSF	562	2U3B	18/May/82	Denpasar

Plus various 747s leased short-term for Hadj flights each year

GLOBAL INTERNATIONAL AIRWAYS (GX) — U.S.A.

Sounding like a fictitious airline in a Hollywood film, Global International leased a lone-flyer 747 from Air Canada (C-FTOA) in June 1983 to operate trans-Atlantic charters to various European destinations. The aircraft, which was painted in the airline's red and white colour scheme with GIA on the tail, was returned to Air Canada in October 1983.

GULF AIR (GF) — BAHRAIN

The impressive Golden Falcon of Gulf Air has appeared on the tails of two 747s. The first was a lone flyer leased for a year from Middle East Airlines (MEA) in March 1984 to operate services on the Bahrain-Bangkok-Manila route. This was then replaced by a 747 leased from Scandinavian Airlines System (SAS) which, because of a reduction in traffic on the route, was threatened with withdrawal several times before it was eventually returned in September 1987.

FLEET

Reg.	Line No.	Model	Delivery Date	Remarks
N203AE	263	2B4B Combi	27/Mar/84	L. from MEA (Orig. OD-AGI) Ret. Aug/85
LN-AET	114	283B	27/Jul/85	L. from SAS/Air Invest Ret. Sep/87

THE HAWAII EXPRESS (LP) — U.S.A.

Using an ex-Alitalia 747 leased from Boeing, The Hawaii Express started a daily low-fare, no-frills service on the Los Angeles-Honolulu route in August 1982. This lone flyer had an all-economy layout for 491 passengers, including 16 in the upper-deck compartment. The aircraft's colour scheme was a multi-colour cheat line terminating in a pineapple yellow tail which earned it the nickname Big Pineapple although it didn't suffer the indignity of having a white pineapple painted on its tail like the DC-10s which replaced it in May 1983.

FLEET

Reg.	Line No.	Model	Delivery Date	Name	Remarks
N355AS	36	143	12/Aug/82	Jason Everest	L. from Boeing Ex Alitalia I-DEMA Ret. May/83

HIGHLAND EXPRESS (VY) — BRITAIN

After a lengthy gestation period, Highland Express Airways started its low-fare, no-frills service from Stansted/Birmingham and Prestwick to New York (Newark) in July 1987 using an ex-American Airlines 747 leased from Citicorp. Another lone flyer, the aircraft had seating for 499 passengers, including 10 business class in the upper-deck compartment, and had the blue and white Scottish flag on its tail. Sadly, the airline ceased operations in December 1987.

FLEET

Reg.	Line No.	Model	Delivery Date	Name (Prefix City of)	Remarks
G-HIHO	87	123	24/Mar/87	Highlander	L. from Citicorp Ex American N9669 Ret. Dec/87

IBERIA (IB/IBE) — SPAIN

Named after famous Spanish writers, the original 747s of Iberia (or Lineas Aereas de Espana, to give it its full title) started Madrid-New York services in December 1970, and had a standard colour scheme in the national colours of red and yellow. However, by the time the 747 fleet was expanded in the early 1980s, a smart new colour scheme had been introduced with a wide red, orange and yellow cheat line sweeping down from the top of the aircraft's upper-deck compartment. With the increase in the fleet came an extension of the 747 route network to other destinations in North America, South America and the Far East.

IBERIA (IB/IBE) (continued)
FLEET

Reg.	Line No.	Model	Delivery Date	Name	Remarks
EC-BRO	76	156	02/Oct/70	Cervantes	S. to TWA N133TW May/80
EC-BRP	91	156	10/Nov/70	Lope de Vega	S. to TWA N134TW Feb/81
EC-BRQ	173	256B	04/Jun/72	Calderon de la Barca	
EC-DIA	450	256B	01/May/80	Tirso de Molina	
EC-DIB	451	256B	22/May/80	Cervantes	
EC-DLC	509	256B Combi	18/Feb/81	Francisco de Quevedo	Cvtd to Combi Dec/85
EC-DLD	515	256B Combi	24/Mar/81	Lope de Vega	Cvtd to Combi Jan/85
EC-DNP	554	256B	26/Feb/82	Juan Ramon Jimenez	
EC-EEK	699	256B Combi	05/Apr/88	Garcia Lorca	
Leased Aircraft					
EC-DXE	121	133	03/May/85	–	L. from Guinness Peat Ex Air Canada C-FTOB Ret. Nov/85

ICELANDAIR (FI) — ICELAND

Although never a 747 operator as such, Icelandair did have a 747 painted in its colour scheme for two months in 1982. The ex-Alitalia aircraft (I-DEME) had been leased from Boeing (registered N356AS) by Scandinavian Airlines System who had sub-leased it to Icelandair to operate Hadj flights for Air Algerie (whose titles appeared on the right-hand side).

IRAN AIR (IR/IRA) — IRAN

Iran Air's 747SPs entered service on the Teheran-London-New York route in May 1976 and the airline appeared set for rapid expansion, with orders for more 747SPs, 200B Combis and 100Bs, but the change of regime in Iran caused some of the 747 orders to be cancelled. Since then some ex-Iranian Air Force 747 Freighters have been added to the fleet, at least three appearing in full Iran Air colour scheme and others still with the IAF cheat line with Iran Air titles, but the situation is confused. The aircraft have retained their blue and white colour scheme through the years but, since the change of regime, have carried a sub-title The Airline of the Islamic Republic of Iran.

Some 747s of other airlines are leased for short terms each year to operate flights during the Hadj season.

IRAN AIR (IR/IRA) (continued)
FLEET

Reg.	Line No.	Model	Delivery Date	Name	Remarks
EP-IAA	275	SP86	12/Mar/76	Kurdistan (Orig. Fars)	
EP-IAB	278	SP86	10/May/76	Khorasan (Orig. Kurdistan)	
EP-IAC	307	SP86	27/May/77	Fars (Orig. Khuzestan)	
EP-IAD	371	SP86	12/Jul/79		
EP-IAG	291	286B Combi	05/Oct/76	Azarabadegan	
EP-IAH	300	286B Combi	14/Mar/77	Khuzestan (Orig. Khorasan)	300th 747 built
EP-IAM	381	186B	02/Aug/79		
EP-ICA	319	2J9F	09/Nov/80		Ex IAF 5-8114
EP-ICB	340	2J9F	24/Sep/80		Ex IAF 5-8115
EP-ICC	343	2J9F	23/Aug/80		Ex IAF 5-8116

IRANIAN AIR FORCE (IAF) IRAN

The Imperial Iranian Air Force (IIAF), as it was originally known, purchased 747-100 passenger aircraft from TWA and Continental in 1975 to be modified with side cargo door for use as 100SF transports and flight-refuelling tanker/transports. They entered service in September 1975 airlifting stores and equipment from the USA and Europe to Iran and were later joined by new Freighters. Soon after the change of regime in Iran some of the new Freighters were transferred to Iran Air and the others had their titles and green, white and red roundles removed and their serial numbers changed to civil registrations.

FLEET

Serial No.	Line No.	Model	Delivery Date	
5-8101	5	131SF	14/Mar/75	Ex TWA N93101. Orig. 5-280 Civil reg. EP-NHJ & V
5-8102	78	131SF	15/Mar/75	Ex TWA N53112. Orig. 5-281 Civil reg. EP-NHT
5-8103	80	131SF	31/Mar/75	Ex TWA N93113. Orig. 5-282 Civil reg. EP-NHS
5-8104	73	131SF	15/Oct/75	Ex TWA N53111. Orig. 5-283 W.O. Nr Madrid 09/May/76
5-8105	85	131SF	03/Nov/75	Ex TWA N93114. Orig. 5-284 Civil reg. EP-NHR
5-8106	8	131SF	14/Nov/75	Ex TWA N93102. Orig. 5-285 Civil reg. EP-NHD
5-8107	151	131SF	14/Nov/75	Ex TWA N93118. Orig. 5-286 Civil reg. EP-NHP
5-8108	9	131SF	12/Dec/75	Ex TWA N93103. Orig. 5-287 Civil reg. EP-NHK
5-8109	153	131	15/Dec/75	Ex TWA N93119. Orig. 5-288 S. back to TWA Dec/76

IRAN/IAN AIR FORCE (IAF) (continued)

Serial No.	Line No.	Model	Delivery Date	Remarks
5-8110	42	124SF	22/Sep/75	Ex Continental N26861 Orig. 5-289 S. to World A/W N750WA Jan/78
5-8111	58	124	15/Oct/75	Ex Continental N26862 Orig. 5-290 S. to Avianca HK-2000 Sep/76
5-8112	64	124SF	30/Oct/75	Ex Continental N26863 Orig. 5-291 S. to El Al 4X-AXZ Apr/77
5-8113	315	2J9F	22/Dec/77	Civil reg. EP-NHN
5-8114	319	2J9F	27/Feb/78	Trs to Iran Air EP-ICA Nov/80
5-8115	340	2J9F	29/Sep/78	Trs to Iran Air EP-ICB Sep/80
5-8116	343	2J9F	23/Oct/78	Trs to Iran Air EP-ICC Aug/80
5-8117	400	2J9F	Not del.	Stored as N1288E 1980/2 S. to Northwest N630US Sep/83

IRAQI AIRWAYS (IA/IAW) IRAQ

The 747-200Cs of Iraqi Airways, which entered service on the Baghdad-London route in July 1976, have retained their pleasing green and white colour scheme, in which the green appears to break over the nose like a wave, descend to a trough mid-way along the fuselage, then rise to another crest up the tail. The aircraft now serve various European destinations plus long-haul routes to Tokyo via Bangkok and to Rio de Janeiro via Amman and Lisbon.

FLEET

Reg.	Line No.	Model	Delivery Date	Remarks
YI-AGN	287	270C	24/Jun/76	First 200C with SCD
YI-AGO	289	270C	17/Aug/76	
YI-AGP	565	270C	15/Jul/82	

IRAQI GOVERNMENT IRAQ

A rare bird is the lone flyer 747SP of the Iraqi Government which is operated for them on VIP flights by Iraqi Airways. The aircraft has the same pleasing green and white colour scheme as the airline's 747s except that the titling is Iraq instead of Iraqi Airways.

FLEET

Reg.	Line No.	Model	Delivery Date	Name
YI-ALM	567	SP70	30/Aug/82	Al-Qadissiya

JAPAN AIR LINES (JL/JAL) — JAPAN

Starting with three 747s on trans-Pacific routes in July 1970, Japan Air Lines now has the world's largest 747 fleet operating world-wide, including non-stop services on the Tokyo-New York and Tokyo-London and Paris routes.

In the early days, the airline's 747s were given the general name of Garden Jet and each zone on the main deck had the decor of a particular Japanese garden, 1st-class passengers being in the Garden of Wisteria with the use in flight of an upstairs lounge called the Teahouse of the Sky. Passenger seating at the time totalled 361, with 40 in 1st class.

JAL also operates high-density domestic services and introduced its first 747SRs in October 1973 on the Tokyo-Sapporo and Tokyo-Fukuoka routes. At the time seating capacity in these aircraft was an all-time high of 498 but the airline has broken its own records in recent years with 550 seats being reached in 1980 and the highest of all time (so far) of 563 in its latest 747-300SRs.

Through the years the aircraft have retained their red and white colour scheme with the distinctive crane logo on their tails but there was a rumour recently that a change was being considered.

FLEET

Reg.	Line No.	Model	Delivery Date	Remarks
JA8101	31	146	22/Apr/70	
JA8102	51	146	18/May/70	
JA8103	54	146	26/Jun/70	Trs to Japan Asia 1982
JA8104	116	246B	11/Feb/71	
JA8105	122	246B	01/Mar/71	
JA8106	137	246B	14/May/71	
JA8107	161	146SF	28/Oct/71	Cvtd from 146 in 1977
JA8108	166	246B	30/Nov/71	
JA8109	180	246B	02/Mar/72	Blown up, Benghazi, 24/Jul/73
JA8110	181	246B	13/Mar/72	
JA8111	182	246B	21/Mar/72	
JA8112	191	146	14/Jun/72	
JA8113	192	246B	29/Jun/72	
JA8114	196	246B	03/Nov/72	
JA8115	197	146	04/Oct/72	
JA8116	199	146	08/Dec/72	
JA8117	221	SR46	26/Sep/73	First 747SR To be S. to Boeing Apr/88
JA8118	229	SR46	21/Dec/73	To be S. to Boeing Apr/88
JA8119	230	SR46	19/Feb/74	W.O. Nr Tokyo 12/Aug/85
JA8120	231	SR46	20/Feb/74	
JA8121	234	SR46	28/Mar/74	
JA8122	235	246B	29/Mar/74	
JA8123	243	246F	17/Sep/74	
JA8124	249	SR46	22/Nov/74	
JA8125	251	246B	17/Dec/74	
JA8126	254	SR46	02/Apr/75	
JA8127	255	246B	12/May/75	
JA8128	259	146	20/Jun/75	Trs to Japan Asia 1986
JA8129	361	246B	06/Mar/79	
JA8130	376	246B	14/Jun/79	

JAPAN AIR LINES (JL/JAL) (continued)

Reg.	Line No.	Model	Delivery Date	Name	Remarks
JA8131	380	246B	28/Jun/79		
JA8132	382	246F	27/Jul/79		
JA8140	407	246B	08/Nov/79		
JA8141	411	246B	03/Dec/79		
JA8142	426	146B/SR	31/Jan/80		
JA8143	427	146B/SR	14/Feb/80		
JA8144	432	246F	17/Mar/80		
JA8149	489B		13/Mar/81		Aloha Express
JA8150	496	246Bçççç			
JA8144	432	246F	17/Mar/80		
JA8149	489	246B	13/Mar/81		Aloha Express
JA8150	496	246B	19/Mar/81		Aloha Express
JA8151	494	246F	15/Apr/81		
JA8154	547	246B	17/Nov/81		
JA8155	548	246B	15/Dec/81		
JA8161	579	246B	16/Jun/83		Executive Express
JA8162	581	246B	06/Jun/83		Executive Express
JA8163	599	346	06/Dec/84		
JA8164	601	146B/SR	04/Dec/84		
JA8166	607	346	04/Feb/85		
JA8169	635	246B	19/Mar/86		Executive Express
JA8170	636	146B/SR SUD	24/Mar/86		
JA8171	654	246F	28/Aug/86		
JA8173	640	346	15/Apr/86		
JA8176	655	146B/SR SUD	09/Sep/86		
JA8177	658	346	02/Oct/86		
JA8178	664	346	15/Dec/86		
JA8179	668	346	05/Feb/87		
JA8180	684	246F	11/Aug/87		
JA8183	692	346SR	10/Dec/87		
JA8184	693	346SR	28/Jan/88		
JA8185	691	346	07/Mar/88		
JA8186	694	346SR	09/Feb/88		
JA8187	695	346SR	19/Feb/88		
N211JL	571	246F	14/Dec/82		
N212JL	588	346	29/Nov/83		
N213JL	589	346	08/Dec/83		

747-400 (General Electric CF6-80C2 Engines)

JA		446	Due Aug/89		

Plus four more on order for 1990

Second-hand Aircraft

JA8160	392	221F	29/Oct/82		Ex Pan Am N905PA Trs to Japan Asia 1986
JA8165	384	221F	20/Dec/83		Ex Pan Am N904PA

JAPAN ASIA AIRWAYS (EG/JAA) — JAPAN

Originally a charter subsidiary of Japan Air Lines, Japan Asia started 747 operations on the Tokyo-Taipei route in November 1982 and now operates scheduled passenger and cargo services on the route and also passenger services on the Osaka-Taipei route. Until recently the airline's aircraft were ex-Japan Air Lines but Japan Asia has now ordered its own 747-300.

FLEET

Reg.	Line No.	Model	Delivery Date	Remarks
JA8102	51	146	10/Dec/82	Ex JAL. Ret. Nov/86
JA8103	54	146	24/Nov/82	Ex JAL
JA8128	259	146	25/Mar/86	Ex JAL
JA8160	392	246F	Oct/86	Ex JAL
JA8189		346	Due Oct/88	

JAPANESE GOVERNMENT — JAPAN

A surprise order for two 747-400s came in December 1987 from the Japanese Government. Due to be delivered in 1991, the aircraft will be used to carry members of the government and other VIPs and are to be operated by the Japanese Air Self Defence Force (JASDF). No engine choice has so far been specified but it is likely to be for General Electric engines in common with the 747-400s ordered by Japan Air Lines.

JET 24 INTERNATIONAL AIRWAYS (TJ) — U.S.A.

The Miami-based charter company Jet 24 leased an ex-American Airlines 747 (N9663) from the leasing company Citicorp in March 1986 to operate trans-Atlantic charters to Madrid. The aircraft was painted in Jet 24 colours, with a dark blue lower fuselage trimmed with a red cheat line just below the door sills extending up the tail, which carried the Jet 24 titles. The aircraft was returned to Citicorp in June 1986 and was leased to Cargolux (as LX-KCV) who then sub-leased it to various airlines in the following months, still in the basic Jet 24 colour scheme.

KABO AIR (QN) — NIGERIA

The Nigerian airline Kabo Air occasionally leases 747s from other airlines or leasing companies (including Cargolux) during the annual Hadj season, sometimes operating them on behalf of Nigeria Airways. In the past (particularly 1982 and 1983) some of the aircraft (such as ex-Alitalia N359AS subleased from Cargolux) carried Kabo Air titles and had their tails painted in the airline's two-tone blue colour scheme.

KENYA AIRWAYS (KQ) — KENYA

When Kenya Airways took over from East African Airways in 1977 it continued to wet lease a 747 from Aer Lingus to operate a weekly London-Frankfurt-Rome-Nairobi service during the annual peak safari/tourist season (December to March), a service the former airline had started in 1974. From 1980 the service was operated by various KLM 747s, carrying a sticker In Service for Kenya Airways, and when the airline was considering getting its own wide-body aircraft in the mid-1980s it was reported to be in favour of a 747 but eventually opted for Airbus A310s.

KLM (KL/KLM) — NETHERLANDS

The early 747s of KLM (Koniklijke Luchvaart Maatschappij) had a white-top colour scheme when they entered service in February 1971 on the Amsterdam-New York route, and later took over other trans-Atlantic routes and services to Australia and the Far East. These aircraft were powered by Pratt & Whitney engines but those delivered since 1975 are powered by General Electric engines, and by that time the current blue-top colour scheme had been introduced. KLM now operate a mixed fleet of all-passenger and Combi aircraft, the former named after the great rivers of the world and the latter after aviation pioneers. During 1985/86 the General Electric powered 747-200Bs were modified to have the stretched upper deck (SUD) to match three 747-300 Combis delivered since 1983.

FLEET

Reg.	Line No.	Model	Delivery Date	Name	Remarks
Pratt & Whitney Powered Aircraft					
PH-BUA	96	206B	16/Jan/71	The Mississippi	
PH-BUB	118	206B	05/Mar/71	The Danube Donau	
PH-BUC	138	206B	21/May/71	The Amazon Amazone	
PH-BUD	152	206B	31/Aug/71	The Nile Nijl	
PH-BUE	156	206B	30/Sep/71	Rio de la Plata	
PH-BUF	157	206B	19/Oct/71	The Rhine Rijn	W.O. Ground collision Tenerife 27/Mar/77
PH-BUG	170	206B	15/Dec/71	The Orinoco	
General Electric Powered Aircraft					
PH-BUH	271	206B Combi	19/Oct/75	Dr Albert Plesman	Cvtd to SUD Aug/85
PH-BUI	276	206B Combi	15/Dec/75	Wilbur Wright	Cvtd to SUD Oct/85
PH-BUK	336	206B Combi	01/Sep/78	Louis Bleriot	Cvtd to SUD Apr/85
PH-BUL	344	206B Combi	03/Nov/78	Charles A. Lindbergh	Cvtd to SUD Jun/85

KLM (KL/KLM) (continued)

Reg.	Line No.	Model	Delivery Date	Name	Remarks
PH-BUM	369	206B Combi	15/May/79	Sir Charles E. Kingsford Smith	Cvtd to SUD Dec/85
PH-BUN	389	206B Combi	17/Aug/79	Anthony H. G. Fokker	Cvtd to SUD Mar/86
PH-BUO	397	206B	21/Sep/79	The Missouri	Cvtd to SUD Jan/85
N1295E	474	206B	11/Sep/80	The Ganges	Orig. allot. PH-BUP Cvtd to SUD Dec/84
N1298E	491	206B	15/Dec/80	The Indus	Orig. allot. PH-BUR Cvtd to SUD Mar/85
N1309E	539	206B Combi	29/Sep/81	Admiral Richard E. Byrd	Orig. allot. PH-BUT Cvtd to SUD Jan/86
N4548M	587	306 Combi	30/Sep/83	Sir Frank Whittle	Orig. allot. PH-BUU
N4551N	600	306 Combi	13/Sep/84	Sir Geoffrey de Havilland	600th 747 built Orig. allot. PH-BUV
PH-BUW	657	306 Combi	03/Oct/86	Leonardo da Vinci	

747-400 (General Electric CF6-80C2 Engines)

PH-BFA		406	Due Feb/89*
PH-BFB		406	Due /89
PH-BFC		406 Combi	Due /89

Plus three more for delivery in 1990

KOREAN AIR (KE/KAL) KOREA

The original two 747s of Korean Air lines entered service on the Seoul-Tokyo-Honolulu-Los Angeles route in May 1973 but it was not until the late 1970s and early 1980s that the 747 fleet grew into its present size with a mixture of 200Bs, 200Fs, SPs and 300s. With the increase in the size of the fleet came an extension of the 747 route network which now includes, in addition to the original route, services from Seoul to New York, via Anchorage or non-stop with the 747SPs, Frankfurt and Paris via Anchorage, Manila, Tokyo, and Zurich via Bahrain and Jeddah. It is expected that a service from Seoul to London via Anchorage will be started in 1988 to coincide with the demand for travel to the Olympic Games.

FLEET

Reg.	Line No.	Model	Delivery Date	Remarks
HL7410	213	2B5B	01/May/73	S. to Boeing Apr/81 L. back as HL7463
HL7411	215	2B5B	12/Jul/73	S. to Boeing Nov/81 L. back as HL7464
HL7443	363	2B5B	23/Mar/79	
HL7445	366	2B5B	11/Apr/79	W.O. Seoul 18/Nov/80
HL7451	448	2B5F	25/Jun/80	

KOREAN AIR (KE/KAL) (continued)

Reg.	Line No.	Model	Delivery Date	Name	Remarks
HL7452	454	2B5F	25/Jun/80		
HL7454	484	2B5B	13/Nov/80		
HL7458	513	2B5B	13/Apr/81		
HL7459	520	2B5F	08/May/81		Del. in Saudia Colours
HL7468	605	3B5	12/Dec/84		
HL7469	611	3B5	15/Apr/85		
747SP					
HL7456	501	SPB5	22/Jan/81		
HL7457	507	SPB5	18/Mar/81		
747-400 (Pratt & Whitney PW4256 Engines)					
HL		4B5	Due Apr/89		
HL		4B5	Due May/89		
HL		4B5	Due Aug/89		
Second-hand Aircraft					
HL7471	211	273C	12/Aug/85		Ex World A/W N748WA & National A/L
Leased Aircraft					
HL7440	132	230B	08/Dec/78		L. from Itel Air Ex Lufthansa D-ABYD
HL7441	168	230F	20/Dec/78		L. from Itel Air Ex Lufthansa D-ABYE
HL7442	186	230B	07/Feb/79		L. from Itel Air Ex Condor D-ABYH Shot down by Russians Sakhalin Is 01/Sep/83
HL7447	128	230B	01/Jul/79		L. from Itel Air Ex Condor D-ABYF
HL7463	213	2B5B	27/Jul/82		L. from Orient Leasing Orig. HL7410
HL7464	215	2B5B	30/Jul/82		L. from Orient Leasing Orig. HL7411
HL7474	472	2S4F	May/85		L. from Japan Leasing Ex Air Afrique TU-TAP
N749WA	237	273C	12/Jun/74		L. from World A/W Ret. Mar/79

KUWAIT AIRWAYS (KU/KAC) — KUWAIT

The 50th operator to buy 747s from Boeing, Kuwait Airways introduced its first aircraft on the Kuwait-London route in August 1978, extending this service to New York in 1980. The following year the route network was extended in the opposite direction, to Bangkok and Manila. Originally, the aircraft had seating for 380 passengers with 40 in 1st class, and surprisingly the current total is still 380 but the mix is different with 34 in 1st class and 24 in business class.

KUWAIT AIRWAYS (KU/KAC) (continued)

FLEET

Reg.	Line No.	Model	Delivery Date	Name	Remarks
9K-ADA	332	269B Combi	28/Jul/78	Al Sabahiya	L. to Egyptair Nov/87
9K-ADB	335	269B Combi	17/Aug/78	Al Jaberiya	
9K-ADC	359	269B Combi	28/Feb/79	Al Mubarakiya	
9K-ADD	553	269B Combi	20/Jan/82	Al Salmiya	

LIBYAN ARAB AIRLINES (LN) — LIBYA

Three 747-200B Combis were built for Libyan Arab Airlines in 1980 and two of them were actually painted in the airline's gold and red colour scheme before the US government stopped the sale. The aircraft were line No. 435, 443 and 469, and were allotted registrations 5A-DIJ, 'K and 'L, respectively. All three were later sold to Varig.

LIONAIR — LUXEMBOUG

Lionair plans to operate passenger services for other airlines or tour companies. Two ex-Pan Am 747s are at present being used for these operations, which began in February 1988.

FLEET

Reg.	Line No.	Model	Delivery Date	Remarks
LX-FCV	47	121	20/Jan/88	Ex Pan Am N754PA
LX-GCV	50	121	13/Jan/88	Ex Pan Am N770PA

LUFTHANSA (LH/DLH) — WEST GERMANY

The German airline Deutsche Lufthansa started 747 operations on the Frankfurt-New York route in April 1970, and the route network was extended to the Far East and South Africa as more of the Pratt & Whitney powered aircraft were delivered. In April 1972, Lufthansa became the first airline to operate a 747 Freighter, using it on the Frankfurt-New York route.

From the mid-1970s the original fleet was replaced with aircraft powered by General Electric engines, and the current fleet comprises all-passenger 200Bs, 200B Combis and Freighters operating a world-wide route network. Typical seating capacities are, for all-passenger aircraft, 345 including 33 in 1st class and 108 in business class, and for Combis, 236 including 21 1st class and 84 in business class, plus cargo pallets.

LUFTHANSA (LH/DLH) (continued)

FLEET

Reg.	Line No.	Model	Delivery Date	Name	Remarks
Original Pratt & Whitney Powered Aircraft					
D-ABYA	12	130	10/Mar/70	Nordrhein-Westfalen	S. to Itel Air Nov/78 To Braniff N610BN & Tower Air N603FF
D-ABYB	29	130	13/Apr/70	Hessen	W.O. Nairobi 20/Nov/74
D-ABYC	44	130	23/May/70	Bayern	S. to Itel Air Jan/79 To Aer Lingus EI-BED
D-ABYD	132	230B	05/May/71	Baden-Wurttemberg	S. to Itel Air Nov/78 To Korean HL7440
D-ABYE	168	230F	09/Mar/72	Cargonaut	First 747-200F S. to Itel Air Dec/78 To Korean HL7441
D-ABYG	179	230B	25/Feb/72	Niedersachsen	S. to Itel Air May/79 To Braniff N611BN & B. Cal G-BJXN
Later General Electric Powered Aircraft					
D-ABYJ	294	230B Combi	23/Nov/76	Hessen	
D-ABYK	299	230B Combi	15/Dec/76	Rheinland-Pfalz	
D-ABYL	320	230B Combi	16/Mar/78	Saarland	
D-ABYM	342	230B Combi	20/Oct/78	Schleswig-Holstein	
D-ABYN	345	230B	10/Nov/78	Baden-Wurttemberg	
D-ABYO	347	230F	22/Nov/78	America	
D-ABYP	348	230B	07/Mar/79	Niedersachsen	
D-ABYQ	350	230B	13/Dec/78	Bremen	
D-ABYR	352	230B Combi	11/Jan/79	Nordrhein-Westfalen	
D-ABYS	356	230B Combi	08/Feb/79	Bayern	
D-ABYT	490	230B Combi	19/Nov/80	Hamburg	
D-ABYU	538	230F	04/Sep/81	Asia	
D-ABYW	549	230B Combi	23/Dec/81	Berlin	
D-ABYX	550	230B Combi	25/Feb/82	Koln	
D-ABYY	574	230B Combi	20/Dec/82	Munchen	
D-ABYZ	614	230B Combi	24/May/85	Frankfurt	
D-ABZA	617	230B Combi	28/Jun/85	Dusseldorf	

LUFTHANSA (LH/DLH) (continued)

Reg.	Line No.	Model	Delivery Date	Name	Remarks
D-ABZB	625	230F	25/Oct/85	Europa	
D-ABZC	633	230B Combi	14/Feb/86	Hannover	
D-ABZD	639	230B	10/Apr/86	Kiel	
D-ABZE	663	230B Combi	16/Jan/87	Stuttgart	
D-ABZF	660	230F	24/Oct/86	Africa	
D-ABZH	665	230B	17/Feb/87	Bonn	
D-ABZI		230F	Due Jul/88		

747-400 (General Electric CF6-80C2 Engines)

D-ABVA	700	430	Due Feb/89		
D-ABVB		430	Due Mar/89		

Plus four more for delivery in 1990/1

LUXAIR (LG/LGL) LUXEMBOURG

In 1980, Luxair planned to operate 747SP flights from Luxembourg to Johannesburg and leased a South African Airways aircraft (ZS-SPF), which was given the Luxair green and white colour scheme and registered LX-LTM. This was then swapped for an earlier aircraft (ZS-SPA) which was also painted in Luxair's colour scheme, but the plan was dropped, resulting in two South African 747SPs operating for a while in a green and white colour scheme until eventually re-painted.

In November 1987, Luxair had another go and again leased a 747SP from South African Airways in full Luxair colours for services from Luxembourg to Johannesburg.

FLEET

Reg.	Line No.	Model	Delivery Date	Remarks
LX-LGX	282	SP44	01/Nov/87	L. from South African ZS-SPB

MALAYSIA AIRLINES (MH/MAS) MALAYSIA

Malaysian Airline System (MAS), as it was originally known, introduced its first two 747s on the Kuala Lumpur-London route in April 1982, calling at various places on the way, then extended its 747 services to Los Angeles via Tokyo when it took delivery of a 300 Combi in July 1986. During the years, other 747s were leased short term for Hadj flights, often with the MAS tail colours.

In November 1987, the airline and its aircraft were given a new image, the titling being changed to simply Malaysia and the original red and white colour scheme being replaced with a red and blue cheat line and the same colours used for the familiar Malaysian kite logo on a white tail.

MALAYSIA AIRLINES (MH/MAS) (continued)

FLEET

Reg.	Line No.	Model	Delivery Date	Remarks
9M-MHI	502	236B	12/Mar/82	Orig. British A/W G-BDXL
9M-MHJ	526	236B	08/Apr/82	Orig. British A/W G-BDXN
9M-MHK	650	3H6 Combi	17/Jul/86	
747-400 (General Electric CF6-80C2 Engines)				
9M-		4H6 Combi	Due Mar/89	
9M-		4H6 Combi	Due May/89	

MARTINAIR HOLLAND (MP/MPH) NETHERLANDS

A newcomer to the 747 scene, Martinair introduced its lone flyer 200 Convertible on cargo services from Amsterdam to Hong Kong via Dubai and Muscat in February 1987; for these flights the aircraft also had accommodation in the upper-deck compartment for 14 1st class passengers. In June 1987, the aircraft was converted to an all-passenger configuration (530 all-economy, 11 abreast, with 45 in the upper-deck compartment) to operate summer-season trans-Atlantic charters to the USA and Canada, plus holiday flights to the Mediterranean. Then in November the aircraft was converted back to a freighter for winter, and the airline plans to continue these progammes in future.

FLEET

Reg.	Line No.	Model	Delivery Date	Name
PH-MCE	669	21AC	23/Feb/87	Prins van Oranje
PH-MCF	712	21AC	Due Oct/88	

METRO INTERNATIONAL AIRWAYS (FT) U.S.A.

Formed as a passenger-charter subsidiary of Flying Tigers, Metro International took over three ex-Singapore Airlines 747s from Flying Tigers in January 1981 to operate a service from New York to Tel Aviv and other trans-Atlantic charters. In February 1983 the aircraft were swapped for three Pan Am 747 Freighters for Flying Tigers, and Metro International continued to operate the New York-Tel Aviv service using various leased 747s until November 1983 when the service was taken over by Tower Air.

The aircraft had a simple colour scheme of a dark blue cheat line and tail. The Metro International titling was originally in small lettering on the forward fuselage but later Metro appeared in large letters in this position and Metro International was added in white up the tail.

METRO INTERNATIONAL AIRWAYS (FT) (continued)

FLEET

Reg.	Line No.	Model	Delivery Date	Remarks
N747FT	218	212B	Jan/81	Ex Singapore 9V-SIA Orig. N747TA S. to Pan Am Feb/83 as N728PA
N748FT	219	212B	Jan/81	Ex Singapore 9V-SIB Orig. N748TA S. to Pan Am Feb/83 as N729PA
N749FT	240	212B	Jan/81	Ex Singapore 9V-SQC Orig. N749TA S. to Pan Am Feb/83 as N730PA

MIDDLE EAST AIRLINES (ME/MEA) LEBANON

An unhappy trio, the three 200B Combis of Middle East Airlines (MEA) entered service on the Beirut-London and Beirut-Persian Gulf routes in June 1975 but civil war in the Lebanon forced the airline to transfer its base to Paris in July 1976 and offer the 747s for lease, initially on Hadj flights but later on longer leases, and all three spent a few years with Saudia. When conditions returned to near normal, the aircraft were back in the red and white MEA colours with a cedar tree logo on their tails to operate a Beirut-New York service via Paris from March 1983, with seating for 322 passengers, including 50 1st class and 62 business (Cedar) class. More problems at home ended the service in 1984 when the three 747s were sold to an American leasing company and leased back, since when they have been sub-leased to other airlines.

FLEET

Reg.	Line No.	Model	Delivery Date	Remarks
N202AE	262	2B4B Combi	30/May/75	Orig. OD-AGH L. to British A/W G-BLVE
N203AE	263	2B4B Combi	20/Jun/75	Orig. OD-AGI L. to British A/W G-BLVF
N204AE	264	2B4B Combi	20/Aug/75	Orig. OD-AGJ L. to Air France

Leased Aircraft

Reg.	Line No.	Model	Delivery Date	Remarks
EI-BPH	104	133	24/Jun/85	L. from Guinness Peat Ex Air Canada C-FTOA Ret. Sep/85
EI-BRR	121	133	30/May/86	L. from Guinness Peat Ex Air Canada C-FTOB Ret. Sep/86

MINERVE (FQ/MIN) FRANCE

One of the latest operators to introduce a lone-flyer 747 is the French airline Minerve, who leased an ex-Scandinavian Airlines System (SAS) aircraft in December 1987. The aircraft is likely to be used mainly for flights from Paris to Reunion and also Pointe-a-Pitre, Guadeloupe, in the West Indies, which the airline had been operating with DC-8s.

FLEET

Reg.	Line No.	Model	Delivery Date	Remarks
F-GHBM	114	283B	08/Dec/87	L. from Guinness Peat Ex SAS LN-AET

NATIONAL AERONAUTICS & SPACE ADMINISTRATION (NASA) U.S.A.

The bulkiest payload carried by a 747 is a space shuttle Orbiter, mounted on top of a NASA aircraft, an ex-American Airlines 747-100 which has had its fuselage strengthened and equipped with support pylons to which the Orbiter is attached. Initially, the aircraft was used in 1977 to carry Orbiter *Enterprise* into the air so that it could be released from high altitude to check its handling and landing characteristics. Later, the 747 was used to ferry Orbiters from their usual landing airfield in California back to the launch site in Florida, starting with Orbiter *Columbia* in April 1981. When carrying the Orbiter, detachable end-plate fins are fitted to the 747's tailplane to restore directional stability. For many years the aircraft retained its American Airline's red, white and blue cheat line but when it flew across the Atlantic with Orbiter *Enterprise* to visit the Paris Air Show and Britain in June 1983 it was given a white-top scheme with a blue cheat line and red NASA titles.

FLEET

Reg.	Line No.	Model	Delivery Date	Remarks
N905NA	86	123	18/Jul/74	Ex American N9668

NATIONAL AIRLINES (NA) U.S.A.

Famous in their time as subjects of "Fly Me" advertisements, and carrying the names of selected stewardesses of the airline, the two 747s of National Airlines were introduced on the Miami-New York and Miami-Los Angeles routes in October 1970. Painted in a yellow and orange colour scheme with the Sun King symbol of sunny Florida on their tails, they also operated services on the Miami-London route during summer months from May 1972. Both aircraft were withdrawn from service in September 1975 at the start of a prolonged strike suffered by the airline and were then sold.

NATIONAL AIRLINES (NA) (continued)

FLEET

Reg.	Line No.	Model	Delivery Date	Name	Remarks
N77772	68	135	08/Sep/70	Jacquelyn (Orig. Patricia)	S. to Northwest N620US May/76
N77773	81	135	20/Oct/70	Linda (Orig. Elizabeth)	S. to Northwest N621US May/76

NATIONAL AIRLINES (OV) U.S.A.

Not as colourful as the original National Airlines, the second National Airlines was formed in December 1983 by changing the name of Overseas National Airways (ONA) after the title had been bought from Pan Am who had taken over the original airline in 1980. The second National Airlines then continued the ONA trans-Atlantic and other passenger charters using mainly leased 747s, and sub-leasing these aircraft to other airlines until flying operations ceased in December 1985.

Most of the aircraft operated by the airline were leased from Citicorp and retained their blue cheat line on an otherwise unpainted fuselage, with National Airlines' titles on the forward fuselage.

FLEET

Reg.	Line No.	Model	Delivery Date	Remarks
N747WR	209	273C	17/Nov/83	Ex World A/W L. to Fl. Tigers 1985/6 S. to Evergreen Mar/86
N748WA	211	273C	05/Nov/83	Ex World A/W L. to Fl. Tigers 1983/5 S. to Korean HL7471 Aug/85
Leased Aircraft				
N358AS	134	243B	01/Dec/83	L. from Boeing Ex Alitalia I-DEMU Ret. to Boeing Feb/85
N749R	104	133	28/Jul/84	L. from Guinness Peat Ex Air Canada C-FTOA Ret. Oct/84
N9663	59	123	06/Jun/84	L. from Citicorp Ex American A/L Ret. Nov/85
N9666	77	123	15/Jun/84	L. from Citicorp Ex American A/L Ret. Sep/85
N9667	79	123	23/Jul/84	L. from Citicorp Ex American A/L Ret. May/85
N9669	87	123	27/Jul/84	L. from Citicorp Ex American A/L Ret. Sep/85

NIGERIA AIRWAYS (WT/NGA) — NIGERIA

The flying elephant logo of Nigeria Airways first appeared on the tail of a 747 in March 1982 when the airline wet-leased an aircraft from Scandinavian Airlines System (SAS) to operate services on the Lagos-Kano-London route. In June 1983 the airline added a SAS 200B Combi, also in the full green and white colour scheme of Nigeria Airways, to operate services on the Lagos-New York route but both aircraft were returned in 1984. The SAS 200B Combi was leased again in July 1986 and currently shares its time between the London and New York routes, plus services to Jeddah.

Various other 747s have been leased during the past few years, usually on a short-term basis for operation during the Hadj period and only with the airline's titles displayed.

FLEET

Reg.	Line No.	Model	Delivery Date	Name	Remarks
LN-AEO	167	283B	31/Mar/82		L. from SAS Ret. Jun/83
N4502R	540	283B	03/Jun/83		L. from SAS Ret. Mar/84
SE-DFZ	358	283B Combi	03/Jun/83		L. from SAS Ret. Jun/84
			24/Jul/86	Spirit of Courage	L. from SAS Re-reg. N9727N Feb/87 but later cancelled

NIPPON CARGO AIRLINES (KZ/NCA) — JAPAN

The first two 747 Freighters of Nippon Cargo Airlines (NCA), in their smart two-tone blue colour scheme, entered service on the Tokyo-San Francisco-New York route in May 1985. After the third aircraft was delivered, the frequency of the services was increased to eight a week and a service was started from Tokyo to Hong Kong. With the delivery of the fourth Freighter, the airline is planning to extend its route network to Amsterdam in 1988. This airline is an associate of All Nippon Airways, hence the model number of the aircraft is the same.

FLEET

Reg.	Line No.	Model	Delivery Date
JA8167	604	281F	13/Dec/84
JA8168	608	281F	28/Feb/85
JA8172	623	281F	15/Oct/85
JA8188	689	281F	27/Jan/88

NORTHWEST AIRLINES (NW/NWA) U.S.A.

One of the famous original U.S. airlines which has survived de-regulation intact, Northwest has been a 747 operator since the earliest days and through the years has built up one of the biggest fleets, with 100s, 200Bs and 200Fs, and was the first customer for 747-400s. Justifying its original title of Northwest Orient, initial 747 services from July 1970 were to Tokyo, Manila, Taipei, Hong Kong and Seoul from its base at Minneapolis/St Paul and New York, Washington, Chicago, Seattle, Los Angeles and San Francisco via either Anchorage or Honolulu. Trans-Atlantic services were added from 1979, initially to Scandinavia via Prestwick, and the following year from Minneapolis/St Paul and Boston to London and Frankfurt. Development of the latter services led to a recent change in title to simply Northwest.

Originally, the aircraft had accommodation for 362 passengers, including 58 in 1st class who had the use in flight of an upper-deck lounge. Configurations have changed with the fashions through the years and, typically, accommodation is now provided for a total of 386 passengers, including 18 in 1st class and 84 in business class.

Through the years, Northwest's aircraft have retained their unusual colour scheme of a plain red tail and a very broad white and dark blue cheat line, leaving an unpainted top to the fuselage. The airline's Freighters have the red tail but a totally unpainted fuselage with only the titles, originally in red but more recently in red and black.

FLEET

Reg.	Line No.	Model	Delivery Date	Remarks
N601US	27	151	30/Apr/70	
N602US	40	151	11/May/70	
N603US	45	151	22/May/70	
N604US	55	151	24/Jun/70	
N605US	62	151	24/Jul/70	
N606US	71	151	30/Aug/70	
N607US	74	151	09/Sep/70	
N608US	75	151	17/Sep/70	
N609US	83	151	28/Oct/70	
N610US	93	151	11/Nov/70	
N611US	88	251B	26/Mar/71	First 747-200B
N612US	135	251B	15/May/71	
N613US	141	251B	22/Jun/71	
N614US	163	251B	22/Oct/71	
N615US	165	251B	23/Nov/71	
N616US	258	251F	03/Jul/75	
N617US	261	251F	09/Jul/75	
N618US	269	251F	29/Aug/75	
N619US	308	251F	27/Jun/77	
N622US	357	251B	24/Sep/79	
N623US	374	251B	25/May/79	
N624US	377	251B	06/Jun/79	
N625US	378	251B	17/Jun/79	
N626US	379	251B	28/Jun/79	

NORTHWEST AIRLINES (NW/NWA) (continued)

Reg.	Line No.	Model	Delivery Date	Name	Remarks
N627US	412	251B	02/Jan/80		
N628US	442	251B	08/Apr/80		
N629US	444	251F	18/Apr/80		
N631US	594	251B	02/Apr/84		
N632US	595	251B	01/May/84		
N636US	642	251B	06/May/86		
N637US	644	251B	19/May/86		
N638US	651	251B	18/Jul/86		
N639US	680	251F	03/Jun/87		
N640US	682	251F	01/Jul/87		

747-400 (Pratt & Whitney PW4256 Engines)

N301US	696	451	Due Dec/88		First 747-400
N302US		451	Due Dec/88		
N303US		451	Due /89		
N304US		451	Due /89		
N305US		451	Due /89		
N306US		451	Due /89		

Plus four more for delivery in 1990

Second-hand Aircraft

N620US	68	135	May/76		Ex National N77772
N621US	81	135	May/76		Ex National N77773
N630US	400	2J9F	15/Sep/83		Ex Iranian A/F 5-8117 & Boeing N1288E
N633US	437	227B	19/Apr/84		Ex Braniff N605BN & Air Algerie N8284V
N634US	465	227B	29/May/84		Ex Braniff N1607B & Air Algerie N8285V
N635US	375	227B	28/Dec/84		Ex Braniff N602BN & People Ex N602PE

OLYMPIC AIRWAYS (OA/OAL) GREECE

Carrying on their tails a set of multi-coloured linked rings similar to the flag of the Olympic Games, the Olympic Airways' 747s entered service on the Athens-New York route in July 1973. For the time, they had an unusual seating arrangement of 12 1st class passengers in the upper-deck compartment and 377 economy on the main deck. The 747 fleet was increased in 1985 and the route network extended to include services to Singapore, Melbourne and Sydney, Montreal and Toronto, and Nairobi and Johannesburg.

FLEET

Reg.	Line No.	Model	Delivery Date	Name	Remarks
SX-OAA	216	284B	21/Jun/73	Olympic Zeus	S. to TWA Apr/85 as N305TW
SX-OAB	223	284B	07/Dec/73	Olympic Eagle	
SX-OAC	387	212B	01/Sep/84	Olympic Spirit	Ex Singapore 9V-SQH
SX-OAD	391	212B	01/Apr/85	Olympic Flame	Ex Singapore 9V-SQI
SX-OAE	399	212B	23/Dec/85	Olympic Peace	Ex Singapore 9V-SQJ

OMANI GOVERNMENT — OMAN

Not the best way to treat a beautiful aircraft, the ex-Braniff 747SP bought by the Omani Government in 1984 for use by the Royal Flight of Oman, has been fitted with a satellite communications dish aerial beneath a large fairing behind the upper-deck compartment as part of a complex communications system. The aircraft spent several years being fitted out for its VIP role but eventually made an appearance in 1987.

FLEET

Reg.	Line No.	Model	Delivery Date	Remarks
A40-SO	405	SP27	02/Jul/84	Ex Braniff N603BN & Boeing N351AS

OVERSEAS NATIONAL AIRWAYS (OV) — U.S.A.

The original Overseas National Airways was a well-established U.S. charter company, active during the 1960s and 1970s, which ceased operations in 1978. The airline's name was then bought by an American leasing company, United Air Carriers, and the second ONA started trans-Atlantic passenger charters from New York in June 1983 using ex-Alitalia 747s leased from Boeing. This airline changed its name again, to National Airlines, in December 1983, when the title was bought from Pan Am after the latter had taken over the original National Airlines.

Two of the aircraft (N356AS and N359AS) retained their Alitalia cheat line and N359AS had a two-tone blue tail after sub-lease to the Nigerian airline Kabo Air, while N358AS was in a yellow primer overall.

FLEET

Reg.	Line No.	Model	Delivery Date	Remarks
N356AS	56	143	29/Jul/83	Ex Alitalia I-DEME Ret. to Boeing Oct/83
N358AS	134	243B	01/Aug/83	Ex Alitalia I-DEMU Trs to National Dec/83
N359AS	190	243B	14/Jun/83	Ex Alitalia I-DEMB Ret. to Boeing Nov/83

PAKISTAN INTERNATIONAL AIRLINES (PK/PIA) — PAKISTAN

Pakistan International Airlines (PIA) started 747 services on the Karachi-London-New York route in May 1976 with two ex-TAP (Portugal) aircraft, but additions to the fleet in recent years has enabled the 747s to take over other routes including services to Manila and Tokyo and to Kuala Lumpur and Singapore.

FLEET

Reg.	Line No.	Model	Delivery Date	Remarks
AP-AYV	239	282B	22/Apr/76	Ex TAP CS-TJC
AP-AYW	256	282B	12/Apr/76	Ex TAP CS-TJD
AP-BAK	383	240B Combi	26/Jul/79	
AP-BAT	429	240B Combi	07/Mar/80	
AP-BCL	247	217B	18/Dec/85	Ex CP Air C-FCRE
AP-BCM	226	217B	08/May/86	Ex CP Air C-FCRB
AP-BCN	225	217B	25/Sep/86	Ex CP Air C-FCRA
AP-BCO	244	217B	06/Nov/86	Ex CP Air C-FCRD

PAN AMERICAN WORLD AIRWAYS (PA/PAA) — U.S.A.

Few airlines have done more to advance the development of air travel than Pan Am and it is sad to see such a great airline suffering from the effects of de-regulation. It achieved fame before World War II with its trans-Pacific and trans-Atlantic flying boat services and continued pioneering after the war with its launch orders for both the Boeing 707 and 747. Pan Am's 747s were the first to enter service, on the New York-London route in January 1970, and its big initial fleet soon took over the airline's other major trans-Atlantic, trans-Pacific, Polar and round-the-world services. Pan Am was also the launch customer for the 747SP and for many years it operated the largest 747 fleet. Following the sale of the Pacific route network and the 747SP fleet to United Airlines in 1986, Pan Am 747s are now concentrated on trans-Atlantic, Polar and Latin American services.

The Pan Am colour scheme underwent small changes in the early years, such as larger black lettering for the titling in the mid-1970s and a wider blue cheat line in the early 1980s, but the big change came more recently with the introduction of the very large blue titling and deletion of the cheat line. The names of the aircraft have also had some changes, the biggest in 1980 when most names were changed to those relating to the sea or oceans, although there have been exceptions in recent allocations, and temporary names are sometimes applied for a particular charter service.

Aircraft allocated to the U.S. Air Force's Civil Reserve Air Fleet (CRAF) are now having a side cargo door (SCD) fitted.

FLEET

Reg.	Line No.	Delivery Date	Name (Prefix Clipper)	Remarks
747-121A				
N652PA	103	25/Apr/71	Mermaid (Orig. Pacific Trader)	
N653PA	106	08/Apr/71	Pride of the Ocean (Orig. Unity)	Cvtd CRAF/SCD 1985
N654PA	110	27/Apr/71	Pacific Trader (Orig. White Wing)	Cvtd to 121SF 1977 S. to Fl. Tigers N817FT 1983
N655PA	117	28/May/71	Sea Serpent (Orig. Wild Fire)	Cvtd CRAF/SCD 1985
N656PA	127	18/Jun/71	New Horizons (Orig. Live Yankee & Empress of the Seas)	
N657PA	129	19/Jun/71	Seven Seas (Orig. Arctic)	
N658PA	131	02/Jul/76	Fortune (Orig. High Flyer)	Stored 1971/6 Cvtd to 121SF 1976 S. to Fl. Tigers N818FT 1983
N659PA	142	20/Dec/73	Romance of the Seas (Orig. Plymouth Rock)	Stored 1971/3
N731PA	4	11/Jul/70	Ocean Express (Orig. Bostonian)	Ret. to leasing co. 1986
N732PA	3	13/Jul/70	Ocean Telegraph (Orig. Storm King)	Ret. to leasing co. 1986
N733PA	6	12/Dec/69	Pride of the Sea (Orig. Young America, Constitution & Washington)	
N734PA	7	19/Dec/69	Champion of the Seas (Orig. Flying Cloud)	Cvtd CRAF/SCD 1986
N735PA	10	09/Jan/70	Spark of the Ocean (Orig. Constitution & Young America)	
N736PA	11	20/Jan/70	Victor	W.O. Tenerife 27/Mar/77
N737PA	13	21/Jan/70	Ocean Herald (Orig. Red Jacket)	
N738PA	14	05/Feb/70	Belle of the Sea (Orig. Defender)	W.O. Karachi 04/Aug/83
N739PA	15	15/Feb/70	Maid of the Seas (Orig. Morning Light)	Cvtd CRAF/SCD 1987
N740PA	16	24/Feb/70	Ocean Pearl (Orig. Rival)	
N741PA	17	28/Feb/70	Sparking Wave (Orig. Kit Carson)	
N742PA	18	02/Mar/70	Neptune's Car (Orig. Rainbow)	

Reg.	Line No.	Model	Delivery Date	Name	Remarks
N743PA	24		28/Mar/70	Black Sea (Orig. Derby)	Cvtd CRAF/SCD 1986
N744PA	25		21/Mar/70	Ocean Spray (Orig. Star of the Union)	
N747PA	2		03/Oct/70	Juan T. Trippe (Orig. America & Sea Lark)	
N748PA	26		31/Mar/70	Crest of the Wave (Orig. Hornet)	
N749PA	30		10/Apr/70	Dashing Wave (Orig. Intrepid)	
N750PA	32		26/Apr/70	Neptune's Favorite (Orig. Rambler)	
N751PA	33		24/Apr/70	Gem of the Seas (Orig. Midnight Sun)	
N752PA	34		02/May/70	Fortune	Blown up, Cairo 06/Sep/70
N753PA	37		30/Apr/70	Queen of the Seas (Orig. Westwind)	
N754PA	47		26/May/70	Ocean Rover	Ret. to leasing co. 1986
N755PA	49		31/May/70	Sovereign of the Seas	Ret. to leasing co. 1986
N770PA	50		31/May/70	Queen of the Pacific (Orig. Great Republic, Bald Eagle & Express)	Ret. to leasing co. 1986
N771PA	70		07/Aug/70	Messenger (Orig. Donald McKay)	Cvtd to 121SF 1975 S. to Fl. Tigers N819FT 1983

747 SP21

Reg.	Line No.	Model	Delivery Date	Name	Remarks
N530PA	265		26/Apr/76	Mayflower	N747SP for test prog. S. to United N140UA 1986
N531PA	268		17/May/76	Freedom	N247SP for test prog. S. to United N141UA 1986
N532PA	270		29/Mar/76	Constitution	N347SP for test prog. S. to United N142UA 1986
N533PA	273		05/Mar/76	Young America (Orig. Freedom, Liberty Bell & New Horizons)	N40135 for test prog. & world tour S. to United N143UA 1986
N534PA	286		28/May/76	Great Republic	S. to United N144UA 1986
N536PA	306		06/May/77	Lindbergh	S. to United N145UA 1986
N537PA	325		09/Jun/78	Washington (Orig. High Flyer)	S. to United N146UA 1986
N538PA	331		12/Jul/78	Plymouth Rock (Orig. Fleetwing)	S. to United N147UA 1986
N539PA	367		20/Apr/79	Liberty Bell (Orig. Black Hawk)	S. to United N148UA 1986
N540PA	373		11/May/79	China Clipper (Orig. White Falcon)	S. to United N149UA 1986

Reg.	Line No.	Model	Delivery Date	Name	Remarks
747 SP27 Second-hand					
N529PA	447		23/Sep/83	America	Ex Braniff N606BN S. to United N150UA 1986
747-221F					
N904PA	384		25/Jul/79	Bald Eagle	S. to Japan A/L JA8165 1983
N905PA	392		28/Aug/79	Golden Eagle	S. to Japan A/L JA8160 1982
Second-hand Aircraft (Standard)					
N723PA	312		16/Jan/85	China Clipper II (Orig. Fleetwing)	Ex Singapore 212B 9V-SQG & Boeing N747BK
N724PA	309		31/Aug/84	Fairwind	Ex Singapore 212B 9V-SQF & Boeing N747BJ
N725PA	94		01/May/84	Mandarin	Ex Delta 132 N9898 & China B-1860 & Guinness Peat EI-BOS Cvtd CRAF/SCD 1986
N726PA	253		08/Jun/84	Cathay	Ex Singapore 212B 9V-SQD & Boeing N747BC
N727PA	283		26/Jun/84	Belle of the Sky	Ex Singapore 212B 9V-SQE & Boeing N747BH
N728PA	218		24/Feb/83	Water Witch	Ex Singapore 212B 9V-SIA & Metro N747FT Cvtd CRAF/SCD 1986
N729PA	219		24/Feb/83	Wild Wave	Ex Singapore 212B 9V-SIB & Metro N748FT Cvtd CRAF/SCD 1987
N730PA	240		24/Feb/83	Gem of the Ocean	Ex Singapore 212B 9V-SQC & Metro N749FT Cvtd CRAF/SCD 1987
N901PA	143		28/Jun/77	Carrier Dove	Ex TMA 123SF OD-AGC S. to Fl. Tigers N820FT 1983
N902PA	72		09/May/78	Seamen's Bride (Orig. Mandarin)	Ex Delta 132 N9896 & China B-1868 Cvtd CRAF/SCD 1986
N4703U	52		Feb/86	Nautilus	Ex United 122 N4703U
N4704U	60		Dec/85	Belle of the Sea	Ex United 122 N4704U
N4710U	61		Dec/85	Sea Lark	Ex United 122 N4710U
N4711U	66		Dec/85	Witch of the Wave	Ex United 122 N4711U
N4712U	67		Dec/85	Tradewind	Ex United 122 N4712U
N9670	90		29/May/84	Empress of the Skies	Ex American 123
N9674	133		01/Dec/83	Beacon Light	Ex American 123
Leased Aircraft					
N535PA	209		20/Oct/74	Mercury	L. from World (273C) N747WA Ret. Dec/79
N903PA	46		08/Jan/78	Express	L. from Fl. Tigers (123SF) N800FT Ret. Aug/79

PEOPLE EXPRESS AIRLINES (PE) — U.S.A.

A child of de-regulation, People Express was often compared with Laker Airways for its low-fare, no-frills service, but like Braniff it grew too big, too fast and went broke. The airline's 747 operations started on the New York (Newark)-London (Gatwick) route in May 1983 with extensions to Los Angeles and Oakland/San Francisco in 1984, Brussels in 1985 and Honolulu in 1986. People Express was bought by Texas Air in November 1986 and its existing aircraft and routes were absorbed by another of Texas Air's airlines, Continental Airlines, in February 1987.

FLEET

Reg.	Line No.	Model	Delivery Date	Remarks
N602PE	375	227B	08/May/83	Ex Braniff N602BN S. to Northwest N635US Dec/84
N603PE	36	143	27/Jun/84	Ex Alitalia I-DEMA
N604PE	120	243B	06/Jun/84	Ex Alitalia I-DEMO
N605PE	190	243B	15/Jun/84	Ex Alitalia I-DEMB
N606PE	56	143	17/Jun/85	Ex Alitalia I-DEME
N607PE	162	238B	10/Jul/85	Ex Qantas VH-EBC
N608PE	171	238B	27/Sep/85	Ex Qantas VH-EBD
N609PE	195	238B	01/May/86	Ex Qantas VH-EBE
N610PE	217	238B	26/Jan/87	Ex Qantas VH-EBF

PHILIPPINE AIRLINES (PR/PAL) — PHILIPPINES

Introduced on trans-Pacific services from Manila to San Francisco via Honolulu in January 1980, the 747s of Philippine Airlines (PAL) soon took over the multi-stop service to Amsterdam, followed by a new service to London in April 1980. The aircraft had an unusual feature in the form of 14 proper beds (some double-tiered) in the upper-deck compartment (called Cloud Nine) which were available to 1st class passengers for a small surcharge and could be occupied throughout a multi-stop flight as they were stressed for landings and take-offs. PAL's 747s are currently having a new colour scheme which features a golden sun burst on the usual red, white and blue tail, and an all-white fuselage with the revised title of Philippines.

FLEET

Reg.	Line No.	Model	Delivery Date	Remarks
N741PR	421	2F6B	21/Dec/79	
N742PR	423	2F6B	22/Feb/80	
N743PR	425	2F6B	21/Mar/80	
N744PR	498	2F6B	12/Dec/80	
N4501Q	500	283B Combi	20/Feb/88	L. from Guinness Peat Ex SAS
N4502R	540	283B	04/Nov/87	L. from Guinness Peat Ex SAS

QANTAS AIRWAYS (QF/QFA) AUSTRALIA

Sporting a new colour scheme with a winged kangaroo on their red tails, the first Qantas 747s were introduced on the Sydney-Melbourne-Singapore route in September 1971 and operated their first service to London in November 1971. An unusual feature of these aircraft was a lower-deck galley, from which meals were delivered to the main deck via elevators (lifts). The 747 fleet has grown a lot since then, with a mix of 200Bs, 200B Combis, SPs and 300s, and the route network has been extended to include trans-Pacific services to Los Angeles and San Francisco, via Honolulu or non-stop with SPs, plus additional destinations in Europe and a one-stop (eastbound only) London-Sydney service via Bangkok taking 21¼ hours.

When first introduced, the Qantas 747-200Bs had accommodation for 356 passengers, with 56 in 1st class who had the use of an upstairs Captain Cook Lounge, the first to have the extended interior. A typical seating arrangement now, in the airline's 300s, is for a total of 415, including 30 1st class in zone A and half of zone B, and 63 business class, 38 of whom are in the stretched upper-deck compartment (which is called zone F and is self-contained with its own galley and toilets), and the remainder in the rear of zone B.

Another new colour scheme was introduced in 1984 with a larger, wingless kangaroo on the tail and an all-white fuselage.

FLEET

Reg.	Line No.	Model	Delivery Date	Name (Prefix City of except *)	Remarks
Pratt & Whitney Powered Aircraft					
VH-EBA	147	238B	30/Jul/71	Canberra	S. to Guinness Peat Jun/84 To Air Lanka 4R-ULF
			01/Sep/86	–	L. from Guinness Peat
VH-EBB	149	238B	14/Aug/71	Melbourne	S. to Guinness Peat Jul/84 To Air Lanka 4R-ULG
			17/Jul/87	–	L. from Guinness Peat L. to Air Pacific
VH-EBC	162	238B	21/Oct/71	Sydney	S. to Boeing Dec/84 To People Ex. N607PE
VH-EBD	171	238B	08/Dec/71	Perth	S. to Boeing Mar/85 To People Ex. N608PE
VH-EBE	195	238B	10/Aug/72	Brisbane	S. to Boeing Jun/85 To People Ex. N609PE
VH-EBF	217	238B	01/Aug/73	Adelaide	S. to Boeing Nov/85 To People Ex. N610PE
VH-EBG	233	238B	19/Mar/74	Fremantle (Orig. Hobart)	S. to El Al Nov/87
VH-EBH	238	238B	24/May/74	Parramatta (Orig. Newcastle)	
VH-EBI	241	238B	10/Oct/74	Dubbo (Orig. Darwin)	

QANTAS AIRWAYS (QF/QFA) (continued)

Reg.	Line No.	Model	Delivery Date	Name	Remarks
VH-EBJ	260	238B	30/May/75	Newcastle (Orig. Geelong)	
VH-EBK	267	238B	07/Nov/75	Wollongong	L. to Air Pacific
VH-EBL	285	238B	29/Jun/76	Ballaarat (Orig. Townsville)	
VH-EBM	310	238B	15/Aug/77	Gosford (Orig. Parramatta)	
VH-EBN	316	238B	20/Dec/77	Albury	
VH-EBO	339	238B	18/Sep/78	Elizabeth	
VH-EBP	341	238B	16/Oct/78	Adelaide (Orig. Fremantle)	
VH-ECA	314	238B Combi	27/Oct/77	Sale	S. to Air Canada C-GAGC Jan/88

Rolls-Royce Powered Aircraft

VH-EBQ	410	238B	11/Dec/79	Bunbury	
VH-EBR	464	238B	30/Sep/80	Hobart (Orig. Dubbo)	
VH-EBS	543	238B	30/Nov/81	Longreach*	
VH-EBT	602	338	13/Nov/84	Canberra	
VH-EBU	606	338	24/Jan/85	Sydney	
VH-EBV	610	338	15/Apr/85	Melbourne	
VH-EBW	638	338	31/Mar/86	Brisbane	
VH-EBX	662	338	12/Nov/86	Perth	
VH-EBY	678	338	01/May/87	Darwin	
VH-ECB	409	238B Combi	14/Nov/79	Swan Hill	
VH-ECC	483	238B Combi	15/Oct/80	Shepparton	

747SP

VH-EAA	505	SP38	19/Jan/81	Gold Coast/Tweed	
VH-EAB	537	SP38	31/Aug/81	Winton*	

747-400 (Rolls-Royce RB211-524G Engines)

VH-		438	Due Apr/89		
VH-		438	Due May/89		
VH-		438	Due Jun/89		
VH-		438	Due Sep/89		

Leased Aircraft

EI-BED	44	130	30/Nov/87		L. from Aer Lingus Ret. Feb/88
N93117	113	131	01/Nov/87		L. from Tower Air Ret. Feb/88
VH-EEI	87	123	08/Feb/88		L. from Citicorp

ROYAL AIR MAROC (AT/RAM) — MOROCCO

Introduced initially on Hadj flights from Rabat to Jeddah in October 1978, the lone flyer 200B Combi of Royal Air Maroc (RAM) was transferred to the airline's scheduled services in December 1978 operating on the routes from Casablanca to New York and Montreal, and from Casablanca to Paris. In 1985 the aircraft was joined by an ex-South African Airways 747SP, which shared the North American services with the Combi and also operated a weekly Casablanca-Rio de Janeiro service, although recently the 747SP has been operating most of the services while the Combi has been used for charters, including a weekly flight to Helsinki.

Both aircraft have the usual red and green colour scheme with the shooting star on their tails.

Other 747s are sometimes leased on a short-term basis for operation of Hadj flights.

FLEET

Reg.	Line No.	Model	Delivery Date	Remarks
CN-RME	338	2B6B Combi	29/Sep/78	
CN-RMS	293	SP44	14/Mar/85	Ex South African ZS-SPD

ROYAL ATLANTIC AIRWAYS — BRITAIN

A proposed British airline with really big ideas is Royal Atlantic Airways, which plans to provide an all-business-class service between London (Stansted) and New York (Newark). The airline originally planned to start the service in 1987 with a Boeing 707 configured to seat 50 passengers but was delayed awaiting approval from the aviation authorities in both countries. Now the airline has even bigger plans and has decided to start the service in 1988 with two 747s, each configured to seat just 80 passengers. Reports state that these passengers will be in fully-reclining sleeper seats, or private suites, and will have the use in flight of a library and fully-equipped business centre. Needless to say, fares will be set at 1st class level.

ROYAL JORDANIAN (Formerly ALIA) (RJ/RJA) — JORDAN

There has been no shortage of variety where the national airline of Jordan has been concerned in recent years. Under its original name of Alia, the airline's first two 747s entered service in April 1977 on the Amman-London and Amman-Amsterdam-New York routes. At that time the aircraft had a regal red and gold colour scheme, but in the early 1980s Alia tried out various strange colour schemes on its Lockheed TriStars before settling on a red tail with gold crown and a multi-coloured cheat line. Its 747s were given this scheme, and then the airline changed its name to Royal Jordanian and introduced yet another colour scheme, this time with an unusual charcoal grey top and tail, and a gold cheat line, crown and titles.

Of Alia's original three 747s, two have been sold to leave a lone flyer 200B Combi, which now spends most of its time on Royal Jordanian's Amman-Vienna-New York route.

FLEET

Reg.	Line No.	Model	Delivery Date	Name	Remarks
JY-AFA	296	2D3B Combi	13/Apr/77	Prince Ali	
JY-AFB	297	2D3B Combi	11/May/77	Princess Haya	S. to Br. Caledonian G-HUGE Mar/85
JY-AFS	514	2D3B	26/Mar/81	Prince Hamzah	S. to Br. Caledonian G-CITB Sep/87

SABENA (SN/SAB) BELGIUM

Sabena (or S.A. Belge d'Exploitation de la Navigation Aerienne, to give its full title) introduced its first two 747s on the Brussels-New York route in February 1971. The airline then became the first to realise the advantages of a Combi and, at the beginning of 1974, had both aircraft modified with a side cargo door, so that cargo pallets could be carried in zone E and allow mixed-traffic operations. Taking this flexibility of operation a stage further, the airline then devised a quick-change technique whereby 116 seats mounted on pallets could be installed in zone E when it was required to operate the aircraft in an all-passenger configuration during summer peaks.

A 300 Combi joined the fleet in 1986, and the 747 route network now includes New York, Johannesburg, Kinshasa and Lagos. Sabena 747s were also used for a daily Brussels-London (Gatwick)-Atlanta service in association with British Caledonian Airways but this was discontinued when the airline was taken over by British Airways.

Sabena's blue and white colour scheme has changed little through the years except that the long and lean S in white on the blue tail is now a shorter blue S on a white disc and the black titling is now larger and in blue.

FLEET

Reg.	Line No.	Model	Delivery Date	Remarks
OO-SGA	92	129 Combi	19/Nov/70	Cvtd from 129 Feb/74
OO-SGB	95	129 Combi	04/Dec/70	Cvtd from 129 Mar/74
OO-SGC	646	329 Combi	10/Jun/86	

SAUDIA (SV/SDI) **SAUDI ARABIA**

Saudi Arabian Airlines (or Saudia for short) started 747 operations on the Riyadh-London route in June 1977 using 200B Combis leased from Middle East Airlines, but in 1981 the airline went on a spending spree and bought 10 new aircraft (eight 100Bs and two SPs), following this in 1985/6 with the purchase of 10 300s. Strangely, Saudia has up to now not bought any 747 Freighters and yet for the past few years has always had at least one leased aircraft in service. Current 747 passenger services extend from Jeddah, Riyadh and Dhahran to New York in the west and Jakarta, Manila, Seoul and Singapore in the east.

Saudia's colour scheme has remained basically unchanged through the years, being in the national colours of green and white with a blue underline on the cheat line and the crossed-swords logo on the tail.

FLEET

Reg.	Line No.	Model	Delivery Date	Remarks
HZ-AIA	512	168B	24/Apr/81	
HZ-AIB	517	168B	02/Apr/81	
HZ-AIC	522	168B	20/May/81	
HZ-AID	525	168B	21/May/81	
HZ-AIE	530	168B	31/Jul/81	
HZ-AIG	551	168B	Jan/82	
HZ-AIH	555	168B	17/Mar/82	
HZ-AII	557	168B	02/Apr/82	
HZ-AIK	616	368	12/Jul/85	
HZ-AIL	619	368	02/Aug/85	
HZ-AIM	620	368	21/Aug/85	
HZ-AIN	622	368	20/Dec/85	
HZ-AIO	624	368	24/Oct/85	
HZ-AIP	630	368	17/Jan/86	
HZ-AIQ	631	368	14/Mar/86	
HZ-AIR	643	368	24/Jul/86	
HZ-AIS	645	368	20/Aug/86	
HZ-AIT	652	368	10/Nov/86	
747SP				
HZ-AIF	529	SP68	23/Jun/81	
HZ-AIJ	560	SP68	25/May/82	
Leased Aircraft				
F-GPAN	337	2B3F	01/Mar/84	L. from UTA via National Ret. Apr/85
HL7447	128	230B	22/Jun/79	L. from Korean Ex Condor D-ABYF Ret. Nov/80
HL7451	448	2B5F	27/May/86	L. from Korean
HL7452	454	2B5F	17/Feb/83	L. from Korean Ret. Feb/84
HL7459	520	2B5F	08/May/81	L. from Korean Ret. Feb/84

SAUDIA (SU/SDI) (continued)

Reg.	Line No.	Model	Delivery Date	Name	Remarks
HL7471	211	273C	08/May/85		L. from Korean Ex World A/W N748WA Ret. May/86
N743TV	524	271C	14/Apr/85		L. from Transamerica Ret. Mar/86
OD-AGH	262	2B4B Combi	01/Jun/77		L. from MEA Ret. Jun/81
			Apr/84		L. from MEA Ret. Apr/85
OD-AGI	263	2B4B Combi	01/Jun/77		L. from MEA Ret. Jun/81
OD-AGJ	264	2B4B Combi	17/Sep/78		L. from MEA Ret. Dec/80
TU-TAP	472	2S4F	01/Mar/84		L. from Air Afrique Ret. Apr/85

SAUDI ARABIAN GOVERNMENT — SAUDI ARABIA

When the Saudi Arabian Government took delivery of a 747SP for the exclusive use of the late King Khaled and the Saudi Arabian royal family in 1979 it was thought to be the ultimate in VIP aircraft. Little has been reported about the interior of this aircraft except that at the time it had a hospital room wired for telemetry communications with a Cleveland, Ohio, hospital which had fitted the King with a heart pacemaker. However, following King Fahd's accession in 1982, the 747SP was relegated to second place because a 747-300 was ordered for the new King's use. Described by newspapers as a flying palace, this aircraft is reported to have living and working areas on all three decks with elevators (lifts) connecting the three floors. Apart from the plush upholstery and gold fittings, there is a fully-equipped medical centre and a world-wide telecommunications system utilising satellite links, which accounts for the satellite communications dish aerial beneath the large fairing on top of the fuselage behind the stretched upper deck.

The colour scheme on the aircraft is basically the same as that of Saudia except for different titling on the fuselage and no titles on the tail.

FLEET

Reg.	Line No.	Model	Delivery Date	Remarks
HZ-HM1A	592	3G1	22/Dec/83	
HZ-HM1B	329	SP68	11/Jul/79	Orig. HZ-HM1

SCANAIR (DK) — DENMARK, NORWAY & SWEDEN

Associated with Scandinavian Airlines System (SAS), the Scandinavian charter airline Scanair leased at least two 747s from SAS for short periods in the early 1980s to operate inclusive-tour flights from various Scandinavian cities to Mediterranean resorts and further afield, in between periods with DC-10s and Airbus A300s. The aircraft retained most of their old-style SAS colour scheme but their tails carried the golden yellow sun symbol and title of Scanair.

FLEET

Reg.	Line No.	Model	Delivery Date	Remarks
LN-RNA	311	283B Combi	Mar/82	L. from SAS Ret. Jul/82
SE-DDL	114	283B	15/Sep/82	L. from SAS Ret. Mar/83

SCANDINAVIAN AIRLINES SYSTEM (SAS) (SK) — DENMARK, NORWAY & SWEDEN

After numerous attempts to phase out its 747s, SAS appeared to have operated its final flight with them in August 1987. The airline had introduced its first 747 – SE-DDL, well known because of its name *Huge Viking* – on the Copenhagen-New York route in April 1971 and through the years that followed had built up a small fleet, even taking delivery in 1981 of the 500th 747 to be built. These aircraft spent most of their time on trans-Atlantic routes, which included Copenhagen to Montreal, Chicago and Los Angeles as well as New York. Currently, those that have not been sold have been leased out to leave a confusing situation.

The aircraft's original blue and white colour scheme had a cheat line which started at the nose in the form of a stylised bow of an ancient viking sailing ship, and to support the theme the aircraft were named after characters from Norse mythology and the sagas. Later the aircraft were given the current white fuselage with bands of colour which appear to decorate more of the underside of the fuselage than the top but are a clever use of all the colours of the three owner-nations' flags.

FLEET

Reg.	Line No.	Model	Delivery Date	Name	Remarks
LN-RNA	311	283B Combi	27/Oct/77	Magnus Viking	L. to Avianca HK2910X Aug/82 W.O. Madrid 27/Nov/83
N4501Q	500	283B Combi	17/Feb/81	Dan Viking	500th 747 built Orig. allot. OY-KHB L. to Guinness P. Feb/88 To Philippine A/L
N4502R	540	283B	22/Oct/81	Huge Viking	Orig. allot. LN-RNB L. to Guinness P. Nov/87 To Philippine A/L

SCANDINAVIAN AIRLINES SYSTEM (SAS)(SK) (continued)

Reg.	Line No.	Model	Delivery Date	Name	Remarks
OY-KHA	167	283B	12/Nov/71	Ivar Viking	S. to Air Invest Jan/82 L. back as LN-AEO (See Leased Aircraft)
SE-DDL	114	283B	22/Feb/71	Bjarne Viking (Orig. Huge Viking)	S. to Air Invest Oct/83 L. back as LN-AET (See Leased Aircraft)
SE-DFZ	358	283B Combi	02/Mar/79	Knut Viking	L. to Nigeria 1983/4 & again Jul/86

Leased Aircraft

Reg.	Line No.	Model	Delivery Date	Name	Remarks
LN-AEO	167	283B	01/Feb/82	Ivar Viking	L. from Air Invest Orig. OY-KHA Ret. Mar/86 To Br. Airtours G-BMGS Mar/86
LN-AET	114	283B	10/Oct/83	Bjarne Viking	L. from Air Invest Orig. SE-DDL Ret. Jul/85 To Minerve Dec/87
N356AS	56	143	26/Jul/82	–	L. from Boeing Ex Alitalia I-DEME Ret. Dec/82

SEABOARD WORLD AIRLINES (SB) U.S.A.

The American cargo carrier Seaboard World introduced the first of its 747 Freighters (called *Containerships*) in August 1974 on the New York-Paris-London-New York route. Following delivery of the second aircraft, a New York-Frankfurt service was started in May 1976 and from October 1978 the aircraft on this route carried cargo containers on the main deck and passengers in the upper-deck compartment. The latter was called the Captain's Deck and was equipped with 16 seats for the carriage of military personnel and their dependents. The airline had plans to extend the service to the general public, charging economy-class fares, but it was taken over by Flying Tigers in October 1980.

FLEET

Reg.	Line No.	Model	Delivery Date	Remarks
N701SW	242	245F	31/Jul/74	Trs to Flying Tigers as N811FT Oct/80
N702SW	266	245F	30/Apr/76	Trs to Flying Tigers as N812FT Oct/80
N703SW	394	245F	06/Sep/79	Trs to Flying Tigers as N813FT Oct/80
N704SW	396	245F	26/Sep/79	Trs to Flying Tigers as N814FT Oct/80
N705SW	476	245F	Not delivered	Del. to Flying Tigers as N815FT Oct/80

SEABOARD WORLD AIRLINES (SB) (continued)

Reg.	Line No.	Model	Delivery Date	Name	Remarks
N706SW	478	245F	Not delivered		Del. to Flying Tigers as N816FT Oct/80

Leased Aircraft

N748WA	211	273C	01/Oct/78		L. from World A/W Ret. Oct/80

SINGAPORE AIRLINES (SQ/SIA) SINGAPORE

Considering the small size of its island home, Singapore Airlines has certainly made a big impression in the air-travel world, with the advertising of its Singapore Girls and its award-winning cabin service. The airline's first 747s entered service on the Singapore-Tokyo route in October 1973, later extending their activities to Australia, Europe and the U.S.A. as the fleet grew. Another important feature is the way Singapore Airlines frequently up-dates its 747 fleet, replacing the original 200Bs with Super Bs (200Bs with improved engines) in 1979/80 and introducing the Big Tops (300s) from 1983 and, coming shortly, 400s from 1989. With the extra endurance of the 400s, the airline should be able to fly from Singapore to London non-stop, which it already operates non-stop in the opposite direction taking 12½ hours.

All aircraft had the midnight blue and rich yellow colour scheme with a stylised bird logo (symbolising flight) on the tail until 1987 when, to mark the airline's 40th anniversary, the yellow of the cheat line and the bird were given the golden treatment.

FLEET

Reg.	Line No.	Delivery Date	Remarks
747-212B			
9V-SIA	218	31/Jul/73	S. to Tiger Air Nov/79 as N747TA/N747FT To Fl. Tigers & Metro
9V-SIB	219	29/Aug/73	S. to Tiger Air Jul/80 as N748TA/N748FT To Fl. Tigers & Metro
9V-SQC	240	29/Jul/74	S. to Tiger Air Sep/80 as N749TA/N749FT To Fl. Tigers & Metro
9V-SQD	253	06/Feb/75	S. to Boeing Jun/83 To Pan Am as N726PA
9V-SQE	283	30/Mar/76	S. to Boeing Jul/83 To Pan Am as N727PA

Reg.	Line No.	Model	Delivery Date	Name	Remarks
9V-SQF	309		27/Jun/77		S. to Boeing Jul/84 To Pan Am as N724PA
9V-SQG	312		14/Sep/77		S. to Boeing Dec/84 To Pan Am as N723PA
9V-SQH	387		02/Aug/79		S. to Olympic Sep/84 as SX-OAC
9V-SQI	391		16/Aug/79		S. to Olympic Apr/85 as SX-OAD
9V-SQJ	399		25/Sep/79		S. to Olympic Dec/85 as SX-OAE
9V-SQK	401		01/Oct/79		S. to Air India May/87 as VT-ENQ
9V-SQL	419		01/Feb/80		
9V-SQM	436		10/Apr/80		
9V-SQN	449		29/May/80		
9V-SQO	457		27/Jun/80		
9V-SQP	470		12/Sep/80		
9V-SQQ	471		25/Sep/80		
9V-SQR	475		30/Oct/80		
9V-SQS	510		19/Mar/81		

747-312

9V-SKA	580		29/Apr/83		
N116KB	583		21/Jun/83		Orig. allot. 9V-SKB
N117KC	584		30/Jun/83		Orig. allot. 9V-SKC
N118KD	590		22/Nov/83		Orig. allot. 9V-SKD
N119KE	593		24/Feb/84		Orig. allot. 9V-SKE
N120KF	598		28/Jun/84		Orig. allot. 9V-SKF
N121KG	603		30/Oct/84		Orig. allot. 9V-SKG
N122KH	609		20/Mar/85		Orig. allot. 9V-SKH
N123KJ	612		30/Apr/85		Orig. allot. 9V-SKJ
N124KK	621		24/Sep/85		Orig. allot. 9V-SKK
N125KL	626		11/Dec/85		Orig. allot. 9V-SKL

747-312 Combi

9V-SKM	637		25/Mar/86		
9V-SKN	653		27/Aug/86		
9V-SKP	666		20/Mar/87		

747-212F

9V-SKQ			Due Aug/88		

747-412 (Pratt & Whitney PW4256 Engines)

9V-SMA			Due Feb/89		
9V-SMB			Due /89		
9V-SMC			Due /89		
9V-SMD			Due /89		

Plus 10 more for delivery 1990/3

SOUTH AFRICAN AIRWAYS (SA/SAA) — SOUTH AFRICA

The Flying Springbok logo of South African Airways (SAA)/Suid-Afrikaanse Lugdiens (SAL) appeared as a small black silhouette in the airline's original colour scheme on its 747s when they entered service on the Johannesburg-London route in December 1971, but it has since been enlarged and given a more prominent place on their orange tails.

South African Airways' current 747 fleet comprises 200Bs, 200B Combis, 300s and 747SPs, and the route network from Johannesburg, Cape Town and Durban extends to Hong Kong, Taipei (Taiwan) and Rio de Janeiro as well as various destinations in Europe.

In the early days, the airline referred to its 747s as Gentle Giants and named them after mountain ranges of South Africa, but the two 300s are named after major cities. Originally, the 200Bs had accommodation for 341 passengers with 34 in 1st class who had the use in flight of an upstairs Penthouse Lounge, while at present the 300s have seating for 370 passengers, still with 34 in 1st class but now including 64 in business class (called Gold Class).

FLEET

Reg.	Line No.	Model	Delivery Date	Name	Remarks
747-200B					
ZS-SAL	154	244B	26/Jan/72	Tafelberg	
ZS-SAM	158	244B	13/Dec/71	Drakensberg	L. to Varig Apr/87 as PP-VNW
ZS-SAN	160	244B	22/Oct/71	Lebombo	
ZS-SAO	194	244B	07/Aug/72	Magaliesberg	
ZS-SAP	198	244B	29/Sep/72	Swartberg	
ZS-SAR	486	244B Combi	06/Nov/80	Waterberg	Orig. allot. ZS-SAA
ZS-SAS	488	244B Combi	24/Nov/80	Helderberg	Orig. allot. ZS-SAB W.O. Nr Mauritius 28/Nov/87
747-300					
ZS-SAT	577	344	02/May/83	Johannesberg	
ZS-SAU	578	344	14/Apr/83	Cape Town Kaapstad	
747SP					
ZS-SPA	280	SP44	19/Mar/76	Matroosberg	L. to Air Mauritius as 3B-NAJ Apr/87
ZS-SPB	282	SP44	22/Apr/76	Outeniqua	L. to Luxair as LX-LGX Nov/87
ZS-SPC	288	SP44	16/Jun/76	Maluti	L. to Air Mauritius as 3B-NAG Oct/84
ZS-SPD	293	SP44	10/Sep/76	Majuba	S. to Royal Air Maroc as CN-RMS Sep/86 (leased from Mar/85)
ZS-SPE	298	SP44	22/Nov/76	Hantam	
ZS-SPF	301	SP44	31/Jan/77	Soutpansberg	

SWAN AIRLINES — BRITAIN

A proposed new British charter operator, Swan Airlines plans to start services from London (Stansted) to the Far East, including Bangkok, Hong Kong, Kuala Lumpur and Singapore. Initially, the airline expects to operate a lone flyer 747-200B with seats for 440 passengers.

SWISSAIR (SR/SWR) — SWITZERLAND

Starting in a small way, Swissair introduced two 747-200Bs on the Zurich-Geneva-New York route in April 1971, but later became the launch customer for the 747-300, ordering five of them, including three Combis. These replaced the original 200Bs in 1983 and extended the 747 route network to include Boston, Chicago, Hong Kong, Seoul and Tokyo.

The 200Bs started life with a simple colour scheme, comprising an ordinary red cheat line and a red and white Swiss flag which covered the top half of the tail, but in 1979 they were given the current colour scheme which has a brown and black cheat line below the windows and a red and white Swiss flag which covers the whole of the tail. All the 747s are named after Swiss cantons (states).

Swissair's 200Bs originally had accommodation for 353 passengers, 32 of whom were in 1st class with the use in flight of an upstairs lounge. Nowadays, the airline's all-passenger 300s have seating for 384 passengers, with 24 in 1st class, 84 in business class and 276 in economy class, 69 of whom are seated six-abreast in the upper-deck compartment.

FLEET

Reg.	Line No.	Model	Delivery Date	Name	Remarks
Original 747-200B					
HB-IGA	112	257B	29/Jan/71	Geneve	S. to Salenia Jan/84 To Air National LX-SAL & TWA N303TW
HB-IGB	126	257B	25/Mar/71	Zurich	S. to Kansa Jan/84 To Egyptair SU-GAK & TWA N304TW
747-300					
HB-IGC	570	357 Combi	19/Mar/83	Bern	
HB-IGD	576	357 Combi	05/Mar/83	Basel	
N221GE	585	357	16/Dec/83	Geneve	Orig. allot. HB-IGE
N221GF	586	357	30/Nov/83	Zurich	Orig. allot. HB-IGF
HB-IGG	686	357 Combi	04/Dec/87	Ticino	

SYRIANAIR (RB/SYR) — SYRIA

One of the first airlines to order 747SPs, Syrian Arab Airlines (or Syrianair for short) introduced the first of its two aircraft on the Damascus-London route in June 1976, later extending their activities to include other European cities, India and Pakistan.

In the current political climate, London is no longer served, the aircraft operating from Damascus to Paris via Munich, Bombay via Abu Dhabi, Delhi via Sharjah, and Dhahran and Jeddah.

The aircraft have a simple blue and white colour scheme with a white bird-in-flight logo on their blue tails.

FLEET

Reg.	Line No.	Model	Delivery Date	Name
YK-AHA	284	SP94	21/May/76	November 16
YK-AHB	290	SP94	16/Jul/76	Arab Solidarity

TAP — AIR PORTUGAL (TP) — PORTUGAL

The Portuguese national airline Transportes Aereos Portugueses (or TAP for short) had four 747s in service for a few years, the first two operating on the Lisbon-New York route from March 1972. When the full fleet was in operation, the 747 route network was extended from Lisbon to Rio de Janeiro, Luanda (Angola), Mozambique and Johannesburg, but problems in the old Portuguese empire led to a reduction in services, resulting in two aircraft being disposed of in 1976, and the remaining two being withdrawn from service in 1983.

All four 747s originally had a mainly red and white colour scheme, comprising a red cheat line and titling with TAP in large red letters on a white tail, plus a small green bird-in-flight logo. In 1979, the airline changed its name to TAP – Air Portugal and at the same time introduced a wide red and thin green cheat line (the national colours) extending up the white tail to end with the letters TAP in red.

FLEET

Reg.	Line No.	Model	Delivery Date	Name	Remarks
CS-TJA	178	282B	16/Feb/72	Portugal	S. to TWA Jun/84 as N301TW
CS-TJB	189	282B	16/May/72	Brasil	S. to TWA Oct/84 as N302TW
CS-TJC	239	282B	07/Jun/74	Luis de Camoes	S. to Pakistan Int. Apr/76 as AP-AYV
CS-TJD	256	282B	17/Oct/75	Bartolomeu de Gusmao	S. to Pakistan Int. Apr/76 as AP-AYW

THAI AIRWAYS INTERNATIONAL (TG/THA) THAILAND

In their very pleasing purple, mauve and gold colour scheme, matching the Royal Orchid service they provided, the first 747s of Thai Airways International started operations on the route from Bangkok to Copenhagen, Frankfurt, Paris and Amsterdam in November 1979, and on the trans-Pacific route to Los Angeles (later changed to Dallas) via Tokyo and Seattle in April 1980. Services to London started in November 1980, and to Sydney and Melbourne in 1981.

Business class was already in fashion when the Thai 747s were introduced so they started with accommodation for 371 passengers, including 24 in 1st class, who could opt for a divan in the upper-deck compartment, and 39 business class in zone B. The only changes that have occurred since reflect the general trend, with a reduction in 1st class to 16 passengers and an increase in space for business class passengers who now number 40; the economy-class zones remain the same.

As befits these fine ladies, the aircraft are named after famous women from Thai history.

FLEET

Reg.	Line No.	Model	Delivery Date	Name
747-200B				
HS-TGA	402	2D7B	02/Nov/79	Visuthakasatriya
HS-TGB	417	2D7B	15/Dec/79	Sirisobhakya
HS-TGC	424	2D7B	23/Feb/80	Dararasmi
HS-TGF	449	2D7B	24/Sep/80	Phimara
HS-TGG	504	2D7B	16/Mar/81	Sriwanna
HS-TGS	597	2D7B	01/Jan/84	Chainarai
747-300				
HS-TGD	681	3D7	16/Dec/87	Suchada
HS-TGE	688	3D7	03/Dec/87	Chutamat
747-400 (General Electric CF6-80C2 Engines)				
HS-		4D7	Due Oct/89	
HS-		4D7	Due Nov/89	

TOWER AIR (FF/TOW) U.S.A.

Formed in 1983 to take over the New York-Brussels-Tel Aviv route from Metro International, Tower Air started operations on the route with second-hand 747s in November 1983. The airline also operates U.S. military and other passenger charters.

Originally, the aircraft were in the colour scheme of the previous operators but later were given a fashionable white fuselage and tail, with a dark blue belly, and very large titling of the same colour.

TOWER AIR (FE/TOW) (continued)

FLEET

Reg.	Line No.	Model	Delivery Date	Name	Remarks
N601BN	100	127	01/Nov/83		Ex Braniff
N602FF	58	124	31/May/84	Rena	Ex Continental N26862 & Avianca HK-2000 L. to Air Jamaica
N603FF	12	130	22/Nov/85	Suzie	Ex Lufthansa D-ABYA & Egyptair N480GX & Transamerica N780T

Leased Aircraft

Reg.	Line No.	Model	Delivery Date	Name	Remarks
N731PA	4	121	10/May/87		L. from Manu. Hanover Ex Pan Am Ret. Oct/87
N93117	113	131	21/Apr/87		L. from GATX Ex TWA Ret. Oct/87

TRANSAMERICA AIRLINES (TV) U.S.A.

Trans International Airlines (TIA), a charter airline based in Oakland, California, changed its name to Transamerica Airlines just before it introduced the first of its 747 Convertibles in December 1979, planning to extend operations to include scheduled services. Although some trans-Atlantic services were started in 1980 and later, including New York-Amsterdam, these were operated mainly with DC-8s while the 747s were generally on trans-Atlantic and trans-Pacific charters, having accommodation for 488 passengers, 10-abreast all-economy, with 32 in the upper-deck compartment. By the mid-1980s the 747s were spending most of their time leased out and the airline ceased operations in September 1986.

The aircraft had the usual Transamerica green and white colour scheme with a two-tone blue tip to the tail which was also repeated on the wing tips.

FLEET

Reg.	Line No.	Model	Delivery Date	Remarks
N741TV	416	271C	21/Dec/79	S. to Int. Lease Finance Jun/87 To Cargolux as LX-ACV
N742TV	438	271C	26/Mar/80	S. to Cargolux Jun/87 as LX-ECV
N743TV	524	271C	01/Jun/81	S. to Int. Lease Finance Dec/86 To Cargolux as LX-BCV

Leased Aircraft

Reg.	Line No.	Model	Delivery Date	Remarks
N780T	12	130	01/Jun/84	L. from GATX Ex Lufthansa D-ABYA Ret. Nov/85 To Tower Air as N603FF

TRANSCONTINENTALE — FRANCE

Yet another French charter company planning to operate a 747 in 1988 is a new airline called Transcontinentale, which is intending to start trans-Atlantic services from France to the French Antilles (Caribbean) and the USA.

TRANS MEDITERRANEAN AIRWAYS (TL) — LEBANON

One of the more colourful of 747 operators, Trans Mediterranean Airways (TMA) had two Freighters in service for a short period during the mid-1970s. Both aircraft were in the full TMA colour scheme, with a green fuselage and a yellow tail, and spent most of their time on the Beirut-Amsterdam-New York route with occasional visits to London and other charter work. The aircraft were ex-American Airlines' passenger 747-100s converted into Freighters with side cargo doors. Like Middle East Airlines, TMA suffered from problems related to the civil war in the Lebanon and 747 operations ceased in June 1977.

FLEET

Reg.	Line No.	Model	Delivery Date	Remarks
OD-AGC	143	123SF	15/May/75	Ex America A/L N9676 S. to Pan Am Jun/77 as N901PA
OD-AGM	136	123SF	30/May/76	Ex American A/L N9675 S. back to American A/L in Dec/76

TRANS WORLD AIRLINES (TW/TWA) — U.S.A.

Another of the famous old U.S. airlines that has not enjoyed the best of good fortune in recent years, Trans World Airlines (TWA) was one of the original customers for 747s and introduced its first aircraft on the domestic coast-to-coast route between New York and Los Angeles in February 1970; its first trans-Atlantic service from New York to London was operated the following month. Other European destinations were soon added to the route network, served from both East and West Coasts of the U.S.A., but the fuel crisis of the 1973/4 winter hit the airline hard and nine of its original 19 aircraft were sold. However, the purchase of various second-hand 747s in recent years has almost restored the fleet to its original state. TWA was also a 747SP operator for a few years in the early 1980s but never seemed to be able to find suitable routes for them and they were later sold.

The early TWA 747s had a red and white colour scheme in which the red cheat line was in the shape of a long, sleek arrowhead (a reminder of the arrow in the colour scheme of the airline's pre-war originating companies) and on the tail a logo with TWA in red letters surrounded by gold interlocking hemispheres, symbolising the airline's world-wide activities. Then came a change to the current colour scheme in which the tapered cheat line lost its arrowhead shape and a red panel was added to the tail to carry the TWA titling in white; at first the airline made the mistake of having the Trans

TRANS WORLD AIRLINES (TW/TWA) (continued)

World titling on the fuselage in outline lettering, which was not clearly visible from a distance, but this was quickly changed to solid lettering.

When first introduced TWA's 747s had seating for 342 passengers, 58 of whom were in 1st class and had the use in flight of an upstairs lounge. Currently, the aircraft can accommodate 431 passengers, with only 21 in 1st class but 52 in business class (called Ambassador class).

FLEET

Reg.	Line No.	Delivery Date	Remarks
747-131			
N93101	5	18/Aug/70	S. to Iranian A/F Mar/75 as 5-280/5-8101
N93102	8	31/Dec/69	S. to Iranian A/F Nov/75 5-285/5-8106
N93103	9	08/Jan/70	S. to Iranian A/F Dec/75 5-287/5-8108
N93104	20	20/Feb/70	
N93105	21	09/Mar/70	
N93106	28	03/Apr/70	
N93107	35	29/Apr/70	
N93108	38	07/May/70	
N93109	43	23/May/70	
N53110	63	10/Aug/70	
N53111	73	26/Sep/70	S. to Iranian A/F Oct/75 as 5-283/5-8104
N53112	78	04/Oct/70	S. to Iranian A/F Mar/75 as 5-281/5-8102
N93113	80	22/Oct/70	Ordered as Eastern N7401Q S. to Iranian A/F Mar/75 as 5-282/5-8103
N93114	85	02/Nov/70	Ordered as Eastern N7402Q S. to Iranian A/F Nov/75 as 5-284/5-8105
N93115	98	20/May/71	Ret. to leasing co. May/86
N53116	102	22/May/71	Ret. to leasing co. May/86
		01/May/87	Leased back
N93117	113	24/May/71	Ret. to leasing co. May/86
N93118	151	02/Sep/71	Ordered as Eastern N7403Q S. to Iranian A/F Nov/75 as 5-286/5-8107
N93119	153	27/Oct/71	Ordered as Eastern N7404Q S. to Iranian A/F Dec/75 as 5-288/5-8109
		16/Dec/76	Bought back
747-SP31			
N58201	415	14/Apr/80	S. to United Arab Emirates as A6-SMR Feb/85

TRANS WORLD AIRLINES (TW/TWA) (continued)

Reg.	Line No.	Model	Delivery Date	Name	Remarks
N57202	439		21/Mar/80		S. to Jet Aviation Jul/84 for Brunei Gvmt (not del.) S. to American as N601AA
N57203	441		08/May/80		S. to American Oct/86 as N602AA
Second-hand Aircraft					
N133TW	76		01/May/80		Ex Iberia 156 EC-BRO
N134TW	91		17/Feb/81		Ex Iberia 156 EC-BRP
N301TW	178		04/Jun/84		Ex TAP 282B CS-TJA
N302TW	189		30/Oct/84		Ex TAP 282B CS-TJB
N303TW	112		17/May/85		Ex Swissair 257B HB-IGA & Salenia LX-SAL
N304TW	126		26/Mar/85		Ex Swissair 257B HB-IGB & Egyptair SU-GAK
N305TW	216		11/Apr/85		Ex Olympic 284B SX-OAA
N17125	172		25/Mar/81		Ex British A/W 136 G-AWNI
N17126	184		30/May/81		Ex British A/W 136 G-AWNK

UNITED AIRLINES (UA/UAL) U.S.A.

Already the biggest airline in the West, United Airlines became even bigger when it took over the Pacific routes of Pan Am in February 1986. United had previously been the major operator on U.S. domestic routes with an extensive route network including coast-to-coast and services from New York, Los Angeles and San Francisco to Hawaii, which are treated as domestic routes. It was on the San Francisco-Honolulu route that United introduced its first 747s in July 1970 and, as the original fleet grew to 18, the aircraft took over the coast-to-coast and other domestic routes.

The airline's first venture on to international routes was some trans-Atlantic charter flights in the early 1980s, which were operated during summer months, and in 1983 included flights from New York to Frankfurt, London and Paris. Also, in April 1983, United started its first international scheduled services, from Portland and Seattle to Hong Kong and Tokyo, but it was not until the Pan Am routes had been taken over in 1986 that the trans-Pacific services really developed. These were from all the important places like Los Angeles, New York and San Francisco to Auckland, Hong Kong, Singapore, Sydney, Taipei and Tokyo. With the routes came Pan Am's fleet of 747SPs plus some TriStars which have since been swapped for more standard 747s.

In the early days, the 747s had a simple red and white, blue trimmed, cheat line with a flash up the tail which started as blue at the base, broke for United titles mid-way, and carried on up in red. The airline then tried adding to this, first with the sub-title 747 Friend Ship, and later with four blue stars on the forward fuselage and base of the fin. However, the airline changed its image in June 1974 and introduced a revised full title of United Airlines (Airlines as one word) and a new colour scheme. This time it was a bolder approach, with a broad orange, red and blue cheat line and a red and blue double U logo on the tail.

Some of the early 747-100s were given names, usually those of past executives of the airline but with one exception, The Original Eight. This name was given to N4712U as a reminder of the eight nurses who flew the San Francisco-Chicago route from May 1930, when hired by Boeing Air Transport (a predecessor of United Airlines) as the world's first airline stewardesses — Ellen Church joined first and the other women were listed in the order in which they joined the airline.

FLEET

Reg.	Line No.	Delivery Date	Name	Remarks
747-122				
N4703U	52	30/Jun/70	William Allen	Ret. to leasing co. Jun/85 To Pan Am
N4704U	60	04/Aug/70		Ret. to leasing co. Aug/85 To Pan Am
N4710U	61	08/Aug/70		Ret. to leasing co. Aug/85 To Pan Am
N4711U	66	28/Aug/70	Charles F. McErlean	Ret. to leasing co. Aug/85 To Pan Am
N4712U	67	31/Aug/70	The Original Eight Ellen Church Ellis Crawford Inez Keller Margaret Arnott Cornelia Peterman Harriet Fry Jessie Carter Alva Johnson	Ret. to leasing co. Aug/85 To Pan Am
N4713U	89	03/Nov/70		
N4714U	97	28/Nov/70	Justin Dart	
N4716U	99	11/Dec/70		
N4717U	101	28/Dec/70	Edward E. Carlson	
N4718U	139	27/May/71	Thomas F. Gleed	
N4719U	145	26/Jun/71		
N4720U	148	23/Jul/71		
N4723U	175	06/Jan/72	William A. Patterson	
N4727U	193	27/Jun/72	Robert E. Johnson	
N4728U	205	27/Apr/73	Gardner Cowles	
N4729U	206	24/Apr/73		
N4732U	207	19/Mar/73		
N4735U	208	30/May/73		

UNITED AIRLINES (UA/UAL) (continued)

Reg.	Line No.	Model	Delivery Date	Name	Remarks
747-SP21 (Second-hand)					
N140UA	265		11/Feb/86		Ex Pan Am N530PA
N141UA	268		12/Feb/86		Ex Pan Am N531PA
N142UA	270		11/Feb/86		Ex Pan Am N532PA
N143UA	273		11/Feb/86		Ex Pan Am N533PA
N144UA	286		12/Feb/86		Ex Pan Am N534PA
N145UA	306		13/Feb/86		Ex Pan Am N536PA
N146UA	325		13/Feb/86		Ex Pan Am N537PA
N147UA	331		12/Feb/86		Ex Pan Am N538PA
N148UA	367		12/Feb/86		Ex Pan Am N539PA
N149UA	373		12/Feb/86		Ex Pan Am N540PA
N150UA	447		09/Feb/86		Ex Braniff SP27 N606BN & Pan Am N529PA
747-222B					
N151UA	673		19/Mar/87		
N152UA	675		02/Apr/87		
747-123 (Second-hand)					
N153UA	59		01/Sep/87		Ex American A/L N9663 & Citicorp N14943 & Cargolux LX-KCV
N154UA	65		01/Sep/87		Ex American A/L N9664 & Avianca N9664 & Cargolux LX-NCV
N155UA	69		01/Sep/87		Ex American A/L N9665 & Dominicana HI-472
N156UA	77		01/Sep/87		Ex American A/L N9666 & Citicorp N14936 & Cargolux LX-LCV
N157UA	79		01/Sep/87		Ex American A/L N9667 & Citicorp N14937 & Cargolux LX-MCV
747-422 (Pratt & Whitney PW4256 Engines)					
N			/89		
N			/89		
N			/89		
N			/89		

Plus 11 more for delivery 1990/2

UNITED ARAB EMIRATES (U.A.E. ROYAL FLIGHT) UNITED ARAB EMIRATES

Formerly known as the Trucial States, the United Arab Emirates are seven Skeikdoms – Abu Dhabi, Ajman, Dubai, Fujairah, Ras al-Khaimah, Sharjah and Umm al-Qaiwain – located on the Persian (Arabian) Gulf. To serve these, the U.A.E. Royal Flight has a variety of VIP aircraft and in February 1985 these were joined by an ex-TWA 747SP. The aircraft went into service almost immediately, with only a change of colour scheme, so it was not surprising to learn that it was to be flown to Hamburg in January 1987 to spend a year having a VIP interior installed.

At a time when it was thought that the last 747SP had been built, a new one appeared on the flight line at Everett in March 1987 destined for an anonymous private owner, who has since been identified as the U.A.E. Royal Flight. Delivered later in green primer/anti-corrosion treatment, this one is also likely to spend some time having its VIP interior installed.

FLEET

Reg.	Line No.	Model	Delivery Date	Remarks
A6-SMR	415	SP31	21/Feb/85	Ex TWA N58201
A6-	676	SP		N60659 before del.

UNITED PARCEL SERVICE (UPS) U.S.A.

Another of the fast-growing number of express-package carriers with an extensive overnight delivery service in the U.S.A., United Parcel Service (UPS) added six ex-American Airlines' 747 Freighters to its large fleet of smaller aircraft during 1984. The carrier's main operating hub (consolidation centre) is at Louisville, Kentucky, but there are various other hubs around the country and its 747 activities extend as far as Hawaii.

All the 747s are operated for United Parcel Service by Orion Air but are painted in the full (and unusual) dark brown and white UPS colour scheme with the UPS shield and parcel logo in gold on their tails.

FLEET

Reg.	Line No.	Model	Delivery Date	Remarks
N671UP	115	123SF	13/Nov/84	Ex American A/L N9671
N672UP	119	123SF	02/Oct/84	Ex American A/L N9672
N673UP	125	123SF	28/Aug/84	Ex American A/L N9673
N674UP	46	123SF	20/Dec/84	Ex American A/L N9661
N675UP	136	123SF	12/Sep/84	Ex American A/L N9675
N676UP	57	123SF	18/Dec/84	Ex American A/L N9676

UNITED STATES AIR FORCE (USAF) U.S.A.

The United States Air Force (USAF) already has four 747s in service (E-4Bs) and has two more on order (VC-25As), plus an interest in up to 19 more which have been allocated to its Civil Reserve Air Fleet (CRAF).

E-4B

The first 747s to enter USAF service were three E-4As, which looked externally similar to civil 200Bs when they were delivered in 1973/4. The first two were powered by Pratt & Whitney JT9D engines but the third had General Electric CF6 engines and the two earlier aircraft were re-engined to this standard later. The aircraft serve as Airborne Command Posts and were originally equipped with command and control communications equipment transferred from EC-135s (Boeing 707s). Operated by the 1st ACCS (Airborne Command and Control Squadron), their main base is at Offutt Air Force Base, Nebraska, and until recently one was kept on 24-hour readiness at Andrews Air Force Base near Washington, D.C., but it was reported recently that its base is now further inland to avoid attack from off-shore submarines. In addition, one aircraft always follows the U.S. President when he makes visits overseas.

During the early years, the aircraft underwent several modification programmes, including the addition of an in-flight refuelling receptacle in the nose to allow maximum endurance of 72 hours with flight refuelling. The fourth aircraft (also powered by General Electric CF6 engines) underwent several years of intensive development and was eventually delivered in December 1979 as the final E-4B version equipped with the latest command and control communications equipment, including a super high frequency (SHF) satellite communications dish aerial beneath a large fairing behind the upper-deck compartment. The three earlier aircraft were then modified, one at a time, to bring them up to E-4B standard.

All four E-4Bs are currently painted in anti-radiation white overall with a blue cheat line, a U.S. flag on the fin and United States of America titles on the fuselage.

FLEET

Serial No.	Line No.	Model	Delivery Date	Remarks
31676	202	E-4B	16/Jul/73	Cvtd from E-4A
31677	204	E-4B	03/Oct/73	Cvtd from E-4A
40787	232	E-4B	15/Oct/74	Cvtd from E-4A
50125	257	E-4B	04/Aug/75	

VC-25A

The next two 747s to be delivered to the USAF will also be special, being replacements for the U.S. President's personal Boeing 707s (VC-137Cs), known popularly as Air Force One and Air Force Two. These 747-200Bs will become VC-25As, and they will have a VIP interior, but probably not as plush or gold-plated as the aircraft used by the Saudi Arabian King.

Rolled out from the Everett factory in April and September 1987, respectively, the aircraft are currently with Boeing Military Airplane Company at Wichita, Kansas, for fitting out.

FLEET

Serial No.	Line No.	Model	Delivery Date
68000	679	VC-25A	Due Nov/88
	685	VC-25A	Due May/89

CIVIL RESERVE AIR FLEET (CRAF)

In the event of an emergency, the USAF would be able to commandeer civil 747s and, to make some of the all-passenger aircraft more suitable as military transports, up to 19 of Pan Am's 747s are due to be modified with side cargo doors and a strengthened main deck. This long-term programme started in 1985 and it is known that the following aircraft have been modified, with others likely to be added during the 1987/8 winter months.

FLEET

Reg.	Line No.	Modification Date
N653PA	106	1985
N655PA	117	1985
N725PA	94	1986
N728PA	218	1986
N729PA	219	1987
N730PA	240	1987
N734PA	7	1986
N739PA	15	1987
N743PA	24	1986
N902PA	72	1986

UTA (UT/UTA) FRANCE

The first airline to give its aircraft the now popular all-white fuselage with very large titles was the French airline UTA (Union de Transports Aeriens), who applied its blue-tailed colour scheme to two 747 Freighters it introduced on routes from Paris to Africa from September 1978.

An unusual job for the first aircraft was to serve as a 'conveyor belt' in a car assembly line. The parts for Peugeot 504 cars were made in Sochaux, France, and transferred to Lyon where they were loaded aboard the UTA 747 (enough for 120 cars at a time) for the flight to Kano, Nigeria. The parts were then transferred by road to a factory at Kaduna for assembly.

When two 200B Combis were introduced in 1981, they had the blue-tailed colour scheme plus green passenger doors as on the airline's DC-10s. This scheme can now be seen on UTA's two new 300 Combis and the two

UTA (UT/UTA) (continued)

look-alike Combis, which are the original 200B Combis which have been modified by Boeing to have the stretched upper deck (SUD). All four aircraft have been given the name Big Boss, and have accommodation for 262 passengers, with 18 in 1st class and 42 in business class, plus cargo pallets. They are used on the airline's routes from Paris to Sydney and Noumea (New Caledonia) via Singapore and Jakarta, and to numerous destinations in Central, South and West Africa.

FLEET

Reg.	Line No.	Model	Delivery Date	Remarks
F-BTDG	518	2B3B Combi	23/Apr/81	Cvtd to SUD Mar/86
F-BTDH	521	2B3B Combi	05/May/81	Cvtd to SUD May/86
F-GBOX	388	2B3F	06/Aug/79	
F-GDUA	573	3B3	01/Mar/83	W.O. by fire, Paris, 16/Mar/85
F-GETA	632	3B3 Combi	31/Jan/86	
F-GETB	641	3B3 Combi	24/Apr/86	
F-GPAN	337	2B3F	26/Sep/78	S. to Air France Mar/86

747-400 (General Electric CF6-80C2 Engines)

F-		4B3	Due Apr/89	

Plus one more for delivery in 1991

Leased Aircraft

N741TV	416	271C	03/May/85	L. from Transamerica Ret. Mar/86

VARIG (RG/VRG) BRAZIL

Varig (or Viacao Aerea Rio-Grandense, to give the Brazilian airline its full title) started 747 operations in February 1981 on the Rio de Janeiro to New York route using three 200B Combis which had been built for Libyan Arab Airlines but which had been refused an export licence by the U.S. government. Services to Europe were begun in April 1981 and, with the addition to the fleet of two 300 Combis in 1985, the 747 route network was extended to include Rio de Janeiro to Tokyo via Los Angeles. Three more 300s are due for delivery in 1988.

All aircraft have the usual Varig blue and white colour scheme with the compass logo on their tails. The 300 Combis have seating for 259 passengers, with 43 in 1st class and 56 in business class, plus cargo pallets.

VARIG (RG/URG) (continued)

FLEET

Reg.	Line No.	Model	Delivery Date	Remarks
747-200B				
PP-VNA	435	2L5B Combi	30/Jan/81	Ex Libyan Arab 5A-DIJ
PP-VNB	443	2L5B Combi	09/Feb/81	Ex Libyan Arab 5A-DIK
PP-VNC	469	2L5B Combi	05/Mar/81	Ex Libyan Arab 5A-DIL
747-300				
PP-VNH	627	341 Combi	10/Dec/85	
PP-VNI	629	341 Combi	19/Dec/85	
PP-VOA	701	341	30/Apr/88	
PP-VOB		341	Due Apr/88	
PP-VOC		341	Due May/88	
Leased Aircraft				
PP-VNW	158	244B	11/Apr/87	L. from South African ZS-SAM

VIASA (VA) — VENEZUELA

VIASA (or, to give the airline its full title, Venezolana Internacional de Aviacion SA) caused some confusion among aircraft spotters for a couple of years from January 1972 when it operated a 747 with double identity. The aircraft was a KLM 747 (PH-BUG) which retained its full KLM white-top colour scheme on the left-hand side and had the full VIASA colour scheme on the right-hand side. It usually operated on the Caracas-Madrid-Paris and Caracas-Madrid-Rome routes and was returned to KLM in June 1974 when DC-10s took over.

Apart from VIASA stickers appearing on Seaboard World Freighters in 1979 and 1980, operating a load-sharing scheme, there were no further VIASA 747 operations until July 1981 when a 200C (N749WA) was leased from World Airways for two years in the full VIASA colour scheme (this time on both sides). This aircraft appeared to spend its time operating as a Freighter between Caracas and Miami or New York and was joined for short periods by two other leased 747s carrying VIASA stickers. The airline ceased 747 operations in November 1983.

The VIASA colour scheme remained basically the same throughout, with a blue cheat line and orange tail, but the VIASA title logo on the tail was later in white instead of orange on a white background.

VIASA (VA) (continued)

FLEET

Reg.	Line No.	Model	Delivery Date	Remarks
PH-BUG	170	206B	01/Jan/72	L. from KLM Ret. Jun/74
N480GX	12	130	12/Jul/82	L. from GATX Ex Lufthansa D-ABYA & Braniff N610BN Ret. Sep/82 To Egyptair
N747WR	209	273C	07/Dec/82	L. from World A/W Ret. Jan/83
N749WA	237	273C	01/Jul/81	L. from World A/W Ret. Nov/83

VIRGIN ATLANTIC AIRWAYS (VS/VIR) BRITAIN

Virgin Atlantic started a low-fare scheduled service between London (Gatwick) and New York (Newark) in June 1984 using a lone-flyer 747 which had previously served with Aerolineas Argentinas. Accommodation was devoted mainly to 465 economy-class passengers but 14 business class were carried in the upper-deck compartment. The aircraft was joined by an ex-Alitalia 200B in 1986 when a London (Gatwick) to Miami service was added.

Outside of the peak summer months (June, July and August) business class (called Upper Class) is extended to the front of the main deck, providing accommodation for 14 passengers in the upper-deck compartment, 55 business class on the main deck and 411 economy class.

The colour scheme for both aircraft is a thin red cheat line on an all-white fuselage, and a red tail; the Virgin title logo appears in red on the nose and larger in white on the tail. The first aircraft originally had the picture on the tail of a painter falling from his suspended platform and spilling a can of red paint on the fuselage but, presumably being in no fit state after falling from that height, he did not appear on the second aircraft.

FLEET

Reg.	Line No.	Model	Delivery Date	Name	Remarks
G-VGIN	134	243B	31/Jan/86	Scarlet Lady	Ex Alitalia I-DEMU & Boeing N358AS
G-VIRG	274	287B	14/Jun/84	Maiden Voyager	Ex Aero. Argentinas LV-LZD & Boeing N354AS

WARDAIR CANADA (WD/WDA) — CANADA

A well-established Canadian charter airline, Wardair introduced its first 747 in May 1973 on trans-Atlantic flights from various Canadian cities to London and other European destinations. With additions to the fleet, 747 activities were extended to include 'winter sunshine' flights to Florida and Hawaii. The aircraft had at that time seating for 456 passengers, with 16 in the upper-deck compartment. Scheduled services were started in 1985 and, although most of these are now operated with the airline's Airbus A300/A310s and DC-10s, the 747s are used on some Toronto-Vancouver services and occasionally on some Toronto-London or Manchester services in summer months.

The Wardair colour scheme has changed little through the years, with a red, white and blue cheat line, the red of which extends up the tail and is broken mid-way by the Wardair title logo, which has been changed to bolder lettering in recent years.

FLEET

Reg.	Line No.	Model	Delivery Date	Name	Remarks
C-FDJC	123	1D1	23/Apr/73	Phil Garratt	Built as Braniff N602BN but not delivered
C-FFUN	146	1D1	15/Dec/74	Romeo Vachon	Ex Continental A/L N26864
C-FTOB	121	133	09/Oct/86	H.A. 'Doc' Oaks	Ex Air Canada & Guinness Peat EI-BRR
C-GXRA	326	211B	09/Jun/78	Herbert Hollick-Kenyon	S. to Br. Caledonian G-GLYN Oct/86
C-GXRD	368	211B	25/Apr/79	H.A. 'Doc' Oaks	S. to Br. Caledonian G-NIGB Mar/87

WORLD AIRWAYS (WO) — U.S.A.

World Airways was first to order the 200C (Convertible) version of the 747 and the airline's first two aircraft entered service in May 1973 on trans-Atlantic passenger charters. Passenger accommodation at the time was for a total of 461 in a 10-abreast, all-economy arrangement, with 16 in the upper-deck compartment. The following winter the aircraft were converted into Freighters for use on trans-Pacific military cargo charters. A third 200C was leased to Korean Air Lines on delivery in 1976, and the first two then became subject to short and long term leases to various airlines, appearing only occasionally in the World Airway's colour scheme. A second-hand 100SF Freighter, purchased in 1978, was also leased out. All four aircraft had been sold by May 1987.

WORLD AIRWAYS (WO) (continued)

FLEET

Reg.	Line No.	Model	Delivery Date	Remarks
N749WA	237	273C	10/Jun/74	L. to Korean 1974/9 S. to Evergreen Int. May/87
N750WA	42	124SF	09/Feb/78	Ex Continental N26861 & Iranian A/F 5-8110 S. to Avianca Jul/86 as HK-2900

Production

On the following pages is a list of all the Boeing 747s built during the past 20 years. The list is in Line Number order and gives details of each aircraft together with the dates of its Roll Out and First Flight; its Delivery Date and subsequent history are included in the Fleet Lists given for each airline in the Operators' section.

Abbreviations

A/F	Air Force	Con. No.	Construction Number
A/L	Air Lines or Airlines	Gvmt	Government
A/S	Airline(s) System	Int.	International
A/W	Airways	Reg.	Registration

Line No.	Con. No.	Model	Operator	Reg.	Roll Out Date	First Flight
1968						
1	20235	121	Boeing	N7470	30/Sep/68	09/Feb/69
1969						
2	19639	121	Pan Am	N747PA	28/Feb/69	11/Apr/69
3	19638	121	Pan Am	N732PA	16/May/69	10/Jul/69
4	19637	121	Pan Am	N731PA	23/Apr/69	10/May/69
5	19667	131	TWA	N93101	08/May/69	13/Jul/69
6	19640	121	Pan Am	N733PA	18/May/69	24/Oct/69
7	19641	121	Pan Am	N734PA	01/Jun/69	31/Oct/69
8	19668	131	TWA	N93102	13/Jun/69	07/Dec/69
9	19669	131	TWA	N93103	23/Jun/69	05/Dec/69
10	19642	121	Pan Am	N735PA	01/Jul/69	22/Dec/69
11	19643	121	Pan Am	N736PA	09/Jul/69	24/Dec/69
12	19746	130	Lufthansa	D-ABYA	16/Jul/69	18/Feb/70
13	19644	121	Pan Am	N737PA	23/Jul/69	09/Jan/70
14	19645	121	Pan Am	N738PA	30/Jul/69	19/Jan/70
15	19646	121	Pan Am	N739PA	06/Aug/69	25/Jan/70
16	19647	121	Pan Am	N740PA	13/Aug/69	31/Jan/70
17	19648	121	Pan Am	N741PA	21/Aug/69	13/Feb/70
18	19649	121	Pan Am	N742PA	28/Aug/69	18/Feb/70
19	19749	128	Air France	F-BPVA	06/Sep/69	28/Feb/70
20	19670	131	TWA	N93104	12/Sep/69	09/Feb/70
21	19671	131	TWA	N93105	19/Sep/69	23/Feb/70
22	19750	128	Air France	F-BPVB	28/Sep/69	07/Mar/70
23	19761	136	BOAC	G-AWNA	03/Oct/69	15/Mar/70
24	19650	121	Pan Am	N743PA	10/Oct/69	11/Mar/70
25	19651	121	Pan Am	N744PA	17/Oct/69	03/Mar/70
26	19652	121	Pan Am	N748PA	23/Oct/69	15/Mar/70
27	19778	151	Northwest	N601US	30/Oct/69	07/Nov/69

Line No.	Con. No.	Model	Operator	Reg.	Roll Out Date	First Flight
28	19672	131	TWA	N93106	05/Nov/69	20/Mar/70
29	19747	130	Lufthansa	D-ABYB	12/Nov/69	30/Mar/70
30	19653	121	Pan Am	N749PA	18/Nov/69	21/Mar/70
31	19725	146	Japan A/L	JA8101	25/Nov/69	31/Mar/70
32	19654	121	Pan Am	N750PA	08/Dec/69	01/Apr/70
33	19655	121	Pan Am	N751PA	10/Dec/69	06/Apr/70
34	19656	121	Pan Am	N752PA	16/Dec/69	10/Apr/70
35	19673	131	TWA	N93107	22/Dec/69	13/Apr/70
36	19729	143	Alitalia	I-DEMA	31/Dec/69	14/Apr/70
1970						
37	19657	121	Pan Am	N753PA	08/Jan/70	15/Apr/70
38	19674	131	TWA	N93108	14/Jan/70	19/Apr/70
39	19751	128	Air France	F-BPVC	20/Jan/70	26/Apr/70
40	19779	151	Northwest	N602US	26/Jan/70	24/Apr/70
41	19762	136	BOAC	G-AWNB	30/Jan/70	06/May/70
42	19733	124	Continental	N26861	04/Feb/70	02/May/70
43	19675	131	TWA	N93109	10/Feb/70	13/May/70
44	19748	130	Lufthansa	D-ABYC	13/Feb/70	13/May/70
45	19780	151	Northwest	N603US	19/Feb/70	10/May/70
46	20100	123	American A/L	N9661	24/Feb/70	17/May/70
47	19658	121	Pan Am	N754PA	02/Mar/70	15/May/70
48	19763	136	BOAC	G-AWNC	05/Mar/70	28/May/70
49	19659	121	Pan Am	N755PA	11/Mar/70	21/May/70
50	19660	121	Pan Am	N770PA	16/Mar/70	21/May/70
51	19726	146	Japan A/L	JA8102	20/Mar/70	16/May/70
52	19753	122	United	N4703U	25/Mar/70	06/Apr/70
53	19752	128	Air France	F-BPVD	31/Mar/70	06/Jun/70
54	19727	146	Japan A/L	JA8103	03/Apr/70	09/Jun/70
55	19781	151	Northwest	N604US	08/Apr/70	17/Jun/70
56	19730	143	Alitalia	I-DEME	13/Apr/70	13/Jun/70
57	20101	123	American A/L	N9662	16/Apr/70	30/Jun/70
58	19734	124	Continental	N26862	21/Apr/70	02/Jul/70
59	20102	123	American A/L	N9663	24/Apr/70	16/Jul/70
60	19754	122	United	N4704U	29/Apr/70	20/Jul/70
61	19755	122	United	N4710U	04/May/70	24/Jul/70
62	19782	151	Northwest	N605US	07/May/70	11/Jul/70
63	19676	131	TWA	N53110	12/May/70	27/Jul/70
64	19735	124	Continental	N26863	15/May/70	17/Jul/70
65	20103	123	American A/L	N9664	20/May/70	08/Jul/70
66	19756	122	United	N4711U	25/May/70	22/Jul/70
67	19757	122	United	N4712U	28/May/70	18/Aug/70
68	19918	135	National	N77772	03/Jun/70	21/Aug/70
69	20104	123	American A/L	N9665	08/Jun/70	04/Sep/70
70	19661	121	Pan Am	N771PA	11/Jun/70	24/Jul/70
71	19783	151	Northwest	N606US	16/Jun/70	22/Aug/70
72	19896	132	Delta	N9896	19/Jun/70	09/Sep/70
73	19677	131	TWA	N53111	24/Jun/70	15/Sep/70
74	19784	151	Northwest	N607US	29/Jun/70	31/Aug/70
75	19785	151	Northwest	N608US	02/Jul/70	04/Sep/70
76	19957	156	Iberia	EC-BRO	08/Jul/70	18/Sep/70
77	20105	123	American A/L	N9666	13/Jul/70	22/Sep/70

Line No.	Con. No.	Model	Operator	Reg.	Roll Out Date	First Flight
78	19678	131	TWA	N53112	16/Jul/70	24/Sep/70
79	20106	123	American A/L	N9667	21/Jul/70	24/Sep/70
80	20080	131	TWA	N93113	24/Jul/70	05/Oct/70
81	19919	135	National	N77773	29/Jul/70	07/Oct/70
82	19897	132	Delta	N9897	03/Aug/70	12/Oct/70
83	19786	151	Northwest	N609US	06/Aug/70	29/Sep/70
84	19744	148	Aer Lingus	EI-ASI	11/Aug/70	03/Nov/70
85	20081	131	TWA	N93114	14/Aug/70	17/Oct/70
86	20107	123	American A/L	N9668	19/Aug/70	15/Oct/70
87	20108	123	American A/L	N9669	24/Aug/70	28/Oct/70
88	20356	251B	Northwest	N611US	27/Aug/70	11/Oct/70
						First 747-200B
89	19875	122	United	N4713U	01/Sep/70	20/Oct/70
90	20109	123	American A/L	N9670	04/Sep/70	01/Dec/70
91	19958	156	Iberia	EC-BRP	10/Sep/70	29/Oct/70
92	20401	129	Sabena	OO-SGA	15/Sep/70	03/Nov/70
93	19787	151	Northwest	N610US	18/Sep/70	06/Nov/70
94	19898	132	Delta	N9898	23/Sep/70	06/Nov/70
95	20402	129	Sabena	OO-SGB	28/Sep/70	20/Nov/70
96	19922	206B	KLM	PH-BUA	02/Oct/70	13/Dec/70
97	19876	122	United	N4714U	06/Oct/70	13/Nov/70
98	20320	131	TWA	N93115	09/Oct/70	22/Dec/70
99	19877	122	United	N4716U	14/Oct/70	20/Nov/70
100	20207	127	Braniff	N601BN	19/Oct/70	09/Dec/70
101	19878	122	United	N4717U	22/Oct/70	07/Dec/70
102	20321	131	TWA	N53116	27/Oct/70	07/May/71
103	20347	121A	Pan Am	N652PA	30/Oct/70	17/Dec/70
104	20013	133	Air Canada	CF-TOA	04/Nov/70	27/Jan/71
105	20355	128	Air France	F-BPVE	09/Nov/70	02/Feb/71
106	20348	121A	Pan Am	N653PA	17/Nov/70	31/Dec/70
107	19764	136	BOAC	G-AWND	17/Nov/70	20/Jan/71
108	19745	148	Aer Lingus	EI-ASJ	20/Nov/70	04/Mar/71
109	19765	136	BOAC	G-AWNE	25/Nov/70	10/Feb/71
110	20349	121A	Pan Am	N654PA	02/Dec/70	14/Apr/71
111	19766	136	BOAC	G-AWNF	07/Dec/70	13/Feb/71
112	20116	257B	Swissair	HB-IGA	10/Dec/70	15/Jan/71
113	20322	131	TWA	N93117	15/Dec/70	16/May/71
114	20120	283B	Scandinavian A/S	SE-DDL	18/Dec/70	06/Feb/71
115	20323	123	American A/L	N9671	23/Dec/70	10/Feb/71
116	19823	246B	Japan A/L	JA8104	30/Dec/70	29/Jan/71
1971						
117	20350	121A	Pan Am	N655PA	05/Jan/71	03/May/71
118	19923	206B	KLM	PH-BUB	08/Jan/71	15/Feb/71
119	20324	123	American A/L	N9672	13/Jan/71	17/Mar/71
120	19731	243B	Alitalia	I-DEMO	18/Jan/71	20/Feb/71
121	20014	133	Air Canada	CF-TOB	21/Jan/71	01/Mar/71
122	19824	246B	Japan A/L	JA8105	25/Jan/71	12/Feb/71
123	20208	127	Braniff	N602BN	29/Jan/71	22/Mar/71
			Not delivered. Stored 1971-3 then delivered to:			
			Wardair	CF-DJC		
124	19959	237B	Air India	VT-EBD	03/Feb/71	08/Mar/71

Line No.	Con. No.	Model	Operator	Reg.	Roll Out Date	First Flight
125	20325	123	American A/L	N9673	08/Feb/71	31/Mar/71
126	20117	257B	Swissair	HB-IGB	11/Feb/71	13/Mar/71
127	20351	121A	Pan Am	N656PA	16/Feb/71	21/May/71
128	20493	230B	Condor	D-ABYF	22/Feb/71	17/Mar/71
129	20352	121A	Pan Am	N657PA	26/Feb/71	27/May/71
130	19960	237B	Air India	VT-EBE	04/Mar/71	02/Apr/71
131	20353	121A	Pan Am	N658PA	10/Mar/71	02/Jun/71
132	20372	230B	Lufthansa	D-ABYD	16/Mar/71	16/Apr/71
133	20326	123	American A/L	N9674	22/Mar/71	23/Apr/71
134	19732	243B	Alitalia	I-DEMU	26/Mar/71	28/Apr/71
135	20357	251B	Northwest	N612US	01/Apr/71	05/May/71
136	20390	123	American A/L	N9675	07/Apr/71	07/May/71
137	19825	246B	Japan A/L	JA8106	17/Apr/71	29/Apr/71
138	19924	206B	KLM	PH-BUC	19/Apr/71	09/May/71
139	19879	122	United	N4718U	26/Apr/71	16/May/71
140	20135	258B	El Al	4X-AXA	28/Apr/71	15/May/71
141	20358	251B	Northwest	N613US	06/May/71	04/Jun/71
142	20354	121A	Pan Am	N659PA	17/May/71	09/Jul/71
143	20391	123	American A/L	N9676	18/May/71	11/Jun/71
144	20015	133	Air Canada	CF-TOC	24/May/71	11/Jun/71
145	19880	122	United	N4719U	28/May/71	15/Jun/71
146	20305	124	Continental	N26864	02/Jun/71	18/Jun/71
147	20009	238B	Qantas	VH-EBA	10/Jun/71	08/Jul/71
148	19881	122	United	N4720U	16/Jun/71	13/Jul/71
149	20010	238B	Qantas	VH-EBB	22/Jun/71	23/Jul/71
150	20269	136	BOAC	G-AWNG	28/Jun/71	30/Jul/71
151	20082	131	TWA	N93118	02/Jul/71	04/Aug/71
152	20398	206B	KLM	PH-BUD	09/Jul/71	06/Aug/71
153	20083	131	TWA	N93119	15/Jul/71	18/Aug/71
154	20237	244B	South African	ZS-SAL	21/Jul/71	28/Aug/71
155	20246	132	Delta	N9899	27/Jul/71	24/Aug/71
156	20399	206B	KLM	PH-BUE	02/Aug/71	03/Sep/71
157	20400	206B	KLM	PH-BUF	06/Aug/71	14/Sep/71
158	20238	244B	South African	ZS-SAM	12/Aug/71	05/Dec/71
159	20247	132	Delta	N9900	18/Aug/71	22/Sep/71
160	20239	244B	South African	ZS-SAN	24/Aug/71	30/Sep/71
161	20332	146	Japan A/L	JA8107	30/Aug/71	04/Oct/71
162	20011	238B	Qantas	VH-EBC	03/Sep/71	07/Oct/71
163	20359	251B	Northwest	N614US	10/Sep/71	13/Oct/71
164	20274	258B	El Al	4X-AXB	16/Sep/71	29/Oct/71
165	20360	251B	Northwest	N615US	22/Sep/71	13/Nov/71
166	20333	246B	Japan A/L	JA8108	26/Sep/71	25/Oct/71
167	20121	283B	Scandinavian A/S	OY-KHA	04/Oct/71	28/Oct/71
168	20373	230F	Lufthansa	D-ABYE	14/Oct/71	30/Nov/71
						First 747-200F
169	20270	136	BOAC	G-AWNH	13/Oct/71	09/Nov/71
170	20427	206B	KLM	PH-BUG	20/Oct/71	22/Nov/71
171	20012	238B	Qantas	VH-EBD	26/Oct/71	23/Nov/71
172	20271	136	BOAC	G-AWNI	01/Nov/71	03/Dec/71
173	20137	256B	Iberia	EC-BRQ	04/Nov/71	09/Dec/71
174	20376	128	Air France	F-BPVF	12/Nov/71	17/Jan/72
175	19882	122	United	N4723U	22/Nov/71	17/Dec/71
176	20377	128	Air France	F-BPVG	02/Dec/71	07/Jan/72

Line No.	Con. No.	Model	Operator	Reg.	Roll Out Date	First Flight
177	20378	128	Air France	F-BPVH	10/Dec/71	26/Jan/72
178	20501	282B	TAP-Portugal	CS-TJA	20/Dec/71	04/Feb/72
1972						
179	20527	230B	Lufthansa	D-ABYG	05/Jan/72	09/Feb/72
180	20503	246B	Japan A/L	JA8109	13/Jan/72	15/Feb/72
181	20504	246B	Japan A/L	JA8110	21/Jan/72	24/Feb/72
182	20505	246B	Japan A/L	JA8111	01/Feb/72	03/Mar/72
183	20272	136	BOAC	G-AWNJ	10/Feb/72	06/Mar/72
184	20273	136	BOAC	G-AWNK	18/Feb/72	10/Mar/72
185	20459	237B	Air India	VT-EBN	25/Feb/72	18/Mar/72
186	20559	230B	Condor	D-ABYH	01/Mar/72	17/Mar/72
187	20284	136	BOAC	G-AWNL	15/Mar/72	04/Apr/72
188	20558	237B	Air India	VT-EBO	28/Mar/72	14/Apr/72
189	20502	282B	TAP-Portugal	CS-TJB	11/Apr/72	04/May/72
190	20520	243B	Alitalia	I-DEMB	24/Apr/72	11/May/72
191	20528	146	Japan A/L	JA8112	09/May/72	26/May/72
192	20529	246B	Japan A/L	JA8113	23/May/72	09/Jun/72
193	19883	122	United	N4727U	07/Jun/72	16/Jun/72
194	20556	244B	South African	ZS-SAO	21/Jun/72	14/Jul/72
195	20534	238B	Qantas	VH-EBE	06/Jul/72	27/Jul/72
196	20530	246B	Japan A/L	JA8114	20/Jul/72	23/Aug/72
197	20531	146	Japan A/L	JA8115	02/Aug/72	18/Aug/72
198	20557	244B	South African	ZS-SAP	28/Aug/72	15/Sep/72
199	20532	146	Japan A/L	JA8116	15/Sep/72	06/Oct/72
200	20541	128	Air France	N28903	29/Sep/72	26/Oct/72
201	20542	128	Air France	N28888	13/Oct/72	30/Oct/72
202	20682	E4A	US Air Force	73-1676	27/Oct/72	13/Jun/73
203	20543	128	Air France	N28899	10/Nov/72	15/Dec/72
204	20683	E4A	US Air Force	73-1677	28/Nov/72	11/Sep/73
205	19925	122	United	N4728U	12/Dec/72	22/Jan/73
1973						
206	19926	122	United	N4729U	03/Jan/73	30/Jan/73
207	19927	122	United	N4732U	17/Jan/73	14/Feb/73
208	19928	122	United	N4735U	31/Jan/73	16/May/73
209	20651	273C	World A/W	N747WA	28/Feb/73	23/Mar/73
						First 747-200C
210	20708	136	BOAC	G-AWNM	26/Feb/73	06/Apr/73
211	20652	273C	World A/W	N748WA	28/Mar/73	25/Apr/73
212	20704	258B	El Al	4X-AXC	22/Mar/73	05/Apr/73
213	20770	2B5B	Korean	HL7410	05/Apr/73	16/Apr/73
214	20767	133	Air Canada	CF-TOD	19/Apr/73	03/May/73
215	20771	2B5B	Korean	HL7411	08/May/73	01/Jun/73
216	20742	284B	Olympic	SX-OAA	17/May/73	02/Jun/73
217	20535	238B	Qantas	VH-EBF	07/Jun/73	13/Jul/73
218	20712	212B	Singapore A/L	9V-SIA	21/Jun/73	13/Jul/73
219	20713	212B	Singapore A/L	9V-SIB	06/Jul/73	01/Aug/73
220	20809	136	British A/W	G-AWNN	20/Jul/73	29/Sep/73
221	20781	SR46	Japan A/L	JA8117	03/Aug/73	31/Aug/73
						First 747SR

Line No.	Con. No.	Model	Operator	Reg.	Roll Out Date	First Flight
222	20810	136	British A/W	G-AWNO	31/Aug/73	08/Oct/73
223	20825	284B	Olympic	SX-OAB	17/Sep/73	12/Oct/73
224	20798	128	Air France	F-BPVL	01/Oct/73	25/Oct/73
225	20801	217B	CP Air	C-FCRA	15/Oct/73	02/Nov/73
226	20802	217B	CP Air	C-FCRB	29/Oct/73	15/Nov/73
227	20799	128	Air France	N63305	09/Nov/73	30/Nov/73
228	20800	128	Air France	N28366	01/Dec/73	10/Jan/74
229	20782	SR46	Japan A/L	JA8118	02/Dec/73	10/Dec/73
1974						
230	20783	SR46	Japan A/L	JA8119	04/Jan/74	28/Jan/74
231	20784	SR46	Japan A/L	JA8120	18/Jan/74	08/Feb/74
232	20684	E4A	US Air Force	74-0787	01/Feb/74	06/Jun/74
233	20841	238B	Qantas	VH-EBG	15/Feb/74	28/Feb/74
234	20923	SR46	Japan A/L	JA8121	25/Feb/74	14/Mar/74
235	20924	246B	Japan A/L	JA8122	08/Mar/74	21/Mar/74
236	20881	133	Air Canada	C-FTOE	29/Mar/74	19/Apr/74
237	20653	273C	World A/W	N749WA	12/Apr/74	02/May/74
238	20842	238B	Qantas	VH-EBH	26/Apr/74	13/May/74
239	20928	282B	TAP-Portugal	CS-TJC	08/May/74	30/May/74
240	20888	212B	Singapore A/L	9V-SQC	24/May/74	21/Jun/74
241	20921	238B	Qantas	VH-EBI	10/Jun/74	28/Jun/74
242	20826	245F	Seaboard World	N701SW	24/Jun/74	12/Jul/74
243	21034	246F	Japan A/L	JA8123	09/Jul/74	02/Aug/74
244	20927	217B	CP Air	C-FCRD	23/Jul/74	04/Oct/74
245	20887	228F	Air France	N18815	20/Aug/74	11/Sep/74
246	20952	136	British A/W	G-AWNP	03/Sep/74	29/Sep/74
247	20929	217B	CP Air	C-FCRE	18/Sep/74	15/Nov/74
248	20953	136	British A/W	G-BBPU	02/Oct/74	22/Oct/74
249	21032	SR46	Japan A/L	JA8124	16/Oct/74	04/Nov/74
250	20977	233B Combi	Air Canada	C-GAGA	30/Oct/74	18/Nov/74
						First 747-200B Combi
251	21030	246B	Japan A/L	JA8125	13/Nov/74	05/Dec/74
252	20954	128	Air France	F-BPVP	27/Nov/74	18/Dec/74
253	21048	212B	Singapore A/L	9V-SQD	13/Dec/74	20/Jan/75
1975						
254	21033	SR46	Japan A/L	JA8126	08/Jan/75	24/Jan/75
255	21031	246B	Japan A/L	JA8127	22/Jan/75	10/Feb/75
256	21035	282B	TAP - Portugal.	CS-TJD	05/Feb/75	27/Feb/75
257	20949	E4B	US Air Force	75-0125	19/Feb/75	25/Apr/75
258	21120	251F	Northwest	N616US	05/Mar/75	27/May/75
259	21029	146	Japan A/L	JA8128	19/Mar/75	03/Apr/75
260	21054	238B	Qantas	VH-EBJ	02/Apr/75	21/Apr/75
261	21121	251F	Northwest	N617US	16/Apr/75	23/Jun/75
262	21097	2B4B Combi	Middle East A/L	OD-AGH	30/Apr/75	16/May/75
263	21098	2B4B Combi	Middle East A/L	OD-AGI	20/May/75	05/Jun/75
264	21099	2B4B Combi	Middle East A/L	OD-AGJ	10/Jun/75	07/Aug/75
265	21022	SP21	Pan Am	N530PA	19/May/75	04/Jul/75
						First 747SP
266	20827	245F	Seaboard World	N702SW	24/Jun/75	07/Aug/75

Line No.	Con. No.	Model	Operator	Reg.	Roll Out Date	First Flight
267	21140	238B	Qantas	VH-EBK	18/Jul/75	15/Aug/75
268	21023	SP21	Pan Am	N531PA	30/Jun/75	14/Aug/75
269	21122	251F	Northwest	N618US	02/Aug/75	15/Aug/75
270	21024	SP21	Pan Am	N532PA	03/Sep/75	10/Oct/75
271	21110	206B Combi	KLM	PH-BUH	10/Sep/75	26/Sep/75
272	21190	258C	El Al	4X-AXD	02/Oct/75	22/Oct/75
273	21025	SP21	Pan Am	N533PA	08/Oct/75	03/Nov/75
274	21189	287B	Aero.Argentinas	LV-LZD	22/Oct/75	11/Nov/75
275	20998	SP86	Iran Air	EP-IAA	11/Nov/75	20/Feb/76
276	21111	206B Combi	KLM	PH-BUI	11/Nov/75	26/Nov/75
277	21182	237B	Air India	VT-EDU	25/Nov/75	15/Dec/75
278	20999	SP86	Iran Air	EP-IAB	16/Dec/75	22/Apr/76
1976						
279	21141	128	Air France	N40116	12/Jan/76	27/Jan/76
280	21132	SP44	South African	ZS-SPA	27/Jan/76	17/Feb/76
281	21213	136	British A/W	G-BDPV	09/Feb/76	25/Feb/76 **Last 747-100**
282	21133	SP44	South African	ZS-SPB	24/Feb/76	10/Mar/76
283	21162	212B	Singapore A/L	9V-SQE	08/Mar/76	19/Mar/76
284	21174	SP94	Syrianair	YK-AHA	23/Mar/76	15/Apr/76
285	21237	238B	Qantas	VH-EBL	05/Apr/76	14/Jun/76
286	21026	SP21	Pan Am	N534PA	19/Apr/76	07/May/76
287	21180	270C	Iraqi A/W	YI-AGN	03/May/76	27/May/76
288	21134	SP44	South African	ZS-SPC	17/May/76	04/Jun/76
289	21181	270C	Iraqi A/W	YI-AGO	01/Jun/76	21/Jun/76
290	21175	SP94	Syrianair	YK-AHB	15/Jun/76	01/Jul/76
291	21217	286B Combi	Iran Air	EP-IAG	29/Jun/76	21/Jul/76
292	21238	236B	British A/W	G-BDXA	19/Jul/76	03/Sep/76
293	21253	SP44	South African	ZS-SPD	28/Jul/76	27/Aug/76
294	21220	230B Combi	Lufthansa	D-ABYJ	25/Aug/76	24/Sep/76
295	21255	228F	Air France	F-BPVR	09/Sep/76	28/Sep/76
296	21251	2D3B Combi	Alia	JY-AFA	23/Sep/76	12/Oct/76
297	21252	2D3B Combi	Alia	JY-AFB	07/Oct/76	26/Oct/76
298	21254	SP44	South African	ZS-SPE	21/Oct/76	05/Nov/76
299	21221	230B Combi	Lufthansa	D-ABYK	10/Nov/76	04/Dec/76
300	21218	286B Combi	Iran Air	EP-IAH	02/Dec/76	22/Dec/76
301	21263	SP44	South African	ZS-SPF	22/Dec/76	14/Jan/77
1977						
302	21239	236B	British A/W	G-BDXB	19/Jan/77	22/Feb/77
303	21326	228B Combi	Air France	F-BPVS	08/Feb/77	04/Mar/77
304	21300	SP09	China A/L	B-1862	28/Feb/77	18/Mar/77
305	21240	236B	British A/W	G-BDXC	18/Mar/77	08/Apr/77
306	21441	SP21	Pan Am	N536PA	07/Apr/77	25/Apr/77
307	21093	SP86	Iran Air	EP-IAC	27/Apr/77	16/May/77
308	21321	251F	Northwest	N619US	17/May/77	03/Jun/77
309	21316	212B	Singapore A/L	9V-SQF	07/Jun/77	19/Jun/77
310	21352	238B	Qantas	VH-EBM	27/Jun/77	11/Jul/77
311	21381	283B Combi	Scandinavian	LN-RNA	15/Jul/77	24/Aug/77
312	21439	212B	Singapore A/L	9V-SQG	19/Aug/77	31/Aug/77

Line No.	Con. No.	Model	Operator	Reg.	Roll Out Date	First Flight
313	21429	228B Combi	Air France	F-BPVT	02/Sep/77	21/Sep/77
314	21354	238B Combi	Qantas	VH-ECA	19/Sep/77	04/Oct/77
315	21486	2J9F	Iranian A/F	5-8113	01/Oct/77	28/Nov/77
316	21353	238B	Qantas	VH-EBN	11/Nov/77	06/Dec/77
317	21241	236B	British A/W	G-BDXD	12/Dec/77	09/Jan/78
1978						
318	21446	237B	Air India	VT-EFJ	12/Jan/78	26/Jan/78
319	21487	2J9F	Iranian A/F	5-8114	26/Jan/78	16/Feb/78
320	21380	230B Combi	Lufthansa	D-ABYL	09/Feb/78	02/Mar/78
321	21350	236B	British A/W	G-BDXE	23/Feb/78	14/Mar/78
322	21454	209B Combi	China A/L	B-1864	09/Mar/78	29/Mar/78
323	21351	236B	British A/W	G-BDXF	23/Mar/78	10/Apr/78
324	21468	2Q2B Combi	Air Gabon	F-ODJG	06/Apr/78	25/Apr/78
325	21547	SP21	Pan Am	N537PA	20/Apr/78	05/May/78
326	21516	211B	Wardair	C-GXRA	28/Apr/78	15/May/78
327	21594	258C	El Al	4X-AXF	08/May/78	07/Jun/78
328	21536	236B	British A/W	G-BDXG	16/May/78	02/Jun/78
329	21652	SP68	Saudi Arab Gvmt	HZ-HM1	24/May/78	28/Aug/78
330	21473	237B	Air India	VT-EFO	02/Jun/78	19/Jun/78
331	21548	SP21	Pan Am	N538PA	12/Jun/78	30/Jun/78
332	21541	269B Combi	Kuwait A/W	9K-ADA	20/Jun/78	17/Jul/78
333	21537	228B Combi	Air France	N1252E	28/Jun/78	21/Jul/78
334	21576	228F	Air France	F-BPVV	10/Jul/78	27/Jul/78
335	21542	269B Combi	Kuwait A/W	9K-ADB	18/Jul/78	03/Aug/78
336	21549	206B Combi	KLM	PH-BUK	26/Jul/78	17/Aug/78
337	21515	2B3F	UTA	F-GPAN	03/Aug/78	21/Aug/78
338	21615	2B6B Combi	Royal Air Maroc	CN-RME	11/Aug/78	06/Sep/78
339	21657	238B	Qantas	VH-EBO	21/Aug/78	08/Sep/78
340	21507	2J9F	Iranian A/F	5-8115	29/Aug/78	18/Sep/78
341	21658	238B	Qantas	VH-EBP	07/Sep/78	20/Sep/78
342	21588	230B Combi	Lufthansa	D-ABYM	14/Sep/78	03/Oct/78
343	21514	2J9F	Iranian A/F	5-8116	21/Sep/78	11/Oct/78
344	21550	206B Combi	KLM	PH-BUL	28/Sep/78	17/Oct/78
345	21589	230B	Lufthansa	D-ABYN	05/Oct/78	25/Oct/78
346	21604	181B/SR	All Nippon	JA8133	12/Oct/78	03/Nov/78
347	21592	230F	Lufthansa	D-ABYO	19/Oct/78	10/Nov/78
348	21590	230B	Lufthansa	D-ABYP	26/Oct/78	22/Nov/78
349	21725	287B	Aero.Argentinas	LV-MLO	02/Nov/78	08/Dec/78
350	21591	230B	Lufthansa	D-ABYQ	09/Nov/78	01/Dec/78
351	21605	181B/SR	All Nippon	JA8134	16/Nov/78	09/Dec/78
352	21643	230B Combi	Lufthansa	D-ABYR	27/Nov/78	16/Dec/78
353	21614	2B2B Combi	Air Madagascar	5R-MFT	04/Dec/78	12/Jan/79
354	21650	2R7F	Cargolux	LX-DCV	11/Dec/78	23/Jan/79
355	21627	233B Combi	Air Canada	C-GAGB	18/Dec/78	16/Jan/79
1979						
356	21644	230B Combi	Lufthansa	D-ABYS	03/Jan/79	23/Jan/79
357	21704	251B	Northwest	N622US	10/Jan/79	15/Feb/79
358	21575	283B Combi	Scandinavian A/S	SE-DFZ	17/Jan/79	17/Feb/79
359	21543	269B Combi	Kuwait A/W	9K-ADC	24/Jan/79	14/Feb/79

Line No.	Con. No.	Model	Operator	Reg.	Roll Out Date	First Flight
360	21606	181B/SR	All Nippon	JA8135	30/Jan/79	21/Feb/79
361	21678	246B	Japan A/L	JA8129	05/Feb/79	24/Feb/79
362	21737	258F	El Al	4X-AXG	12/Feb/79	07/Mar/79
363	21772	2B5B	Korean	HL7443	15/Feb/79	08/Mar/79
364	21731	228B Combi	Air France	F-BPVX	21/Feb/79	15/Mar/79
365	21635	236B	British A/W	G-BDXH	27/Feb/79	19/Mar/79
366	21773	2B5B	Korean	HL7445	05/Mar/79	23/Mar/79
367	21648	SP21	Pan Am	N539PA	09/Mar/79	30/Mar/79
368	21517	211B	Wardair	C-GXRD	15/Mar/79	02/Apr/79
369	21659	206B Combi	KLM	PH-BUM	21/Mar/79	09/Apr/79
370	21745	228B	Air France	F-BPVY	27/Mar/79	13/Apr/79
371	21758	SP86	Iran Air	EP-IAD	02/Apr/79	26/Apr/79
372	21730	259B Combi	Avianca	HK-2300	06/Apr/79	11/May/79
373	21649	SP21	Pan Am	N540PA	12/Apr/79	01/May/79
374	21705	251B	Northwest	N623US	18/Apr/79	11/May/79
375	21682	227B	Braniff	N602BN	14/Apr/79	17/May/79
376	21679	246B	Japan A/L	JA8130	30/Apr/79	31/May/79
377	21706	251B	Northwest	N624US	04/May/79	26/May/79
378	21707	251B	Northwest	N625US	10/May/79	08/Jun/79
379	21708	251B	Northwest	N626US	16/May/79	21/Jun/79
380	21680	246B	Japan A/L	JA8131	22/May/79	20/Jun/79
381	21759	186B	Iran Air	EP-IAM	29/May/79	20/Jun/79
382	21681	246F	Japan A/L	JA8132	04/Jun/79	27/Jun/79
383	21825	240B Combi	Pakistan Int.	AP-BAK	08/Jun/79	02/Jul/79
384	21743	221F	Pan Am	N904PA	14/Jun/79	05/Jul/79
385	21746	267B	Cathay Pacific	VR-HKG	20/Jun/79	09/Jul/79
386	21843	209B	China A/L	B-1866	28/Jun/79	16/Jul/79
387	21683	212B	Singapore A/L	9V-SQH	02/Jul/79	19/Jul/79
388	21835	2B3F	UTA	F-GBOX	06/Jul/79	25/Jul/79
389	21660	206B Combi	KLM	PH-BUN	11/Jul/79	03/Aug/79
390	21829	237B	Air India	VT-EFU	16/Jul/79	03/Aug/79
391	21684	212B	Singapore A/L	9V-SQI	19/Jul/79	09/Aug/79
392	21744	221F	Pan Am	N905PA	24/Jul/79	11/Aug/79
393	21922	181B/SR	All Nippon	JA8136	27/Jul/79	21/Aug/79
394	21764	245F	Seaboard World	N703SW	01/Aug/79	25/Aug/79
395	21923	181B/SR	All Nippon	JA8137	06/Aug/79	25/Aug/79
396	21841	245F	Seaboard World	N704SW	09/Aug/79	16/Sep/79
397	21848	206B	KLM	PH-BUO	14/Aug/79	06/Sep/79
398	21787	228F	Air France	F-BPVZ	17/Aug/79	07/Sep/79
399	21935	212B	Singapore A/L	9V-SQJ	22/Aug/79	17/Sep/79
400	21668	2J9F	Iranian A/F	5-8117	27/Aug/79	17/Sep/79
Not delivered. Stored 1979-83 then delivered to:			Northwest	N630US		
401	21936	212B	Singapore A/L	9V-SQK	30/Aug/79	25/Sep/79
402	21782	2D7B	Thai Int.	HS-TGA	05/Sep/79	01/Oct/79
403	21726	287B	Aero.Argentinas	LV-MLP	10/Sep/79	01/Oct/79
404	21727	287B	Aero.Argentinas	LV-MLR	13/Sep/79	05/Oct/79
405	21785	SP27	Braniff	N603BN	18/Sep/79	07/Oct/79
406	21827	249F	Flying Tigers	N806FT	21/Sep/79	15/Oct/79
407	22064	246B	Japan A/L	JA8140	26/Sep/79	18/Oct/79
408	21828	249F	Flying Tigers	N807FT	01/Oct/79	01/Nov/79
409	21977	238B Combi	Qantas	VH-ECB	04/Oct/79	25/Oct/79
410	22145	238B	Qantas	VH-EBQ	09/Oct/79	28/Nov/79

Line No.	Con. No.	Model	Operator	Reg.	Roll Out Date	First Flight
411	22065	246B	Japan A/L	JA8141	12/Oct/79	12/Nov/79
412	21709	251B	Northwest	N627US	17/Oct/79	21/Dec/79
413	21786	SP27	Braniff	N604BN	22/Oct/79	29/Nov/79
414	21993	237B	Air India	VT-EGA	25/Oct/79	17/Dec/79
415	21961	SP31	TWA	N58201	30/Oct/79	02/Dec/79
416	21964	271C	Transamerica	N741TV	02/Nov/79	30/Nov/79
417	21783	2D7B	Thai Int.	HS-TGB	07/Nov/79	03/Dec/79
418	22254	258B	El Al	4X-AXH	12/Nov/79	06/Dec/79
419	21937	212B	Singapore A/L	9V-SQL	15/Nov/79	14/Jan/80
420	21924	181B/SR	All Nippon	JA8138	20/Nov/79	18/Dec/79
421	21832	2F6B	Philippine A/L	N741PR	27/Nov/79	14/Dec/79
422	21925	181B/SR	All Nippon	JA8139	30/Nov/79	15/Jan/80
423	21833	2F6B	Philippine A/L	N742PR	05/Dec/79	07/Jan/80
424	21784	2D7B	Thai Int.	HS-TGC	10/Dec/79	04/Feb/80
425	21834	2F6B	Philippine A/L	N743PR	11/Dec/79	17/Jan/80
426	22066	146B/SR	Japan A/L	JA8142	18/Dec/79	21/Jan/80
427	22067	146B/SR	Japan A/L	JA8143	20/Dec/79	25/Jan/80
1980						
428	21982	228B	Air France	F-GCBA	03/Jan/80	30/Jan/80
429	22077	240B Combi	Pakistan Int.	AP-BAT	08/Jan/80	02/Feb/80
430	21830	236B	British A/W	G-BDXI	11/Jan/80	16/Feb/80
431	21994	237B	Air India	VT-EGB	16/Jan/80	07/Feb/80
432	22063	246F	Japan A/L	JA8144	21/Jan/80	24/Feb/80
433	21932	SPJ6	CAAC	B-2442	24/Jan/80	14/Feb/80
434	21995	237B	Air India	VT-EGC	29/Jan/80	28/Feb/80
435	22105	2L5B Combi	Libyan Arab	5A-DIJ	01/Feb/80	28/Feb/80
			Order cancelled	Aircraft delivered to:		
			Varig	PP-VNA		
436	21938	212B	Singapore A/L	9V-SQM	06/Feb/80	10/Mar/80
437	21991	227B	Braniff	N605BN	11/Feb/80	25/Mar/80
			Not delivered. Stored 1980-4 then delivered to:			
			Northwest	N633US		
438	21965	271C	Transamerica	N742TV	14/Feb/80	07/Mar/80
439	21962	SP31	TWA	N57202	19/Feb/80	11/Mar/80
440	21831	236B	British A/W	G-BDXJ	22/Feb/80	26/Mar/80
441	21963	SP31	TWA	N57203	27/Feb/80	10/Apr/80
442	22389	251B	Northwest	N628US	03/Mar/80	31/Mar/80
443	22106	2L5B Combi	Libyan Arab	5A-DIK	06/Mar/80	26/Mar/80
			Order Cancelled.	Aircraft delivered to:		
			Varig	PP-VNB		
444	22388	251F	Northwest	N629US	11/Mar/80	02/Apr/80
445	22298	SP09	China A/L	B-1880	14/Mar/80	18/Apr/80
446	21966	267B	Cathay Pacific	VR-HIA	19/Mar/80	07/Apr/80
447	21992	SP27	Braniff	N606BN	24/Mar/80	19/May/80
448	22480	2B5F	Korean	HL7451	27/Mar/80	30/Apr/80
449	21939	212B	Singapore A/L	9V-SQN	01/Apr/80	13/May/80
450	22238	256B	Iberia	EC-DIA	04/Apr/80	23/Apr/80
451	22239	256B	Iberia	EC-DIB	09/Apr/80	02/May/80
452	22246	2U3B	Garuda	PK-GSA	14/Apr/80	12/Jun/80
453	22291	181B/SR	All Nippon	JA8145	17/Apr/80	03/May/80
454	22481	2B5F	Korean	HL7452	22/Apr/80	04/Jun/80

Line No.	Con. No.	Model	Operator	Reg.	Roll Out Date	First Flight
455	21933	SPJ6	CAAC	B-2444	25/Apr/80	06/Jun/80
456	22292	181B/SR	All Nippon	JA8146	23/May/80	
457	21940	212B	Singapore A/L	9V-SQO	05/May/80	12/Jun/80
458	22245	249F	Flying Tigers	N808FT	08/May/80	20/Jun/80
459	22247	2U3B	Garuda	PK-GSB	13/May/80	03/Jul/80
460	22237	249F	Flying Tigers	N810FT	16/May/80	31/Jul/80
461	22248	2U3B	Garuda	PK-GSC	21/May/80	22/Jul/80
462	22299	209F	China A/L	B-1894	27/May/80	11/Jul/80
463	22272	228B Combi	Air France	N1289E	30/May/80	18/Jun/80
464	22614	238B	Qantas	VH-EBR	04/Jun/80	24/Jun/80
465	22234	227B	Braniff	N1607B	09/Jun/80	14/Jan/81
			Not delivered. Stored 1981-4 then delivered to:			
			Northwest	N634US		
466	22149	267B	Cathay Pacific	VR-HIB	12/Jun/80	30/Jun/80
467	21934	SPJ6	CAAC	N1304E	17/Jun/80	11/Jul/80
468	22249	2U3B	Garuda	PK-GSD	20/Jun/80	08/Aug/80
469	22107	2L5B Combi	Libyan Arab	5A-DIL	25/Jun/80	05/Dec/80
			Order Cancelled	Aircraft delivered to:		
			Varig	PP-VNC		
470	21941	212B	Singapore A/L	9V-SQP	30/Jun/80	15/Aug/80
471	21942	212B	Singapore A/L	9V-SQQ	03/Jul/80	11/Sep/80
472	22169	2S4F	Air Afrique	TU-TAP	09/Jul/80	12/Sep/80
473	22302	SP27	Braniff	N1608B	14/Jul/80	02/Dec/80
			Not delivered.	Stored 1981-2 then delivered to:		
			CAAC	N1301E		
474	22376	206B	KLM	N1295E	17/Jul/80	06/Aug/80
475	21943	212B	Singapore A/L	9V-SQR	22/Jul/80	16/Oct/80
476	22150	245F	Flying Tigers	N815FT	25/Jul/80	22/Sep/80
477	22293	181B/SR	All Nippon	JA8147	30/Jul/80	15/Aug/80
478	22151	245F	Flying Tigers	N816FT	04/Aug/80	03/Oct/80
479	22337	2D7B	Thai Int.	HS-TGF	17/Aug/80	11/Sep/80
480	22306	236F	British A/W	G-KILO	12/Aug/80	19/Sep/80
481	22294	181B/SR	All Nippon	JA8148	15/Aug/80	30/Sep/80
482	22390	2R7F	Cargolux	LX-ECV	04/Sep/80	30/Sep/80
483	22615	238B Combi	Qantas	VH-ECC	09/Sep/80	29/Sep/80
484	22482	2B5B	Korean	HL7454	12/Sep/80	17/Oct/80
485	22427	228B Combi	Air France	F-GCBC	17/Sep/80	07/Oct/80
486	22170	244B Combi	South African	ZS-SAR	22/Sep/80	24/Oct/80
487	22297	287B	Aero.Argentinas	LV-OEP	25/Sep/80	04/Nov/80
488	22171	244B Combi	South African	ZS-SAS	30/Sep/80	12/Nov/80
489	22478	246B	Japan A/L	JA8149	03/Oct/80	26/Nov/80
490	22363	230B Combi	Lufthansa	D-ABYT	08/Oct/80	04/Nov/80
491	22379	206B	KLM	N1298E	13/Oct/80	06/Nov/80
492	22506	243B Combi	Alitalia	I-DEMC	16/Oct/80	14/Nov/80
493	22429	267B	Cathay Pacific	VR-HIC	21/Oct/80	05/Dec/80
494	22477	246F	Japan A/L	JA8151	03/Oct/80	26/Nov/80
495	22303	236B	British A/W	G-BDXK	29/Oct/80	16/Jan/81
496	22479	246B	Japan A/L	JA8150	03/Nov/80	13/Dec/80
497	22507	243B Combi	Alitalia	I-DEMD	06/Nov/80	26/Nov/80
498	22382	2F6B	Philippine A/L	N744PR	11/Nov/80	02/Dec/80
499	22508	243B Combi	Alitalia	I-DEMF	14/Nov/80	11/Dec/80
500	22381	283B Combi	Scandinavian A/S	N4501Q	19/Nov/80	20/Dec/80
501	22483	SPB5	Korean	HL7456	24/Nov/80	23/Dec/80

Line No.	Con. No.	Model	Operator	Reg.	Roll Out Date	First Flight
502	22304	236B	British A/W.	G-BDXL	02/Dec/80	24/Jan/81
			Not delivered.	Stored 1981-2 then delivered to:		
			Malaysian A/S	9M-MHI		
503	22428	228B Combi	Air France	N1305E	08/Dec/80	23/Dec/80
504	22471	2D7B	Thai Int.	HS-TGG	12/Dec/80	16/Jan/81
505	22495	SP38	Qantas	VH-EAA	18/Dec/80	11/Jan/81
1981						
506	22305	236B	British A/W	G-BDXL	05/Jan/81	12/Feb/81
507	22484	SPB5	Korean	HL7457	09/Jan/81	30/Jan/81
508	22378	2H7B Combi	Cameroon A/L	TJ-CAB	15/Jan/81	06/Feb/81
509	22454	256B	Iberia	EC-DLC	21/Jan/81	06/Feb/81
510	21944	212B	Singapore A/L	9V-SQS	27/Jan/81	18/Feb/81
511	22594	181B/SR	All Nippon	JA8152	02/Feb/81	18/Feb/81
512	22498	168B	Saudia	HZ-AIA	06/Feb/81	02/Mar/81
513	22485	2B5B	Korean	HL7458	12/Feb/81	06/Mar/81
514	22579	2D3B	Alia	JY-AFS	18/Feb/81	09/Mar/81
515	22455	256B	Iberia	EC-DLD	24/Feb/81	12/Mar/81
516	22595	181B/SR	All Nippon	JA8153	02/Mar/81	29/Mar/81
517	22499	168B	Saudia	HZ-AIB	06/Mar/81	23/Mar/81
518	22514	2B3B Combi	UTA	F-BTDG	12/Mar/81	01/Apr/81
519	22446	209B	China A/L	B-1886	18/Mar/81	07/Apr/81
520	22486	2B5F	Korean	HL7459	24/Mar/81	10/Apr/81
521	22515	2B3B Combi	UTA	F-BTDH	30/Mar/81	17/Apr/81
522	22500	168B	Saudia	HZ-AIC	03/Apr/81	23/Apr/81
523	22722	219B	Air New Zealand	ZK-NZV	09/Apr/81	06/May/81
524	22403	271C	Transamerica	N743TV	15/Apr/81	01/May/81
525	22501	168B	Saudia	HZ-AID	21/Apr/81	08/May/81
526	22442	236B	British A/W	G-BDXN	27/Apr/81	21/May/81
			Not delivered.	Stored 1981-2 then delivered to:		
			Malaysian A/S	9M-MHJ		
527	22723	219B	Air New Zealand	ZK-NZW	01/May/81	22/May/81
528	22724	219B	Air New Zealand	ZK-NZX	07/May/81	12/Jun/81
529	22503	SP68	Saudia	HZ-AIF	13/May/81	04/Jun/81
530	22502	168B	Saudia	HZ-AIE	19/May/81	11/Jun/81
531	22530	267B	Cathay Pacific	VR-HID	28/May/81	15/Jun/81
532	22592	287B	Aero.Argentinas	LV-OOZ	03/Jun/81	24/Jun/81
533	22510	243B	Alitalia	I-DEMG	15/Jun/81	01/Jul/81
534	22547	SPO9	China A/L	N4508H	23/Jun/81	20/Jul/81
535	22678	228F	Air France	N4508E	01/Jul/81	20/Jul/81
536	22511	243B	Alitalia	I-DEML	10/Jul/81	28/Jul/81
537	22672	SP38	Qantas	VH-EAB	20/Jul/81	03/Aug/81
538	22668	230F	Lufthansa	D-ABYU	29/Jul/81	13/Aug/81
539	22380	206B Combi	KLM	N1309E	05/Aug/81	21/Aug/81
540	22496	283B	Scandinavian A/S	N4502R	13/Aug/81	26/Aug/81
541	22709	181B/SR	All Nippon	JA8156	21/Aug/81	21/Sep/81
542	22512	243B	Alitalia	I-DEMN	31/Aug/81	21/Sep/81
543	22616	238B	Qantas	VH-EBS	09/Sep/81	25/Sep/81
544	22710	181B/SR	All Nippon	JA8157	17/Sep/81	15/Oct/81
545	22545	243F	Alitalia	I-DEMR	25/Sep/81	15/Oct/81
546	22513	243B	Alitalia	I-DEMP	05/Oct/81	02/Nov/81
547	22745	246B	Japan A/L	JA8154	13/Oct/81	04/Nov/81

Line No.	Con. No.	Model	Operator	Reg.	Roll Out Date	First Flight
548	22746	246B	Japan A/L	JA8155	21/Oct/81	17/Nov/81
549	22669	230B Combi	Lufthansa	D-ABYW	29/Oct/81	19/Nov/81
550	22670	230B Combi	Lufthansa	D-ABYX	06/Nov/81	01/Dec/81
551	22747	168B	Saudia	HZ-AIG	16/Nov/81	11/Dec/81
552	22593	287B	Aero.Argentinas	LZ-OPA	24/Nov/81	16/Dec/81
553	22740	269B Combi	Kuwait A/W	9K-ADD	10/Dec/81	14/Jan/82
1982						
554	22764	256B	Iberia	EC-DNP	04/Jan/82	25/Jan/82
555	22748	168B	Saudia	HZ-AIH	18/Jan/82	03/Feb/82
556	22447	209B	China A/L	B-1888	01/Feb/82	17/Feb/82
557	22749	168B	Saudia	HZ-AII	15/Feb/82	19/Mar/82
558	22794	228B Combi	Air France	N4506H	01/Mar/82	17/Mar/82
559	22711	181B/SR	All Nippon	JA8158	15/Mar/82	01/Apr/82
560	22750	SP68	Saudia	HZ-AIJ	29/Mar/82	13/Apr/82
561	22768	2U3B	Garuda	PK-GSE	12/Apr/82	24/Apr/82
562	22769	2U3B	Garuda	PK-GSF	26/Apr/82	08/May/82
563	22725	219B	Air New Zealand	ZK-NZY	10/May/82	27/May/82
564	22805	SP09	China A/L	N4522V	24/May/82	10/Jun/82
565	22366	270C	Iraqi A/W	YI-AGP	08/Jun/82	25/Jun/82
566	22872	267B	Cathay Pacific	VR-HIE	22/Jun/82	09/Jul/82
567	22858	SP70	Iraqi Gvmt	YI-ALM	07/Jul/82	02/Aug/82
568	22791	219B	Air New Zealand	ZK-NZZ	21/Jul/82	05/Aug/82
569	22939	228F	Air France	N4544F	10/Aug/82	25/Aug/82
570	22704	357 Combi	Swissair	HB-IGC	15/Sep/82	05/Oct/82
						First 747-300
571	22989	246F	Japan A/L	N211JL	20/Sep/82	07/Oct/82
572	22712	181B/SR	All Nippon	JA8159	08/Oct/82	23/Oct/82
573	22870	3B3	UTA	F-GDUA	10/Nov/82	10/Dec/82
574	22671	230B Combi	Lufthansa	D-ABYY	17/Nov/82	04/Dec/82
575	22969	243B	Alitalia	I-DEMS	08/Dec/82	11/Feb/83
1983						
576	22705	357 Combi	Swissair	HB-IGD	14/Jan/83	14/Feb/83
577	22970	344	South African	ZS-SAT	31/Jan/83	16/Feb/83
578	22971	344	South African	ZS-SAU	16/Feb/83	27/Mar/83
579	22990	246B	Japan A/L	JA8161	25/Mar/83	25/Apr/83
580	23026	312	Singapore A/L	9V-SKA	28/Mar/83	15/Apr/83
581	22991	246B	Japan A/L	JA8162	27/Apr/83	17/May/83
582	23048	267B	Cathay Pacific	VR-HIF	03/May/83	13/May/83
583	23027	312	Singapore A/L	N116KB	23/May/83	12/Jun/83
584	23028	312	Singapore A/L	N117KC	13/Jun/83	23/Jun/83
585	22995	357	Swissair	N221GE	18/Jul/83	22/Sep/83
586	22996	357	Swissair	N221GF	05/Aug/83	12/Sep/83
587	23056	306 Combi	KLM	N4548M	25/Aug/83	15/Sep/83
588	23067	346	Japan A/L	N212JL	15/Sep/83	10/Oct/83
589	23068	346	Japan A/L	N213JL	05/Oct/83	26/Oct/83
590	23029	312	Singapore A/L	N118KD	25/Oct/83	11/Nov/83
591	23071	2J6B Combi	CAAC	B-2446	14/Nov/83	06/Dec/83
592	23070	3G1	Saudi Arab Gvmt	HZ-HM1A	02/Dec/83	15/Dec/83

Line No.	Con. No.	Model	Operator	Reg.	Roll Out Date	First Flight
1984						
593	23030	312	Singapore A/L	N119KE	12/Jan/84	01/Feb/84
594	23111	251B	Northwest	N631US	08/Feb/84	28/Feb/84
595	23112	251B	Northwest	N632US	09/Mar/84	27/Mar/84
596	23120	267B	Cathay Pacific	VR-HIH	04/Apr/84	17/Apr/84
597	22472	2D7B	Thai Int.	HS-TGS	02/May/84	16/May/84
598	23031	312	Singapore A/L	N120KF	31/May/84	18/Jun/84
599	23149	346	Japan A/L	JA8163	28/Jun/84	07/Nov/84
600	23137	306 Combi	KLM	N4551N	27/Jul/84	09/Aug/84
601	23150	146B/SR	Japan A/L	JA8164	10/Sep/84	25/Oct/84
602	23222	338	Qantas	VH-EBT	17/Sep/84	06/Oct/84
603	23032	312	Singapore A/L	N121KG	05/Oct/84	17/Oct/84
604	23138	281F	Nippon Cargo	JA8167	25/Oct/84	19/Nov/84
605	22487	3B5	Korean	HL7468	14/Nov/84	03/Dec/84
606	23223	338	Qantas	VH-EBU	06/Dec/84	21/Dec/84
1985						
607	23151	346	Japan A/L	JA8166	04/Jan/85	17/Jan/85
608	23139	281F	Nippon Cargo	JA8168	24/Jan/85	20/Feb/85
609	23033	312	Singapore A/L	N122KH	13/Feb/85	01/Mar/85
610	23224	338	Qantas	VH-EBV	05/Mar/85	21/Mar/85
611	22489	3B5	Korean	HL7469	19/Mar/85	30/Mar/85
612	23243	312	Singapore A/L	N123KJ	02/Apr/85	19/Apr/85
613	23300	243B Combi	Alitalia	I-DEMT	16/Apr/85	08/May/85
614	23286	230B Combi	Lufthansa	D-ABYZ	30/Apr/85	16/May/85
615	23221	367	Cathay Pacific	VR-HII	14/May/85	31/May/85
616	23262	368	Saudia	HZ-AIK	29/May/85	13/Jun/85
617	23287	230B Combi	Lufthansa	D-ABZA	07/Jun/85	21/Jun/85
618	23301	243B	Alitalia	I-DEMV	26/Jun/85	12/Jul/85
619	23263	368	Saudia	HZ-AIL	14/Jul/85	26/Jul/85
620	23264	368	Saudia	HZ-AIM	25/Jul/85	09/Aug/85
621	23244	312	Singapore A/L	N124KK	08/Aug/85	23/Aug/85
622	23265	368	Saudia	HZ-AIN	22/Aug/85	11/Oct/85
623	23350	281F	Nippon Cargo	JA8172	06/Sep/85	01/Oct/85
624	23266	368	Saudia	HZ-AIO	20/Sep/85	09/Oct/85
625	23348	230F	Lufthansa	D-ABZB	04/Oct/85	15/Oct/85
626	23245	312	Singapore A/L	N125KL	18/Oct/85	05/Nov/85
627	23394	341 Combi	Varig	PP-VNH	01/Nov/85	22/Nov/85
628	23461	2J6B Combi	CAAC	B-2448	12/Nov/85	30/Nov/85
629	23395	341 Combi	Varig	PP-VNI	21/Nov/85	13/Dec/85
630	23267	368	Saudia	HZ-AIP	04/Dec/85	03/Jan/86
631	23268	368	Saudia	HZ-AIQ	13/Dec/85	14/Jan/86
1986						
632	23413	3B3 Combi	UTA	F-GETA	03/Jan/86	23/Jan/86
633	23393	230B Combi	Lufthansa	D-ABZC	14/Jan/86	24/Jan/86
634	23392	367	Cathay Pacific	VR-HIJ	23/Jan/86	08/Feb/86
635	23389	246B	Japan A/L	JA8169	03/Feb/86	01/Mar/86
636	23390	146B/SR SUD	Japan A/L	JA8170	12/Feb/86	26/Feb/86
637	23409	312 Combi	Singapore A/L	9V-SKM	21/Feb/86	10/Mar/86
638	23408	338	Qantas	VH-EBW	04/Mar/86	19/Mar/86

Line No.	Con. No.	Model	Operator	Reg.	Roll Out Date	First Flight
639	23407	230B	Lufthansa	D-ABZD	13/Mar/86	31/Mar/86
640	23482	346	Japan A/L	JA8173	21/Mar/86	06/Apr/86
641	23480	3B3 Combi	UTA	F-GETB	31/Mar/86	14/Apr/86
642	23547	251B	Northwest	N636US	08/Apr/86	22/Apr/86
643	23269	368	Saudia	HZ-AIR	16/Apr/86	01/May/86
644	23548	251B	Northwest	N637US	24/Apr/86	10/May/86
645	23270	368	Saudia	HZ-AIS	02/May/86	19/May/86
646	23439	329 Combi	Sabena	OO-SGC	12/May/86	29/May/86
647	23476	243B Combi	Alitalia	I-DEMW	20/May/86	06/Jun/86
648	23501	281B	All Nippon	JA8174	29/May/86	16/Jun/86
649	23502	281B	All Nippon	JA8175	06/Jun/86	23/Jun/86
650	23600	3H6 Combi	Malaysian A/S	9M-MHK	16/Jun/86	02/Jul/86
651	23549	251B	Northwest	N638US	24/Jun/86	11/Jul/86
652	23271	368	Saudia	HZ-AIT	02/Jul/86	23/Jul/86
653	23410	312 Combi	Singapore A/L	9V-SKN	11/Jul/86	12/Aug/86
654	23391	246F	Japan A/L	JA8171	04/Aug/86	19/Aug/86
655	23637	146B/SR SUD	Japan A/L	JA8176	12/Aug/86	29/Aug/86
656	23611	228B Combi	Air France	F-GCBH	20/Aug/86	08/Sep/86
657	23508	306 Combi	KLM	PH-BUW	28/Aug/86	20/Sep/86
658	23638	346	Japan A/L	JA8177	08/Sep/86	22/Sep/86
659	23534	367	Cathay Pacific	VR-HIK	16/Sep/86	03/Oct/86
660	23621	230F	Lufthansa	D-ABZF	24/Sep/86	14/Oct/86
661	23676	228B Combi	Air France	F-GCBI	02/Oct/86	18/Oct/86
662	23688	338	Qantas	VH-EBX	10/Oct/86	26/Oct/86
663	23509	230B Combi	Lufthansa	D-ABZE	20/Oct/86	12/Nov/86
664	23639	346	Japan A/L	JA8178	28/Oct/86	03/Dec/86
665	23622	230B	Lufthansa	D-ABZH	15/Nov/86	17/Dec/86
666	23769	312 Combi	Singapore A/L	9V-SKP	09/Dec/86	16/Jan/87
667	23698	281B	All Nippon	JA8181	26/Nov/86	13/Dec/86

1987

Line No.	Con. No.	Model	Operator	Reg.	Roll Out Date	First Flight
668	23640	346	Japan A/L	JA8179	08/Jan/87	25/Jan/87
669	23652	21AC	Martinair	PH-MCE	26/Jan/87	05/Feb/87
670	23746	2J6B Combi	CAAC	B-2450	05/Feb/87	20/Feb/87
671	23709	367	Cathay Pacific	VR-HOL	16/Jan/87	01/Feb/87
672	23711	236B Combi	British A/W	G-BDXM	23/Jan/87	13/Feb/87
673	23736	222B	United	N151UA	11/Feb/87	01/Mar/87
674	23735	236B Combi	British A/W	G-BDXN	19/Feb/87	10/Mar/87
675	23737	222B	United	N152UA	03/Mar/87	16/Mar/87
676	23610	SP	United Arab Emirates	N60659	Mar/87	
677	23799	236B	British A/W	G-BDXO	25/Mar/87	10/Apr/87
678	23823	338	Qantas	VH-EBY	06/Apr/87	18/Apr/87
679		VC-25A	US Air Force	N1788B	Apr/87	
680	23887	251F	Northwest	N639US	30/Apr/87	18/May/87
681	23721	3D7	Thai A/W Int.	HS-TGD	18/May/87	22/Jun/87
682	23888	251F	Northwest	N640US	01/Jun/87	18/Jun/87
683	23813	281B	All Nippon	JA8182	12/Jun/87	30/Jun/87
684	23641	246F	Japan A/L	JA8180	01/Jul/87	29/Jul/87
685		VC-25A	US Air Force	N60659	Jul/87	
686	23751	357 Combi	Swissair	HB-IGG	10/Aug/87	26/Aug/87
687	23864	267F	Cathay Pacific	VR-HVZ	24/Aug/87	11/Sep/87

Line No.	Con. No.	Model	Operator	Reg.	Roll Out Date	First Flight
688	23722	3D7	Thai A/W Int.	HS-TGE	08/Sep/87	16/Nov/87
689	23919	281F	Nippon Cargo	JA8188	22/Sep/87	21/Dec/87
690	23920	367	Cathay Pacific	VR-HOM	06/Oct/87	23/Oct/87
691	23969	346	Japan A/L	JA8185	20/Oct/87	15/Feb/88
692	23967	346SR	Japan A/L	JA8183	05/Nov/87	24/Nov/87
693	23968	346SR	Japan A/L	JA8184	19/Nov/87	22/Dec/87
694	24018	346SR	Japan A/L	JA8186	14/Dec/87	21/Jan/88
695	24019	346SR	Japan A/L	JA8187	17/Dec/87	21/Jan/88
1988						
696	23719	451	Northwest	N661US	26/Jan/88	29/Apr/88 **First 747-400**
697	24088	236B Combi	British A/W	G-BDXP	28/Jan/88	13/Feb/88
698	24067	228B Combi	Air France	F-GCBJ	12/Feb/88	02/Mar/88
699	24071	256B Combi	Iberia	EC-EEK	05/Mar/88	25/Mar/88
700	23817	430	Lufthansa	D-ABVB	Mar/88	27/Jun/88
701	24106	341	Varig	PP-VOA	28/Mar/88	23/Apr/88
702	24107	341	Varig	PP-VOB	10/Apr/88	07/May/88
703	24108	341	Varig	PP-VOC	26/Apr/88	18/May/88
704	24161	366 Combi	Egyptair	SU-GAL	06/May/88	07/Jun/88
705	23814	467	Cathay Pacific	VR-HOO	May/88	28/Aug/88
706	24138	230F	Lufthansa	D-ABZI	24/May/88	19/Jun/88
707	24162	366 Combi	Egyptair	SU-GAM	05/Jun/88	23/Jun/88
708	23720	451	Northwest	N662US	Jun/88	
709	24215	367	Cathay Pacific	VR-HON	27/Jun/88	12/Jul/88
710	24177	212F	Singapore A/L	9V-SKQ	14/Jul/88	11/Aug/88
711						
712	24134	21AC	Martinair	PH-MCF	25/Jul/88	15/Sep/88
713	24194	3B5	Korean Air	HL7470	09/Aug/88	21/Aug/88
714	24158	228F	Air France	F-GCBK	14/Aug/88	11/Sep/88

As line numbers generally only come to light once an aircraft has been delivered, our listing is correct to September 1988 with the roll-out and subsequent first flight of the 714th aircraft, a series - 228F for Air France. As of September 1988, outstanding orders for the Boeing 747 exceeded 150 aircraft, the majority attributed to the new - 400 series for delivery from December 1988. Details of ordered aircraft can be found in the Operators section.